Praise for *Joan Garry's Guide to Nonprofit Leadership*

"WOW! I giggled, I pondered, I smiled, I nodded! Awesome! I share Joan's belief that nonprofits can change the world and she has given us the book that will make that happen! What's more, thanks to the way it is written, we'll be smiling as we learn!"

—Caryl Stern, President & CEO,
Executive Director, Walton Family Foundation

"Joan has written a powerful, must-read book for nonprofit leaders. Her experience and compassion will motivate you in your journey to 'experiment your way to success.' Filled with good humor and free of jargon, this book provides readers with valuable lessons from one of the country's most skilled leadership coaches."

—Vikki Spruill, President & CEO,
New England Aquarium

"As an instructor here at The Annenberg School, Joan has proven herself to be a joyful and inspiring educator, igniting student interest in the power of nonprofit communications. How fitting that she has invested time in sharing that joy and inspiration in *Joan Garry's Guide to Nonprofit Leadership*. Among the qualities that make for an effective nonprofit leader, writes Joan, are boldness, joy, a good sense of humor, and the ability to tell a good story. Not coincidentally, these same attributes describe her book perfectly. The arguments and advice are bold and illustrated by a range of engaging and personal stories drawn from her career as one of the nation's most influential nonprofit leaders."

—Michael X. Delli Carpini,
former Dean, The Annenberg School
for Communication, University of Pennsylvania

"When Joan Garry says messy, she really means messy! This book pulls no punches! It's a tell-all expose of the 501c-3 underbelly, a guide from the inside for anyone involved, or thinking of becoming involved, with a non-profit organization. What's a bigger surprise though, is the wit and heart and passion on every page, and the spirit of kindness that comes from someone truly passing on wisdom."

—Alan Cumming, Celebrity

"As an overworked nonprofit ED with one eye twitching due to cash-flow issues, I am always skeptical of people claiming to be 'experts' about nonprofit leadership. Joan, however, proves to be not only an authority on our work, but also no-nonsense, down-to-earth, and hilarious. This book is chock-full of helpful stories and concrete recommendations, delivered in Joan's usual engaging conversational tone, sprinkled with jokes and witticisms. You feel like you're venting with a wise and caring friend at happy hour. There is great advice here for new as well as experienced nonprofit leaders."

—Vu Le, Blogger,
Nonprofit AF and Former Executive Director,
Rainier Valley Corps

"While it may sound idiotic to think about curling up with a good book on management and leadership, that's how great this book is. *Joan Garry's Guide to Nonprofit Leadership* is brilliant, practical, beautifully written, hysterically funny, insightful, moving, entertaining, original, incredibly useful, emotionally satisfying, and right about just about everything. There's something useful and enjoyable on every page, and there is no excuse for not buying it immediately."

—Kenneth Cloke, Author,
Resolving Conflicts at Work and *The End of Management
and the Rise of Organizational Democracy*

JOAN GARRY'S
GUIDE TO
Nonprofit Leadership

Because the World is Counting on You

2nd Edition

Joan Garry

WILEY

For general information on our other products and services or for technical support, please contact our Customer Care Department within the United States at (800) 762-2974, outside the United States at (317) 572-3993 or fax (317) 572-4002.

Wiley publishes in a variety of print and electronic formats and by print-on-demand. Some material included with standard print versions of this book may not be included in e-books or in print-on-demand. If this book refers to media such as a CD or DVD that is not included in the version you purchased, you may download this material at http://booksupport.wiley.com. For more information about Wiley products, visit www. wiley.com.

Library of Congress Cataloging-in-Publication Data is available:

ISBN 9781119730484 (Paperback)

ISBN 9781119730514 (ePDF)

ISBN 9781119730491 (ePub)

AUTHOR PHOTOGRAPHS: JOSEPH MORAN [JOSEPHMORAN.COM]
COVER DESIGN: PAUL MCCARTHY

SKY10022472_111220

Contents

Preface to the Second Edition

March 2017. I stood on a chair (I'm short) to offer remarks to clients, friends, family, and colleagues to celebrate the publication of my first book. Not gonna lie. It was exciting. A book. People saw me as this expert — someone who could help them figure out the gnarly knots that stood between them and the pursuit of their nonprofit mission.

Little did I know then what an imposter I was. Well, maybe that is overstating a bit, but I had no idea how much more there was to know, how many more leaders there were to meet and hear from and, as a result, how much more advice there was to share with you that could be helpful.

In this second edition, I add two major stories and a big dose of hope (in a world that is more than just a little hungry for it).

Story #1: In 2015, I came to understand just how many "small" nonprofits there were. As the popularity of my blog and podcast grew (now reaching folks from 150 countries around the world), I became something of a Dear Abby. And this Abby became totally overwhelmed with dozens of emails weekly from folks with challenges galore. While they often seemed insurmountable to the writer, I felt like I could help — I had advice for them, resources, and I could give them the pat on the back they desperately needed. But I couldn't keep up. And as a pleaser personality, leaving these folks hanging was not OK by me.

Some research quickly unearthed the reason for the flood of emails. Nearly 70% of all nonprofits have budgets under $500,000. And how much do you think these groups budget for professional development? You guessed it. Zero.

Armed with all those emails and a digital marketing partner, I launched The Nonprofit Leadership Lab just two months after the publication of the first edition of this book. The Nonprofit Leadership Lab provides content and community for board and staff leaders of small nonprofits and is the best online resource of its kind. Since its launch we have supported over 5,000 leaders — both board and staff. I feel a great sense of pride that we have been able to help so many folks develop new skills, transform their boards, write kick-ass grant proposals, and feel a sense of community with thousands in the U.S. and around the world.

But it is what these leaders have taught me that is the main reason I wanted to write this second edition. Two-thirds of the sector stares at cash flow and yet is chock-full of passionate and remarkable founders for whom building and growing an organization is simply not the best and highest use of their magic powers. Hundreds of thousands of nonprofits build their boards the best way they know how, and board members are painfully unclear on the significant leading role they play in their organizations' success.

Angela Duckworth's book, *Grit: The Power of Passion and Perseverance* (Scribner), is a first-rate look into the tough stuff people are made of — the role perseverance plays in who we can become. When I spend an hour engaging with our members, that is always the first word that comes to mind, *Grit*, and it compels me to be even more of an advocate and champion for these leaders.

And so a deep dive into small nonprofits: how to be an effective one and what all nonprofits have to learn from the grit and determination of the small nonprofit are additional areas of focus in this edition.

Story #2: Actually, it's many stories. Stories that upset me, stories that anger me, and stories that call me to action to use my platform to work to make things different. These stories are all about the power and responsibilities of boards to fully lead and partner with their organizations to move them from messy to thriving. Our sector does a downright poor job recruiting board members, educating them about what the job really is, and holding them accountable.

In a monthly column for *The Chronicle of Philanthropy,* I spoke the truth about boards' abuse of power — that this may just be responsible for more great staff leader attrition than any other factor. The engagement in that piece was off the charts on every one of my social media platforms. Some folks even sent me videos because someone had asked that I see and hear them.

Since I wrote the first edition of this book, boards' abuse of power is a recurring theme I hear from members of my Leadership Lab and from the dozens of my coaching and strategy clients. This issue was prominent for me in 2016 and led me to write Chapter 3, which reframes nonprofit leadership as copilots flying a twin-engine jet. Today, I feel a greater sense of urgency as these stories continue to come my way. A lack of understanding of board service is the one thing that most often thwarts the success of a nonprofit organization's efforts to do the good work that is so badly needed. And this is as true of nonprofits with multi-million-dollar budgets as it is of the hundreds of thousands of those organizations who struggle to hit $500,000 in revenue. I hope that my new chapter about why boards matter will be a catalyst in a broad and actionable conversation about how to make real and lasting change in this area.

Those two stories represent my "why" about this second edition. Shall we talk about the "why now"?

Since the first edition of this book was published in 2017, we have seen the development of a mindset that is about drawing lines in the sand and building walls (literally and figuratively). We have become a society that is focused on what divides us rather than what unites us. The situation is ugly. People on both sides of the aisle are angry. It seems hopeless.

This divisive society will not magically disappear anytime soon. Hardly. And I guarantee you that every American citizen will be fired up — ready to stand up for what they believe in. Folks who have spent their lives on the sidelines or in the stands will be propelled from their seats.

By you. All you have to do is invite them.

And it isn't just because they feel compelled to do something. It's also because they want to be on the side of hope and possibility. And so they will look to those who are leading.

And they will see you.

And they will want to play for your team: your team that advocates and educates; your team that works to protect our planet and the living creatures who are our neighbors; your team that brings beauty through music and the arts or reminds us of our history and the shoulders we stand on.

I am driven to help you to be the best leader you can be: to fuel your ability to lead well, manage well, and have the greatest possible impact; and to encourage you to take time from repairing our world to take good care of yourself.

I am writing now amid the most terrifying health crisis of our time, the COVID-19 pandemic. I am watching nonprofits struggle so badly, and at the same time, I am watching them do the most heroic things. Eric Cooper, the President and CEO of the San Antonio Food Bank, saw what he never imagined possible. In one week in April 2020, ten thousand cars lined up waiting for food. Many of the drivers never imagined they would ever need the services that Eric's heroic team provided. Listening as Eric Cooper became emotional on the evening news reminded me that there is such humanity in our sector, such deep empathy, and this has been, for me, one of the real the treasures to see in the darkness. I have no crystal ball, but as all of us navigate our way through this crisis, one that reveals so clearly the racial, gender, ability, and class divides in our country, I am certain that nonprofit leaders will continue to need our support and continue to lead us in the direction of a truly civil society.

Eric Cooper's story is one of many; you will meet a host of new characters in this new edition. In the past three years, I have worked with thousands of leaders whose stories affirm much of what I shared the first time around. Many of these leaders enriched my understanding of the superpowers and the kryptonite of the nonprofit leader. You will meet these characters and hear their stories throughout the book, and I hope that the stories and the lessons within them will be as much of a gift to you as they have been to me.

So let's get to it, shall we?

Acknowledgments

We are who we are because of the families that raised us. My mom passed away just after I submitted the manuscript for the first edition. I found a paper copy of the cover art for the book in her purse about a month later. It looked well worn — like the cashiers at Stop & Shop had probably seen it a few times. It made me smile. If I am smart, feisty and a bit of a dog with a bone about issues that feel important to me, it is because I am my mother's daughter. To steal a line from one of my kids, *Thanks for birthing me, Mom.*

My dad taught me the power of being a good coach. I saw him in action during years of being his right hand in Little League dugouts. And I admired him. Offering direction, support, and encouragement, he was not just a coach; he was a champion and an educator. A leader. Everyone wanted to be on his team. I was lucky. I was born into his team.

Father Jim Loughran, SJ, of blessed memory, taught my first philosophy class. He challenged me to consider the value of my moral compass, my own intellectual capacity, and the power of inquiry.

We are who we are because of the people who shape our thinking during our journey. Attorneys Paula Ettelbrick and Suzanne Goldberg represented our family in a precedent-setting case to create a legal connection between our kids and me. These two triggered the activist in me, planting the idea in my head that it was time to get off the sidelines and onto the field.

In 1985, Showtime engaged consultants Joan Goldsmith and Ken Cloke. Joan and Ken were evangelists about making teamwork a reality (not a buzzword) in workplaces. And they taught me about the power of difficult conversations. Much of my work today feels like the baton they passed on to me.

Yes, this was the village that led me from a solid, happy life to a life with real purpose — leading me to the nonprofit sector and never looking back.

During my tenure at GLAAD, I met activists, donors, and volunteers who inspired me to do my best for them. Lessons learned from this journey are too long to list but special thanks to "heart monitor Julie" and the five-star staff and board who partnered with me to build an organization to last. And I hope you are lucky enough to find someone like Karen Magee to step into a board leadership role. I can talk about the power of that partnership because I speak from experience with Karen.

This book is my chance to reach more people with guidance and direction. My deepest thanks to Scott Paley of Abstract Edge for believing that I had something to say and for working tirelessly to ensure that the message reached far and wide. Without a blog and a podcast (both Scott's idea), there would be no book.

The team at my small but very mighty consulting firm has changed and grown since my first edition. I am so grateful to have a team that is as driven to help the "helpers" as I am. To a person, my team is smart, funny, empathetic, and dedicated. Special thanks to Cindy Pereira who runs what we jokingly call "Joanlandia." "I think you should update your book, Joan," she said offhandedly one day. I think it was the next day we had a signed contract. Because that is how Cindy rolls. I'm also deeply grateful to Laura Zielke, the Director of Member Experience for The Nonprofit Leadership Lab. She treats our work together as a vocation and in this, we are kindred spirits. Laura worked closely with me in identifying Lab members whose stories would really bring the lessons to life.

Thank you so much to Arielle Eckstut my "book doctor" and Jim Levine, my agent at Levine Greenberg Rostan Literary Agency. Jim was a nonprofit leader in a former life, and I could not have asked for a better advocate who really understands that nonprofits are messy. And, of course, I am so grateful to my friends and colleagues at Wiley for believing in me.

I am forever grateful to all my clients, members of the Leadership Lab, and the thousands of board and staff leaders who have entrusted their professional development to me and my team through the years. It is a privilege to serve you, and you are all my heroes. Full stop.

Lastly, we are who we are because of the families we create. I never thought I'd be so lucky to have one, and I try never to take it for granted. I keep a small paper note in my desk drawer. It reads simply: *You Have A Colorful Family*. Amen. Thanks to my three kids — Scout, Ben, and Kit for letting me catch you, raise you, annoy you, amuse you, and love you with all my heart.

And of course, to my legal wife of 7 years and spouse for almost 40, Eileen Opatut. In 1996, she casually suggested I leave the for-profit sector and apply for a nonprofit executive director job. We had three kids under 7 and had just bought a big house, the perfect time for a new low paying job. She saw, as she always does, what I often miss completely — I was a leader and an advocate ready for a cause. And so began a new chapter in my life. A life that turned from black and white to color the day we met, like Dorothy's arrival in Oz, complete with three munchkins.

"Of course you're tired. Changing the world is an exhausting business."

Introduction

I could have killed my development director.

And I don't mean it the way you think.

Julie arrived at a quarterly board meeting, but she didn't look quite right. It was hard not to notice that there was something protruding from her blouse.

A heart monitor.

She flew in from Los Angeles to Chicago, and I flew in from New York. We had not seen each other in a few weeks.

Maybe she mentioned something about doctors' appointments, but come on. I was leading a nonprofit trying to save a portion of the world. Who has time for the health and well-being of staff?

Clearly not me.

I'm sure you're wondering. Julie is fine. Today she is a clinical psychologist who no doubt helps clients contend with Type A oblivious bosses who drive their employees to heart problems.

Oh, also in case you are wondering, the board meeting was a big hit. Julie and I were impressive and on our game — as we usually were. I did get a few comments at the breaks like "Hey, how's Julie?" or "Julie looks like the job is taking a toll on her." "No worries," I said. And went on to get an A+ on our board meeting presentation.

But wow. *Who was I?* Why did I not tell Julie to turn on her heels and take the next flight home to Los Angeles?

I am not utterly clueless. I swear. I would never intentionally try to put Julie (or anyone else for that matter) in harm's way.

But nonprofits can cause a person to transform into someone they don't recognize.

> Nonprofits can cause a person to transform into someone they don't recognize. Why? Because nonprofits are messy.

Why?

Because nonprofits are messy.

It's inherent in the formula of the unique beast we call a 501(c)(3).

A + B + C + a big dose of intense passion = MESSY

A. A poorly paid and overworked group (staff) who. . .
B. Rely on the efforts of people who get paid nothing (volunteers) and are overseen by. . .
C. Another group of volunteers who get paid nothing and who are supposed to give and get lots of money (board).

All this is in the service of something that every single one of them cares passionately about. Wow. Now that is a recipe for messy. And that organization you care so deeply about can get messier still if it's not led and managed well.

I learned the messy lesson the hard way.

What did I know? Fifteen years in corporate America and then poof! I'm running a nonprofit (more on the "poof" part in a few).

I felt ever so well equipped with my financial skills, my management skills, and my understanding of how to manage a budget and to deliver results.

I had never met "messy" like this until the day I sat down at my desk at GLAAD, one of the largest gay rights nonprofit organizations. Or so I thought.

Actually, GLAAD was large by reputation, but "large" was not the first word that came to mind when I saw that we had $360 in the bank — that was not at all the word that came to mind.

It was bad. And I'll admit it here — I felt like a bit of a fraud, soon to be unmasked as having neither the grit nor the skills to dig us out.

There was one very bad day the first week on the job. I remember it well.

I was at my computer, writing a solicitation letter to a lapsed donor — trying *everything* to drive cash in the door. I was pleased with the letter. I sent it to print on the serviceable printer, reviewed it, found a typo.

And with that I burst into tears. It may have been my predicament, but I think it was singularly focused. I knew we could not afford to reorder letterhead.

Then there was this other day.

I was in Los Angeles meeting with donors (and praying they would pick up the tab) when my phone rang. It was my Deputy Director in New York. He calmly said that it might be time to look for office space he knew we couldn't afford.

There was an inch of snow on his desk when he arrived for work.

Very very messy.

I'm not sure I knew what to expect when I left corporate America for this job. Not sure I did a lot of thinking. My move from the corporate world to the nonprofit world was more of a "heart" move than a "head" move.

I was not unhappy in the corporate world. Hardly. I'd hit the corporate jackpot. In my first job out of college, I landed on the management team of MTV.

Yes, working at MTV in the early '80s was just as cool as you can imagine. I also learned a ton. I learned about the pace, intensity, and thrill of being a part of a startup (more on that later). I learned how to innovate when I wrote the business plan for the MTV Video Music Awards. And my Harvard MBA boss bought me an HP12c calculator (the calculator that allows people to *assume* you have an MBA) and taught me about budgets and balance sheets.

From MTV I moved to Showtime Networks. There I became a very good manager of people. I became a team player. I learned what it meant to be a good corporate citizen as one of the early gay poster children when Showtime began to walk the walk on diversity. We gave money to worthy causes, and I found myself in the early '90s advocating for corporate sponsorship dollars from Showtime to gay organizations.

While there we built a new business, a now-dinosaur that we called pay-per-view. And it was there that I learned about boxing.

Yes, boxing. Like that thing big sweaty guys do with gloves on in rings.

I learned that people pay a lot of money to watch boxing on TV. And that if you get really good seats at the MGM Grand Hotel in Las Vegas, the flying sweat . . . well, it flies.

The most important gift Showtime gave me was the recognition that I had a voice. I became another kind of poster child — essentially an employee advocate for better communication and transparency from the senior leadership. This work, which included hosting a full staff (800) town meeting, was transformative.

I found my voice as an *advocate* for the employees at Showtime.

I found my wheelhouse.

Now what? I had no idea. I just knew a change was in the offing.

There was no *Aha!* moment for me. There was just a conversation. My now wife but then spouse, partner, longtime companion, (enter other euphemisms here) came home from work and told me that the executive director job at GLAAD was open.

I casually remarked, "You know, somebody like me ought to have a job like that. We have three kids, I drive a minivan, and we really do have a white picket fence. That would shake up America's picture of a gay rights activist, huh?"

Eileen, who knows how to shake things up in just the right way, casually responded to my casual remark, "Well then somebody like you should apply."

I never in a million years thought they would hire me. I had no nonprofit experience, and I had never asked a soul for money before.

So they hired somebody like me. A lot like me. So me it was me. As my good friend Amy says, "Well slap my fanny!"

I guess I should have asked more questions before I took the job. That said, it probably would not have mattered. The Board didn't know either. The GLAAD *brand* may have been big but the problems were way bigger. I impressed myself with a tough salary negotiation that proved meaningless because all they could afford to pay me was $360. But just a one-time payment. That was the sum total in the GLAAD bank account.

How did I manage? Well, nobody handed me a book — that's for sure. I don't even remember anyone telling me that everything was going to be OK. It was *my* job to tell everyone *else* that everything was going to be OK.

There was so much I didn't know. Like *everything* it seemed.

I wish there *had* been a book — one with practical advice about how to untangle this mess, written by someone who had stood in my shoes, written by someone who would be my advocate, help me realize that I was not alone, and maybe even make me laugh that I was sobbing over a piece of stationery.

So I decided to write the book I wish someone had handed me.

Because my experience as a nonprofit leader and then as a board member and major donor and today as the principal in a nonprofit consulting practice has taught me a great deal that I believe will help you as a nonprofit leader become more effective at your job and remind you of the joy you can find in being underpaid and overworked to save even the smallest part of the world.

Maybe you are wondering how I untangled the knots at GLAAD without a book. ☺

We did indeed dig out. I left the organization eight years later with a $1.5 million cash reserve, an $8 million budget and a staff of over 40. But that's not what counts.

We made an impact. Long before marriage equality, GLAAD put same sex couples on the wedding pages of every major newspaper in America. Starting with *the New York Times*.

If you think there are too many gay characters on television, give it to me right between the eyes. Our work at GLAAD brought us there. If the name Matthew Shepard, the young gay man murdered in Wyoming in 1998, is familiar to you, it's because GLAAD shaped that into a national story, ensuring that any discussion about hate crimes be expanded to include sexual orientation, a lasting legacy for a young man from Laramie.

How did we do it?

The recipe is not unique to my leadership or to GLAAD. There are universal constants.

Between my own personal experience and working with hundreds of board and nonprofit staff leaders, these constants are critical to either digging out, stabilizing, or taking your organization to a place of even greater impact.

You need to rely on the strengths and power of those around you and see your varying stakeholder groups as a village, each with an important role to play in the success of your organization.

Then there is the mission. Your passion for it and your ability to articulate it, why it's important, and what impact it is having on the world. (I continue to be stunned by how infrequently leaders get this right.). You have to cultivate your storytelling skills, and in so doing, you will cultivate your fundraising prowess.

You have to recognize the skills and attributes of your staff and manage them with compassion and accountability (now *that* is a delicate balance). You have to be transparent and authentic with successes and with challenges. Recognize that you are slightly more like a tribe than a staff.

See the board as a resource and invest time and energy in building a committed and diverse group. Be an active member of the board recruitment committee from day one. And seek out strong co-chairs and consider them partners. Avoid the "yes" folks. Strong chairs will give you great advice and ask tough questions. Try not to get defensive, and this pushback will make you a more effective leader.

Once your organization stops teetering (see the preceding steps), budget money annually to build a reserve. Once you are able to pull your nose out of the cash flow worksheet, you can actually think ahead. So get to it. Where are the gaps? Are there constituents you are not serving that no other organization can serve as well as you? These conversations can lead to smart and bold strategies and fundable plans for the future.

This is how to dig out, how to stabilize, how to thrive. This is the core of my advice to many of my clients, to the thousands who visit my blog weekly, and to the dozens who write weekly with questions. And this captures the spirit of the advice I hope will be valuable to you.

But the single most important attribute of a nonprofit leader (board member or staff leader) — the attribute that is most critical in helping you to untangle knots, and the one that can move your organization from good to great — is joy.

In my own experience as a staff leader and a board leader along with work with all my clients I have had through the years, it is this attribute that creates standout leaders. They get it. It is a joy to be paid to advocate, feed the hungry, to change laws, to raise money, to create a strong infrastructure — all in the service of others.

I believe deeply in the power of the nonprofit sector to change the world in ways large and small. If you have raised your hand to say "I want to help; I want to work here; I want to volunteer; I want to raise money for you," you are, in my book, *nobility*.

Your work says something important about your character, your spirit, your commitment to a fair and just world, your integrity, your courage, your grit, and your perseverance.

Not everyone makes this choice. Far too many people with time, connections, and capacity sit on the sidelines.

You made a different choice.

Your feet are firmly planted on the high road. And know that you are admired.

By many. Including me.

I speak from experience. Traveling on the high road isn't easy and it's messy, but if you love your organization, it's worth every minute.

Nonprofits are messy. Not enough money. Too many cooks. An overdose of passion.

Leading nonprofits isn't easy.

I'm here to help. I'm offering this book to share some of the most valuable lessons I've learned over my career.

I'm also providing a free collection of valuable templates, checklists and other downloadable resources at JoanGarry.com/resources.

"You want to use X-ray vision to spy on an Executive Session meeting? No, I don't think that's a great idea."

Chapter 1 The Superpowers of Nonprofit Leadership

Dear Joan:

I've been with my organization for nearly 8 years, most recently in a development role. My predecessor has been the voice and face of the organization for nearly 25 years and has just retired. The board has offered me the ED position.

This would be alien territory for me. I've been the relationship guy, and I keep the trains running on time.

And the truth is, I'm not exactly sure what I would be getting into. I want to give this a go but I think I need help and would like to retain you as a coach.

My goal is simple: I want to learn to behave like an executive director.

Signed,
ED "E.T."

"To behave like an executive director." A very good goal for an executive director, I might add.

E.T. became a client, and we teased out exactly what he meant by this.

To be a leader and not a department head. To worry about the whole organization and every stakeholder. To stare at cash flow and wonder about payroll. To take responsibility for partnering with the board so that its members can fulfill their obligations. To stand up at a gala and give an inspiring and motivational speech. To feel an overwhelming sense of responsibility for the communities you serve.

It's a hard role to be in and a hard role to cast for. I am currently working with a board that cannot agree on the role the executive director should play (and they are already interviewing candidates!). (Can *you* say "cart before the horse?")

Who should a board be looking for? What matters? In small organizations, the staff leader really *does* do it all. A person who can inspire a group with her words *and* read a balance sheet? What skills and attributes matter? Do you have them? How do you cultivate them?

And the decision is so important. In my experience, leadership transitions are *the* most destabilizing forces in a nonprofit organization. Try raising money when you are between executive directors. Nuff said.

What's interesting is that all these same issues and questions apply to board chairs as well. What should an organization be looking for in a board chair? (Note: the correct answer is *not* "pray that someone raises her hand and pick her.") How might the skills and attributes of that person complement those of the staff leader? What skills and attributes matter? How do you cultivate them?

A QUIZ

Before I give you the answer to these questions, let's try a little quiz. Are you currently a nonprofit ED, overwhelmed by the idea that you need to be all things to all people? A board chair enthusiastic about leading the board to support the staff? Or someone who aspires to change the world and make the for-profit to nonprofit leap?

The quiz should put things into perspective and begin to reveal the superpowers you need to be an effective leader within a nonprofit.

So riddle me this, Batmen and Batwomen: It's time to pick your next board chair or executive director; here are the finalists! (I just grabbed a few superhero prototypes — lots of others exist out there.)

- Black Panther
- Spider-Man
- Elastigirl
- Kermit the Frog

Let's dissect this, shall we? (Oh, apologies to Kermit — not a good word for frogs.)

Each of these four have amazing strengths. Perhaps at first blush, you figure any of them could be a five-star nonprofit leader.

Black Panther?

This guy has some serious things going for him:

- Sometimes organizations just want someone to fly in and save the day.

- He's dripping with integrity and tells the truth.
- He is very smart.
- Would you say no to him if he asked you for a donation?
- His high-tech, energy-absorbing suit (designed by his STEM-strong sister) is fabulous — not to mention the stylish claw necklace!

Spider-Man?

Lots of appeal here too. He's human, powerful, and nerdy. He's vulnerable but strong. Some comic book fanatics say he is the single greatest superhero of them all.

- He has real humanity — vulnerabilities, guilt, and flaws.
- He's driven. Peter Parker, the man behind Spider-Man, helps people because he understands the price of not doing it — he could have prevented his uncle's death.
- He grows into his power. The responsibility of leadership is not something he asks for, but he accepts it and uses that responsibility to the best of his ability.

Elastigirl?

When I think about Helen Parr (a.k.a. "Mrs. Incredible" and "Elastigirl" and "mom"), I am reminded that not everything is black-and-white and that being flexible is absolutely key to success in any setting. Is Elastigirl your choice?

- She's well rounded.
- Very optimistic — would lead with an optimism that her organization could change the world.
- She's someone you want to be around — kind, warm-hearted, and generous.
- She has real humanity — vulnerabilities, guilt, flaws.

Kermit?

Another guy with some solid skills and attributes for nonprofit leadership:

- A team builder, he can bring a diverse group together. Anyone who can get Gonzo, Fozzie, and Miss Piggy working toward a common goal has a real superpower.
- Kermit is an optimist but not a Pollyanna. He can get down sometimes too, but in the end, he has a vision and rallies the Muppets around it.
- He cares deeply about doing the right thing.
- Kermit is your go-to guy in a crisis.
- Strong planning skills.
- His ego is just the right size — he can and does admit mistakes.

Time to put the four of them to the test. Here's the kind of situation each of them may encounter. Then you get to make your choice.

You need a new board chair. The previous leader didn't want the job — might have been in the restroom during elections. Committees are dormant. The board does a decent job selling tickets to your big gala, but half of them don't want to pay for a ticket themselves. The founder of the organization is a big personality, and when she stepped down two years ago, she offered to join the board; and your previous board chair couldn't say no. She isn't letting go of the job. Your ED is a good performer, but the founder is driving her mad. You are worried she may be recruited away.

Who is the right person for the job?

Black Panther is the command/control nonprofit leader. The world is quite black-and-white for him. He would see board members as "good guys" or "bad guys"; we know it's not that simple. Nonprofit leadership demands both an understanding of and an *appreciation* for *nuance* and the land of the *gray*. We know this type. A good leader to dig you out fast but not the marathon guy.

Spider-Man is a more empathetic, three-dimensional leader. His downfall is the challenge of many leaders — *insecurity*.

Elastigirl? What a nice woman. Who wouldn't want to sit and hear about an organization from somebody like Helen Parr? She is a relationship builder of the highest order. But her fatal leadership flaw? She is a pleaser — a bit too flexible. Now, most nonprofit leaders have some pleaser stuff going on. But if it drives you, you are done for. You have various stakeholders, and pleasing everyone usually means pleasing no one. Your job isn't about pleasing; it's about serving your mission.

OK, so I've given the answer away.

My vote goes to Kermit hands down.

First off, Kermit would have figured out some way to give the founder a big role with no real power—look how he manages Piggy. He would rally the troops without shaming them. He would find the key strength in each board member and bring out the best in each of them. He would not be overly bossy with the ED — he'd offer his support and be more like a coach. And he would help staff and board keep their eyes on the prize, never losing sight of the organization's mission and vision.

Kermit may not thrive in a hierarchical work environment, but he'd be a rock star ED or board chair.

Kermit is not perfect, and he knows it. This trait is key to effective leadership. It makes him a good delegator! He is all about team, and he understands the value each team member brings to the work. He believes in diversity. He likes to work to reach consensus but never loses sight of the end game — he stays true to the cause. He is fair and listens, and he can manage high-maintenance personalities without sacrificing the work. I also think he can disagree, and his team ultimately listens and respects his decisions (decisions they feel were made with their input).

Kermit understands what it takes to be a great leader in the nonprofit sector:

- Understanding that power comes from all around you.
- Recognizing that developing core leadership *attributes* is as important as skills building.

YOU'RE NOT ON TOP OF ANYTHING

In 1997, as the Executive Director of the Gay & Lesbian Alliance Against Discrimination (GLAAD), I was approached by the Coors Brewing Company. Coors was interested in making a $50,000 corporate sponsorship donation to GLAAD. As our organization was still on a financial respirator, I was interested. Very interested.

But I knew the history of Coors and the gay community — the Coors family had deep ties to the Heritage Foundation, a significant funder of organizations leading the opposition to LGBTQ equality. As a result there had been a longstanding boycott in the gay community: drink any beer you like but not Coors.

A discussion with Coors illustrated to me that the company was better on gay issues inside its organization (domestic partner benefits and other nondiscrimination policies) than many other companies who sponsored GLAAD.

Should I accept the sponsorship money and in so doing help rebuild the Coors brand in the gay community? The decision was mine to make.

Or was it?

In Jim Collins's monograph, *Good to Great and the Social Sectors: Why Business Thinking Is Not the Answer*, he makes the case that power and decision-making in the nonprofit sector are different from (and messier than) what they are in the private sector.

FIGURE 1.1 The standard org chart.

To be a great leader, you must erase your preconceived notions of what it means to be in charge, starting with a standard org chart like the one shown in Figure 1.1.

You probably have a piece of paper that shows this kind of hierarchy. Time to recycle.

Is it factually accurate? Yup. Is it how you should look at/ exert your power as a nonprofit leader? Absolutely not.

So now look at the chart shown in Figure 1.2.

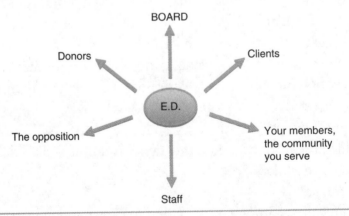

FIGURE 1.2 Deriving power from everyone around you.

In the org chart shown in Figure 1.1, the Coors decision is easy. I make a statement about the changes at Coors, accept the donation, make payroll, and let the chips fall where they may.

In the nonprofit sector a leader is beholden to vast and diverse stakeholders. I was hired to run GLAAD in the service of moving the needle forward on equal rights for the community I served. The bottom line matters, of course, but only to ensure that you have sufficient resources to work in the service of your mission.

In the org chart shown in Figure 1.2, the executive director derives power from all around her. This is why former Girl Scout ED Frances Hesselbein once told a reporter that she saw herself in the center and that she was "not on top of anything."

So what did this mean for the Coors decision? The voices of the stakeholder groups around me were critical. I needed to be well-informed, I needed strong input from different groups, and I needed a thought partner in my board chair to kick around the pros and cons. I knew the decision was ultimately mine, but I never really thought of it that way. We were all in this together.

My development director (the one I'd nearly killed — see this book's Introduction) was outraged and feared we would lose more money than we earned. We did our due diligence and determined that would not be the case. The staff was mixed — some worried I would be eaten alive by the press (given my own corporate background); others thought it was unfair to Coors when in fact by corporate standards, they were leaders.

This kind of power demands that you meet with the leaders of the Coors Boycott Committee — not to empower them, but to ensure their voices are heard — we even invited them to a board meeting.

And this kind of power demands that you see the decision from all sides. We secured a meeting with the most senior people at Coors and garnered commitments from them to do more than just donate money.

And this kind of power demanded that I put myself at a national LGBTQ conference in which several hundred community members could share their distaste with the thought that GLAAD may make this choice. In this setting, you can be sure that I heard them — many of them were yelling at me.

In the end, Coors became a corporate sponsor of GLAAD. Not everyone agreed, but everyone had a voice. All stakeholder groups were heard, and our entire process and strategy was smarter and more effective than any decision I had made on my own. This is what Jim Collins means when he talks about power in the nonprofit sector being *diffuse*. At its best, it creates a staff that feels valued and heard, a supportive board comfortable in challenging, and a membership that sees a process rich with integrity.

Nonprofit decision-making at its best.

*   *   *

So you can see how this can get messy, right — how quickly a staff can become disgruntled? So can your clients. You want them to be engaged in the work, to secure their opinions about decisions and policies, but must you walk a fine line. If you don't, you wind up with angry stakeholders, and you wind up fighting to make decisions that are in the best interest of the entire organization.

How about a board chair that has already made up their mind about the ED annual review process and doesn't ask for input? How valuable does the full board feel? I'm going to go with "not very." Or, how about an ED who has already made a big decision and asks the senior staff to weigh in? That ED better pray the senior staff comes up with the same decision. Then there is the ED who listens to input and finds themself more indecisive than when they first asked.

Each of these scenarios makes things messier.

WHAT DO I *DO* WITH ALL THIS?

Not everyone is Kermit. And no one fits neatly into one of the four superhero profiles. You might identify with someone outside the list. (I hope there are no Darth Vaders among you.)

The key is to recognize attributes that don't serve you well and make adjustments. So, for me, I think I am a "BP/K" — a Black Panther/Kermit combo. (Yes, I am now making fun of every personality profile test to which you've ever been subjected at work or during a retreat.)

I am a fixer. I know this about myself. I love to save the day — that's why I love my work — I have serious Black Panther tendencies. They serve me well in my business but, as a nonprofit leader, not so much. I like to think I have some Kermit going on as well. Like Kermit, I like to think of myself as an orchestra conductor, bringing out the best in my tribe.

So what if you aren't Kermit?

Black Panther Tendencies

Thomas arrived as the new ED of a pretty small organization — budget size a few hundred thousand. Thomas wears a cape and not just on Halloween. He arrived at his organization to fix it, to save the day. The organization had been in disarray for some time.

Thomas started weekly staff meetings and no one came. Well, some did but most didn't. They were too busy. Thomas was angry and he threatened consequences. The following week, attendance was better, still not great. Attitudes were even worse.

What was he missing?

Thomas made several incorrect assumptions:

- **If you tell people what to do, they will just do it.** Now that worked like a charm for me in Catholic grammar school in the 1960s, but in a nonprofit, your staff needs to feel some sense of ownership of the decisions made. This is what they deserve in lieu of that year-end bonus that is coming like, NEVER.

> Your staff needs to feel some sense of ownership of the decisions made.

- **He assumed they understood** — in this case, he assumed they understood the value of a staff meeting. That's not how the previous leader managed (or didn't).

So here are the changes I suggested that he make:

- **Have a meeting about the meeting.** Send an email around; tell folks that this meeting is to talk about how a staff meeting might be valuable to the entire group and to each staffer. Let them figure out the need themselves. And yes, everyone showed up; they built a standing agenda that was more than just reporting out, and staff meetings are now weekly and well attended.
- **Ask more questions.** Cape-wearers are fixers and they know the answers. Maybe they are arrogant or maybe just very self-assured. Thomas liked to just tell staff the answers; he directed them closely because he was clear about what needed to be done. I encouraged Thomas to ask staff members what *they* would do. Have a conversation about strategy. Guide *gently* if they are off base, and more importantly, *listen carefully*. You know, it is possible that *they are right* and you are not (I know — hard to believe).

- **Dip your toe into the world of the "gray."** To Black Panther, things are black-and-white. There are good guys and bad guys. Things need to happen a *certain* way. You need to *try* to appreciate the gray. This might mean you have to own the fact that you are not as open-minded as you need to be. Are you a board chair ready to write off a board member who does nothing? Try having a coffee with said board member. Ask her what success looks like for her, what she needs from the chair to be successful. Don't vote her off the island too quickly. Move from black to gray.

Spider-Man Tendencies

Unlike T'Challa (Black Panther) who is clearly a respected leader of his people, Peter Parker is a three-dimensional teenager — a nerd, an introvert, and an outsider — a sensitive soul who has experienced tragedy and loss. Spidey, on the other hand, owns his brilliance and is all about victory, but both Peter and Spidey share two key things — (a) the importance of the intersection of knowledge and power and (b) a core value to lead a responsible life.

Kim began her job as a board chair deeply insecure about her ability to do a good job (get in line, Kim). She was now in charge of a sizable board filled with some very high-powered folks. If you spent an hour with this group and someone asked you who the chair was, she would not be your obvious choice. She was not a great public speaker and was intimidated by the resumes of those folks around the table, none of whom, by the way, were willing to step into the leadership role. But Kim knew the organization needed someone dedicated — someone who loved the organization — and really wanted the staff leader to succeed.

Kim's challenge was not to be overrun by the bombastic folks in the room — to establish leadership. But Kim doesn't wear a cape.

In our coaching sessions, Kim and I spoke about where her power comes from. I learned that she was deeply empathetic and had a profound and personal connection to the mission. I also learned that she was smart as hell.

The following shifts helped Kim quite a bit:

- **Be the most knowledgeable person in the room.** I'm not talking about smarts; I'm talking about the professional aspects of the role of board chair. I begged her to buy *Robert's Rules of Order*. It is amazing how much respect a board chair can garner when managing a meeting professionally. I also encouraged her to spend time really understanding the nonprofit sector and the complexities and context of the issue the organization was up against.
- **Play to Your Strengths.** Remember Kim's empathy, remember her introvert tendencies? We devised a regular email from the board chair. It opened with a story about the work or something Kim had learned about the broader context of the work, reminding board members why they serve. Then, she was able to call board members to action. She had put the requests into an emotional and intellectual context.

Elastigirl Tendencies

Pleasers cause themselves heaps of trouble. Stretching yourself thin to make everyone happy inevitably backfires in nearly every situation — from a kindergarten class to a boardroom to a staff meeting.

The most important lesson I have learned about Elastigirl leaders is that if you can help them draw a picture of what happens as a result of pleasing, it makes them really unhappy. Elastigirls respond in the moment and do not anticipate well. It's kind of like an automatic camera — "point and shoot." Trouble to the left? Let me fix it. Conflicting trouble to the right? I'll make you happy, too. But they can't look far enough down the road to see the implications.

Tina is an ED of a direct service organization that has a very strong client advocacy group. There had long been a push to put a member of that group on the board. Attempting to please the Client Advocacy Task Force, Tina, as ED, brought the group into a board meeting to talk about it so the group could make the pitch. Now it was time for Tina to please the board. They loved the idea. Meanwhile Ben, Director of Programs, saw the challenge a mile away. He could see that electing the chair of the task force to the board could give that task force undue power. He saw that it would be difficult for this person to be anything other than a representative of the task force rather than someone who could view the organization from 35,000 feet, as an effective board member must.

The outcome was not pleasing. The new board member came to advocate for clients. In and of itself, this was OK, but an idea he brought to the table was not in the best interest of the organization, and the board voted it down. He quit the board and undermined the credibility and reputation of Tina with anyone who would listen, including fellow board members. Tina, displeased with how she, as ED, was being treated, was recruited away. A messy leadership transition ensued (more on that in Chapter 10).

Some advice for the pleasers out there:

- **Tell your board chair (partner) that you have a bit of a blind spot.** Gasp! Am I really suggesting that you tell your board chair that you are imperfect? Yup! You are partners, remember? Ask your board chair to help you think through the implications of decisions because you need help exercising your anticipation muscle.
- **Remember that a pleaser flexes too quickly and consciously slow down.** The word *yes* can come out of your mouth *so*

fast. Please count to 10 (or 20 or more) before saying anything. Even better, practice these words *"Let me go back to
my team and talk about this. They will have an important
perspective on this issue."*

- **Keep Your Eye on the Mission at All Times.** If you do, you
will make better decisions and you will say "no" when you
need to. You will be more effective in the long run, and that
will be pleasing for everyone who cares about your mission.

- **Bonus:** *What Not to Do* — **Do Not Find a Bad Cop!** I have
seen this too many times to count. A Vice Chair who leans
into the board about their fundraising commitment. A Deputy
Director who institutes tough new HR policies while the ED
is out of town. This is unfair to the "bad cop" and a clear sign
of an ineffective leader. If you can't put on your big kid pants
and make tough decisions, please reevaluate your line of work.

WHAT WAS THIS QUIZ REALLY ABOUT?

Think about what we have been talking about here. Have I
mentioned anything about specific fundraising prowess, how
often your board should meet, how effectively your organization measures success, or what role the audit committee should
play in the development of the annual budget?

Nope. Those are skills. I wasn't talking about skills. I was
talking about attributes. Because this is my pet peeve. Far too
often, leaders are selected based on skills. *"Well, David was the
chair of the board of his alma mater — so he knows what the
job is all about."* Does he? Does he have the right attributes to
run a meeting and attempt to build consensus or the discipline
not to roll his eyes when a fellow board member says something awfully stupid?

Attributes matter as much, if not more than skills. Attributes.
Or perhaps given the roll we are on in this chapter, we should
dub them *superpowers*.

THE FIVE KEY SUPERPOWERS

Dear Joan,

I chair the ED search committee for our organization, and we are in the final rounds with two very different candidates. One is well known in our community and would bring gravitas to our organization. He is known to be a great fundraiser; finance and management skills are not his forte and his background in media (our sandbox) slim. The other candidate is from corporate America, basically unknown in our sector, strong in our sandbox, known for strong management and zero fundraising experience.

Oh, and did I mention that we may not hit payroll next week? And that we owe a quarter of a million dollars to vendors?

Who should we hire . . . Help!

Signed,

Conflicted in the Boardroom

Trust me. Any search committee could have written this. And it's not just a board dilemma.

It's universal to anyone inside or outside of an organization considering a move into leadership. Thinking about throwing your hat in the ring for a promotion at your school — you've been a teacher but never a fundraiser? Are you the COO who feels ready for the leadership gig? Are you a current board chair with no fundraising experience? Could you be an ED that won't admit to a soul that the balance sheet is total gibberish to you?

And it's a dilemma for current leaders, working to be the nonprofit leaders their organizations deserve.

A number of years ago, a statewide human rights organization had a similar dilemma. Hire the candidate with deep roots in the issue — well known in the community, strong media skills, and a fundraising track record.

The other finalist — no chops in the sector, not a fundraiser, came from the labor movement. You know, the movement where you need to get lots of people on the same page and then fight for what you believe in? A movement in which your reps have to trust you, allow you to lead — one in which relationship building is key?

They picked the labor candidate. This candidate grabbed the reins and the organization grew in scope and impact in very short order.

How did this hire get made?

> Attributes may in fact be the true superpowers of leadership.

Someone on that search committee encouraged the group to consider the "chopless" candidate through a different lens.

Through the lens of key leadership *attributes*. And in my opinion, attributes may in fact be the true superpowers of leadership. (I know it might be confusing with all these numbers floating around, four superheroes, five superpowers, but math never was my strong suit.)

And yes, I have a list.

- **Conviction:** As each of you knows, nonprofit leadership is no walk in the park. Hey, why should it be? You are moving mountains. But without conviction in the real promise of the organization, no one will follow your lead. When I coach clients who have been leaders for a long period of time, I often ask *"Are you as passionate about the mission of this organization as you were when you arrived?"* When I hear a pause of any sort, we talk about it. A lot.
- **Authenticity:** Real leadership demands it. So too does fundraising. Because it is the foundational attribute of trust.

Ever been to a fundraiser when the head of the school, or board chair is talking to you but not looking at you and not listening to you? Rather, she is, but to spot the next donor on her list — you know, the one who gives more than you do. Icky right? Because there is nothing genuine about your interaction. I'm guessing the leader didn't ask you any questions about you and how you were doing.

Not authentic.

What does authenticity look like?

Working a room? Come on. I like to say that everyone is really interesting for at least 3–5 minutes. So, engage authentically, learn something, and maybe teach something.

Authenticity looks like admitting failure. Everyone makes mistakes, but a person who lives in the world authentically shares her mistakes, or values the role mistakes can make in becoming a more effective and productive organization.

- **Learn to Tell a Good Story:** I drive staff and board clients mad talking about this. A great leader is a great storyteller. In the next chapter, I talk about this at great length, but it is absolutely critical and a key component of my coaching work with clients around commencement addresses and gala remarks. What kind of story? The kind of story that makes folks say "Tell me more." or "Let me get out my checkbook." or "Now THAT is a story I should write about!" or "Will you come talk to my congressperson?"

Have Fun; Be Funny: One of the reasons I started my blog (https://blog.joangarry.com) was that nearly every nonprofit resource was so damned serious. I get it. Saving the world is serious business. But that kind of intensity is unsustainable. You have to have a release valve. I find that behaving like an eight-year-old is often a very good strategy.

FIGURE 1.3   Aasun's other board.

So, we were in the middle of a board meeting and a quite serious discussion about the need for greater investment in technology. Our IT Director, Aasun Eble, who was indeed quite able, was giving a serious and dry presentation. Seemingly out of nowhere, the following slide appeared.

Aasun decided we should all meet his three poodles. The room became weak with laughter, but that is not the end of the story.

From that day forward, you did not give a board presentation at a GLAAD board meeting without a picture of your pets appearing somewhere on a slide. This gimmick brought my senior staff to life for our board in a way that resonated for them. It was no longer the Director of IT or the CFO. It was Kerry, the dad to two adorable kittens, Marilyn and Monroe. And it was unexpected and funny. It brought us together in a different sort of way.

- **Be Bold:** I believe that with authenticity and conviction comes a sense of fearlessness. Now I'm not suggesting that you suggest a bold new strategy or initiative in your first week (that would be stupid, not bold). I'm suggesting that your board, your staff, and your constituents or clients deserve a leader who will make the tough calls, come up with a new idea, and try it. I'm not talking about arrogance here, nor am I talking about a leader who behaves like a lone cowboy. But remember: didn't you step into a leadership role to *change* the status quo?
- **Be Joyful:** Related to but different from humor. This should not be that hard to feel or to project.

I have a beef with Executive Directors who don't see their work as a privilege. To get paid to do something that matters? To make a living making some part of the world a better place? I'm not naive; the work can be hard, painful, and sometimes feel like too steep a climb. But make no mistake. It's a joy and a privilege. The most effective nonprofit leaders see it this way, and their attitudes are palpable.

Did you just read the list and remember wistfully that Dino's Pizzeria is looking for drivers?

Don't give up on me so easily.

Remember:

- Nobody has all these attributes from the start.
- These attributes can be developed, and you can present them in your own way.
- These attributes do not *replace* skills; I am just arguing that attributes are often ignored as you consider your own leadership bag of tricks. Working on cultivating these attributes can have as much if not more of a payoff than a class on how to read a balance sheet or a certificate in nonprofit fundraising.

THE *REAL* POWER OF LEADERSHIP

I saved the most important lesson for last. Understanding how power works as a nonprofit leader is critical. Realizing that developing your core attributes in addition to skills can take your leadership game from good to great.

But never forget where the real power comes from.

It comes from the two to three sentences that you and your board slaved over and nearly wordsmithed to a pulp: Your mission. What is it you do, and *what is it in the service of?*

Your mission statement is your North Star. The big thing that matters most. Your role as a leader is to keep the organization focused on your mission, even when you are deciding about the centerpieces for the gala.

Great nonprofit leaders have certain skills. Work on honing core attributes and develop not only a real understanding of the nature of nonprofit power but an appreciation for it as well — all in the service of your mission — your North Star.

Nonprofit leadership is neither simple nor easy. It's not easy being green. Like I said, you are in the mountain moving business — it couldn't possibly be easy. But with your mission as your beacon, it is worth every single minute.

"Your nonprofit dynamically disseminates an expanded array of potentialities to continually initiate distinctive infrastructures? I don't get it."

Chapter 2 You've Got to Get Me at Hello

Some organizations are easier to explain to folks than others. An organization that helps clients directly would seem to be the easiest to explain; advocacy and lobbying often feel more complex and abstract. School officials can struggle to identify messages that clearly differentiate their school from other choices parents have for their kids.

But get this: even the easy ones don't always get it right.

Cities and towns all across the US have organizations that deliver meals to folks who can't, for one reason or another, get out of the house. Meals on Wheels is the most common name you hear. These organizations offer support to those who are homebound and innumerable opportunities for people to be at their very best — to be plain old good neighbors. And this is what I love about nonprofits.

When I get calls to help organizations raise money, the most common request is this: "Can you teach my board members to ask for money?" I politely tell these folks that I don't do that as part of my work.

Instead, I tell them that I teach board members how to tell stories. They are baffled until I tell them that a check is the organic end result of a great story told by an organization's ambassador.

> A check is the organic end result of a great story told by an organization's ambassador.

When I work with organizations, I begin by describing a cocktail party — no cocktails and the only guest is me. It's a cocktail party for your organization, and the premise is that I know precious little. Like oh-so-many people who attend such events, I show up because of the view of Central Park from the terrace of the fabulous apartment or the open bar or both.

I say to each person, one by one: "Tell me about your organization."

The only direction they are given? Be succinct. Make me care. Make it stick.

Here's how it played out with the staff of a meal delivery organization.

"We deliver hundreds of meals each week."

Good. Data is good, because size *does* matter. But data alone does not stick with me. And this is the single most common statement food delivery nonprofits make, certain that the impressive number of meals served is the key success metric that will inspire me to write a check.

"We pride ourselves on never turning anyone away."

OK, that's impressive. But if you don't have to turn anyone away, tell me again why you need my money.

"Our food is delicious. And we can customize meals for specific kinds of illnesses."

OK, we're getting warmer. We're not just getting food out the door — we care about our clients enough to be sure the food is delicious. More importantly, this organization sees that clients are different and have unique needs. That feels special to me, and I like this a lot.

No one story was wrong. Every staff member spoke passionately about the work. I was inspired, and it was clear that this organization was lucky to have each and every one of them.

I'll be honest: I am not an easy grader. I wanted more. I wanted to touch and feel the work. And I was looking for more context.

Missing elements of the recipe?

- *Emotion.*

    What emotion do clients experience? Or the folks in the kitchen or on the trucks? In 2–3 minutes, can you take me on a tour?

    > "Our organization <u>feeds</u> people, creates a community of caring people who feed and are fed by each other. We bring thousands of families hope each week. We deliver companionship and our delicious food is a gift."

- *Real People.*

    > "For 20 years, Bob has been driving one of our trucks — he has the same route and talks about his families like — well, like family. He returns to the office and stops in the kitchen to tell the crew that Mary (give her a disease and an age) loved the cranberry sauce — she said it tasted like the kind her mom made."

- **Add dose of *Need* and *Urgency*.** (here's where you can add in size and data)

  > "When we started our work, we delivered X meals a year. This coming year, we are budgeted to increase that to Y meals. Government funding has decreased in the last X years, increasing our urgent need for private dollars."

- **Then add *YOU*.** (seal the deal with personal experience)

  > "Today, I'm a staff member, but I started as a kitchen volunteer. The soup I helped prepare was so much more than soup. It's hope, compassion — I know we are really feeding people. I saw it first hand when I rode the truck to make deliveries once a month. We had this one client —Madeline— a feisty woman in her early seventies fighting cancer. She was one tough bird. But when we arrived, she melted. Her whole face lit up. And she told us the soup was almost as good as her own ☺."

- **Stir and *voilà!***

  You have me at hello. I am drawn in. I want to know more. I may be ready to actually *do!*

*　*　*

Even for an organization whose mission is crystal clear and whose impact is quantifiable, it can be tough to tell a good story.

> Anytime someone utters the magic words — "Tell me about your organization" — you're being handed a big, fat opportunity.

I know this in my heart, though: Anytime someone utters the magic words — "Tell me about your organization" — you're being handed a big, fat opportunity.

And if I have anything to say about it, you won't miss out on that opportunity.

TELL ME ABOUT YOUR ORGANIZATION

I just mentioned that the request in this section heading is a big, fat opportunity. Allow me to explain. Whether you're staff, board, faculty, administration, or volunteer, you're a singularly credible messenger and one of the most powerful ambassadors in your organization.

Through your telling, you can bring volunteers, other board members, elected officials, parents, clients, donors, and press to the organization you care about.

So you have to get this right.

Talking about your organization in a way that's compelling, engaging, and memorable is, in my mind, the most important skill you can develop.

Maybe you're thinking, "I don't often have time to tell a whole story." Or, more importantly, "I was asked the question but only have a minute. We're standing in a lobby."

Different settings demand different tellings.

IN THE LOBBY — THE MISSION STATEMENT

Let me be crystal clear. A mission statement is not a story. Neither is it an elevator pitch. A mission statement is a written declaration of purpose. It should state clearly whom you serve, what you do, and why you do it.

> A mission statement is not a story. Neither is it an elevator pitch. A mission statement is a written declaration of purpose. It should state clearly whom you serve, what you do, and why you do it.

A mission statement rarely changes. (If the need for a new one exists, it is as a result of some kind of significant strategic shift. More on that topic in Chapter 5.)

The organization named *charity: water,* for example, will likely always exist to bring "clean and safe drinking water to people in developing countries."

That's to the point, eh? The mission statement articulates the problem and offers hope with charity: water on the job.

Here's part of NPR's mission statement:

The mission of NPR, in partnership with its member stations, is to create a more informed public, one challenged and invigorated by a deeper understanding and appreciation of events, ideas, and culture within the United States and across the globe.

What I like about this one is that it's aspirational. I desperately want the public to be well informed, and I only have to hit the Scan button on the car radio or graze the TV news to know that NPR represents hope. I know what this organization stands for. I know that it will lead me deeper into the news and help me better understand and appreciate the world around me.

Sadly, mission statements often don't rise to the occasion.

That last sentence was oh-so-kind. Many mission statements are simply big, hot messes.

They're developed by a group of type A folks (board and senior staff) who become frighteningly tied to individual words and phrases. Words like *facilitate* (weak), *integrate* (unclear), and *change-agent* (let me guess — you represent people who make change).

It can become ugly. And the outcome, uglier still.

As a result, precious few of the 1.5 million nonprofits in the US have five-star mission statements. Typically, your best hope is that they're clinical and soulless; at worst, they're completely incomprehensible.

So, in that context, how does a mission statement fare in the telling?

Well, first things first. Mission statements often come across sounding a lot like the Girl Scouts' or Boy Scouts' pledge recited with three fingers in the air and hand over heart: memorized, regurgitated, and often lacking meaning.

By the way, try opening any conversation with a possible stakeholder with the words "Our mission is. . . ." and watch the stakeholder's eyes roll into the back of their head — then watch your opportunity fly away.

A clear mission statement is absolutely critical to every single stakeholder group and is one of the key ingredients in a healthy nonprofit.

But a story it is not.

And that's OK. You've only entered the lobby.

A mission statement is OK to present in the lobby. But if your nonprofit is one of the unlucky ones that has a long, incomprehensible mission statement, offer the one you'd write if you were solely in charge.

IN THE ELEVATOR — THE PITCH

OK, now you're in the elevator and the same request is made. You have a greater opportunity — though it's not the kind that presents itself when you're sitting next to someone at a dinner party. It's somewhere in between.

In this situation, a mission statement won't do, especially if you have one of those really bad ones.

Note that you aren't in the full-on solicitation business here. You don't have enough time. So what is the goal? To inform and to *invite*:

> Get out the facts quickly — short and to the point — and then say something compelling that makes them want to know more — that invites them into a conversation.

You have 30 seconds — maybe 60, if you're lucky.
Here are a few pointers:

- **No mission statement.** Do not attempt to impress your listener with a recitation of your mission statement. That is not impressive. It is a bad move or a missed opportunity.
- **Pretend that your audience is a 10-year-old kid.** One time, I asked an executive director to tell me about her organization. We were at a cocktail party (not in an elevator). *Twenty minutes later,* she finally wrapped up.

  I couldn't help myself — I asked her this question next: "Do you think you might answer that question again and, this time, pretend I am 10-years-old?"

  Her response the second time was shorter. She chopped out all the jargon and spoke simply and clearly. And something about my being 10 led her to speak to *me,* to think about *me* and what would engage me. It became much less about her organization and her and much more about me.
- **End with an authentic invitation.** You could put it in the form of a simple question (such as "Would you like to know more?") or ask to exchange business cards or email addresses and then follow up.

Are you thinking "one minute and I'm also supposed to get an email address?" Well, you sure ain't if you don't ask.

STEP OFF THE ELEVATOR AND WORK THE ROOM

As with the fundraising training I describe in Chapter 6, this is the big, fat opportunity. Unconstrained by that short elevator ride or the quick chat in the lobby, you are now free to chat for a few minutes with individuals.

Let's assume you aren't attending a fundraiser for your organization — instead, you're at a cocktail party or a barbeque. You know some folks and not others.

First things first: Put on your organizational glasses. Look at the attendees through the lens of your role with your nonprofit.

Now, I don't mean this in an icky way. I'm not suggesting, for example, that you make a beeline for your neighbor who just landed a lucrative new job. I'm talking about *connections,* not *capacity* (a topic I talk about in Chapter 6).

Though most people are not engaged as board members or donors or volunteers, they very much admire people who are. When you're chatting someone up, remember that the person will find your involvement inspiring.

If you tell a good story.

And if you tell a great story, it may move that person from inspired to motivated. *That* is a home run.

TWO UNIVERSAL CHALLENGES

There are two universal challenges faced by board, staff, and volunteer ambassadors of every single nonprofit.

Fortunately, both are simple challenges that are easy to remedy.

1. The Curse of Knowledge

In 1990, a Stanford graduate conducted a series of experiments revealing information that was quite profound and obvious all at the same time. By completing certain experiments, the graduate was able to unearth evidence indicating that once we humans know something, we find it hard to imagine *not* knowing it. Our knowledge has "cursed" us: We have difficulty sharing it with others, because we can't readily re-create their state of mind.

This curse came to light in the work of brothers Chip and Dan Heath, in a 1990 *Harvard Business Review* article and in a subsequent book that I highly recommend: *Made To Stick: Why Some Ideas Survive and Others Die.*

You'll never guess the antidote to this curse.

The Heath brothers are clear:

"Leaders can thwart the curse of knowledge by 'translating' their strategies into concrete language." They continue: "Stories, too, work particularly well in dodging the curse of knowledge, because they force us to use concrete language."

I rest my first case.

2. The Elements of a Good Story

I come from solid Irish stock. We are hard-wired to tell a good story. (We are also hard-wired to enjoy the story more than the folks we tell it to, but I digress).

First, in order to *tell* a good story, you have to know what *makes* a good story. And not all nonprofit leaders have the gift of Irish gab and the temperament to attempt to enthrall a crowd.

So, allow me to share what I have learned about good storytelling, from my experience, my ancestors, and my remarkable clients.

I'll start with three don'ts.

Don't Assume

Chip and Dan Heath make this point quite clearly in the book I mentioned earlier. Let me offer a personal example. I was working with an organization that fights hunger in my home state of New Jersey. Now, I'm lucky. I live in an affluent suburb there and experience all the privilege that comes with it. My view is also somewhat myopic. If someone from this organization wants to tell me a story to motivate me, yes, a personal story will get me, but that person should not assume that I know the magnitude of this problem in my own backyard.

According to the most recent census, of the
8.8 million residents of New Jersey, nearly
1.2 million of them experience food insecurity.
Then consider that nearly half a million
of those are kids.

If you assume that I already know this information, you miss a huge opportunity to motivate me.

Don't Give Me a List

Lists don't stick. Big things do. Let's look for a minute at AIDS services organizations. At the highest level, we know that these organizations work to fight AIDS. Their vision is a world without it.

Most HIV/AIDS organizations today have a long list of services they provide to folks living with HIV. On the direct service side, you can find legal clinics, mental health services, substance abuse programs, programs aimed specifically at different demographics, HIV testing, syringe access programs, workforce development, and other resources.

Amazing list of services, right? Impressive. But I'm not going to hold on to all of them, and I have no throughline, or common thread.

Don't hit me with a list. Try spelling out what type of problems you can address and what level of assistance you can provide:

"At XYZ organization, we understand that a life with HIV is a journey. We are there every step of the way. We also know that HIV affects every aspect of your life. If your journey involves substance misuse, we are there. Housing discrimination? We are there. Need a hot meal? Join our community for lunch or dinner seven nights a week. At XYZ, we take care of all of you."

Don't Lead with a Vision That Feels out of Reach

I hope your organization has a vision. Sadly, many don't. But let's just say you do. If you start with vision, you can either emotionally paralyze the listener or cause them to shut down.

Try this wording: We are working to end human slavery worldwide.

Of course, I am impressed. In fact, I'm so impressed that I'm nearly speechless. What question can I ask as a follow-up? I don't know how to jump in to make this a conversation. Remember that you're inviting folks to converse about the organization. Try to avoid shutting them down.

Let me be clear: I am all for a story that helps me imagine something new and exciting. That's a good thing, indeed.

Emily Klehm, who leads South Suburban Humane Society in Chicago Heights, Illinois, began her tenure in 2007 when a staff of 15 ran a shelter with a budget of less than $1 million. Her budget is now twice that amount, and she is on the verge of securing a grant of more than $6 million to transform what was once known as "The Little Shelter That Could." This transformation is visionary in all the very best ways.

Emily had me at hello. She talked about the power of pets. I think I made her look at a few photos of my beloved cat Louie and my live stuffed animal dog Charlie. She talked about an animal campus where people and pets can be together, turning shelters into happy places where kids can go to learn about animals on a campus with walking trails. Then she took me to a brand-new place.

"Do you know one of the main reasons that women do not leave abusive relationships?" I'm thinking Emily has gone astray (sorry for the bad pun). "Women don't want to leave their pets." My eyes got really wide. "I want a pet-friendly domestic violence shelter here on our campus," she said. And that was it. I am actually getting goosebumps as I type. Now *that* is a vision I want to support. And I told her so. When the grant comes through, I want to help.

One last thing: The tagline for South Suburban Humane Society is "the little shelter that could." We laughed about needing a new tagline. The organization has outgrown the word *little,* but the word *could* says it all. It speaks to the heart of this organization's growth in scope and impact — it's about imagining what is possible.

A COMPELLING STORY

"If the story is not about the hearer, he will not listen. And here I make a rule — a great and interesting story is about everyone or it will not last." —John Steinbeck, *East of Eden*

I'm going to take my own advice here and not assume.

Let's talk about the elements of a powerful and compelling story. And to make my point, I will tell the story of my friends

Ken and Judy and an organization in New York City called Transportation Alternatives.

- ### Someone to Root For

Judy's story is the story of Transportation Alternatives, the community they have built, and the impact they have had. My friend Judy lost her daughter Ella when Ella was hit by a New York City bus. I've known this family since Ella and our daughter Scout met weekly in a local play group. Ella was special.

Judy is our protagonist. Her story is tragic. And my credibility as a messenger is high because of my personal connection. And you want to know more.

- ### Struggle or Conflict

> "The only thing that kept Judy and Ken 'alive' was a need to do something — anything — to make that Brooklyn intersection safer. It had already been identified as one of the most dangerous in the city. But how could they get anyone to pay attention? So much bureaucracy. So much red tape. And they felt they were fighting the battle alone."

The struggle is clear. They want changes to the intersection; no one is paying attention to them.

- ### Empathy

> "I admire Ken and Judy so much. This could have been my daughter. Or yours. I'd like to think that I would focus on securing a legacy for my daughter."

This is an important part. Put the listener in the shoes of that protagonist. God forbid, if *you* were Judy and Ken, what would you want?

• **How Is Your Organization Working to Solve This Problem?**

> "Transportation Alternatives created an army of the bereaved — a community in which the words *I know what you are going through* really meant something. The organization worked with this group to create a goal, a different one from Ken and Judy's, one that it believed — based on their understanding of NYC politics — was actually achievable. They secured buy-in from the army and in less than three months, the new goal was met. The speed limit in New York City was dropped from 30mph to 25mph."

What have we learned? TA was compassionate and empathetic and worked with this group to help them, to offer them hope, to help them attempt to find some good in unimaginable loss. The organization worked with the group to set a tangible goal and met it in record time. Makes you want to write a check right now, doesn't it?

• **Evidence of Forward Motion with New Goals**

> "Empowered by this remarkable accomplishment, the TA army set new goals. Their next stop is the bus drivers' union and the Taxi and Limousine Commission to tackle the issue of enforcement. And yes, there is talk of replicating this model in other cities".

I totally get this organization. I recognize TA as caring and compassionate and also driven to make a change that honors the legacy of children taken too soon. But not only driven — smart, diplomatic, and intentional, too. It's an organization with measurable impact (speed limit) and immeasurable impact (offering hope to families broken by loss).

This is how it works.

TWO MORE EXAMPLES FOR EMPHASIS

Here are two more examples that I hope will help you in crafting your own story — one from the for-profit sector and one from my very own backyard. Both of these stories are true.

FedEx

We all know the unique selling proposition of FedEx — to paraphrase, "absolutely, positively overnight." Late one afternoon, a driver (let's call her Jamia) had truck trouble and it broke down. FedEx has a plan for such things (of course) and sent a replacement van. But it was stuck in traffic.

Jamia loves working for FedEx and lives its mission every day. She began to deliver a few packages on foot but could see that she would simply run out of time.

Now, I'm not sure what I would do in this circumstance — would I call my boss and say I had tried everything but that, on this day, I could not meet the delivery promise? I'd bet some people would do that.

Not Jamia. She managed to persuade a *competitor's* driver to take her to her last stops.

In My Own Backyard

Our twins, Ben and Kit, are thick as thieves and always have been.

When they were 5 and attended a small, progressive school in suburban New Jersey, the school officials thought maybe they were *too* thick. Their teachers, who knew them each so well, determined that two separate pre-K experiences made sense.

Try telling that to Kit. She was bereft. Miserable. The sweetest kid in the world actually bit a teacher. It got pretty bad.

In other schools, a kid who bites might be removed from the class, and a kid of color might actually wind up in handcuffs when teachers call the police. Certainly, a punishment of some sort was in order.

But Kit's teachers proposed a better solution — one that was so smart, so simple, and so compassionate, I will never forget it.

Twice a week, Kit would get on the phone and call Ben's classroom and invite Ben for snack time. He'd come into the classroom and Kit would already have set out his snack crackers and juice for him. They both lit up. All was well with the world. They would chat for a while and then Ben would toddle back to his class.

I still get goose bumps when I think about how wonderful these teachers were to propose a solution like this. How much they cared.

A story like this one is golden. It speaks to the mission of the school, to what makes it a unique and special place. Even if you don't have kids, you want them to go to a place that makes these kinds of choices. Kit, as the protagonist, is clear about her challenge, and the school solves her problem in a way that honors her.

PRACTICE, KID, PRACTICE

Because storytelling does not come naturally to organizational ambassadors, as I mentioned earlier in this chapter, a nonprofit organization must work with intention to build a culture of storytelling in its organization.

Each board and staff member should understand the elements of a good story and be asked to shape their own. Here are some ideas:

- Set aside time at a board meeting to ask people to share their organization stories. Have them offer each other constructive feedback and ask questions, such as, "Which story stayed with you? Does it bring the work to life? Is the impact clear?"
- Hold quarterly brown bag lunches with staff to practice. Ask the simple question "What do you do, and why is it important?" and have them offer an illustration of tangible impact. Give each staffer two or three minutes, tops. Staff members not only fine-tune their storytelling skills but also hear a variety of stories they themselves could tell.
- Feed your board and staff regularly with new (current) stories about the organization that they can use when at a weekend BBQ or a fundraiser for another organization. Your best ambassadors need good, fresh material!

Ever sat at a tactical, in-the-weeds staff meeting for 90 minutes, then head back to your desk and realize no one told a single great story about the impact of the work of the organization?

When I suggest this to nonprofit EDs, they often seem as if it never crossed their minds. "Oh, that's a good idea!" they tell me.

So just do it. Build a culture of storytelling in your organization and it can make all the difference in the world.

In Chapter 3, I'll focus on the role of the board chair and that person's relationship to the ED, but I'll give you an appetizer here.

It is the shared job of the board chair and the executive director to ensure that the key ambassadors of the organizations are also your best storytellers.

Here's a simple equation. If you keep it on a sticky note on your desk and incorporate it into working with your board, your volunteers, and your staff at all levels, I guarantee you will bring more motivated folks to your organization's table:

Credible Messenger + Compelling Story = A New Stakeholder

"You actually made a piñata of your board chair as a team building exercise at your retreat? That's hilarious. But I think you're going to need extra sessions."

Chapter 3 Copilots in a Twin-Engine Plane

Riddle me this, Batmen and Batwomen. What is the one thing that illustrates that your organization is thriving? Just one. "No fair," you say? Hey! It's my book. Just one. Here's your list:

- A strong mission
- A solid cash reserve
- A charismatic executive director
- The diversity of your revenue streams
- Staff turnover percentage

What? You can't pick just one? I'm going to make it even harder. The answer is actually not even on this list. But I'll give you a hint: It's a *relationship*.

In my experience with hundreds of nonprofits, it's clear to me that the single most important indicator of a healthy nonprofit is the relationship between the staff and the board leader — the executive director/ED and the board chair.

Why?

It's simple.

So EDs reading this chapter are thinking, "Hey, wait! I'm in charge, and things work best when I am left to my own devices to run the organization and the board just raises money." And board chairs are in a different place — "On paper, I am the boss. I'm not buying this 'shared leadership' thing. At the end of the day, I am responsible for hiring and firing our ED That doesn't feel like a partnership to me."

> Shared leadership with an invested thought partner with leadership skills can cut the kind of challenges listed above off at the pass.

I thought perhaps I had dispelled these ideas in Chapter 2 when I spoke about where power comes from in a nonprofit, but we need to keep digging on this one because it is (a) important and (b) a bit counterintuitive.

The ED and the board chair each lead a group of the organization's most vital stakeholders. The ED manages a staff (if the organization is lucky enough to have resources) that is paid to do the critical day-to-day work of the organization. Unlike a corporate board, a nonprofit board adds remarkable horsepower to the organization. (No eye-rolling, please — stay with me!) With the proper recruitment strategy, a board becomes a volunteer army of stakeholders of the highest caliber that brings skills, expertise, and life experience that the organization desperately needs and would not likely be able to afford. And, ideally, each and every board member shares a passion for the mission and the determination to do what it takes to ensure that the organization has the highest degree of impact. Lastly, each understands their role as an ambassador for the organization, always on the lookout for new stakeholders — the best and the brightest staff, donors, sponsors, and other volunteers — to continue to build the capacity of the organization to do its very best work.

It sounds like a great model, doesn't it? Board and staff work as thought partners who, together, drive the organization forward, led by two individuals who understand their roles, both separately and in relation to one another, each of whom is passionate about their job and determined to do right by the organization.

It could be.

It should be.

You're not buying it. And to be blunt, you (and I'm talking to you, board and staff leaders) are not always committed to investing the time and energy into getting it right.

I argue that it is your job. Your clients and the communities you advocate for deserve your best. And while it is messy, this shared leadership model is the key to enabling nonprofits of all sizes to have greater reach and impact.

But here's the thing: in what I consider to be the ultimate irony, these two groups are far too often in tension with one another. Tension. Not just peaceful coexistence. Tension. In fact, it is this tension that led me to become a certified mediator. In working with clients with organizational challenges, it isn't long before I find my way to organizational leadership. And there I often find a relationship that is not working. The roles are not clear, the communication is poor and the expectations are either unrealistic or unstated.

There — I said it. Like a marriage on the rocks.

I'm by no means suggesting that creating and sustaining this kind of partnership is easy. One of my blog subscribers put it well: "The board chair and the ED need to be in step like in a three-legged race." The last time I was in a three-legged race,

I was probably 10 and it wasn't pretty. But the winners managed through the challenge, sometimes caused their partners to fall, helped each other up, and crossed the finish line, joyful about winning and probably laughing about how filthy they were.

> The board chair and the ED need to be in step like in a three-legged race.

THE IDEAL BOARD CHAIR PROFILE

Based on what we have talked about so far, it seems to me that you are looking for someone green (à la Kermit), whose love of the cause is actually greater than their fear of asking for "green," and who actually *wanted* the job. We need someone who has enough of an ego to want to be successful and yet is humble enough to understand that everyone's voice matters and who, as I mentioned in Chapter1, values the power that comes from those around them. Lastly, you want someone who partners with the executive director by asking good questions, by encouraging the discussions of missteps and by supplying the right amount of rope.

At my very first board meeting as an ED, I was delighted to be supported by two co-chairs who, in my mind, fit this bill to a tee. So smart, so strategic, so committed — fundraising champions. The two of them were part of the package that sold me on leaving the for-profit sector to take this great new low-paying job. We had a terrific first meeting that we had designed together; we had a clear sense of what the outcomes needed to be.

Except one.

At the end of the meeting, both co-chairs resigned. I was furious. They had betrayed me.

Nope. They did me a favor. They told the group that they had micromanaged my predecessor as a result of concerns about performance issues and did not believe they could give me sufficient rope. I needed and deserved the right amount of rope to lead and build the organization.

So, what did I do? I had to think on my feet. What did I need to do? (1) Raise cash and (2) build the board. With these as my priorities, I identified two board members who were aggressive fundraisers and who were invested in my success and knew a million people. If we could do these two things *together*, we could stabilize the organization and begin to attract board prospects who would see board leadership as a privilege. The strategy paid off. Within a year, I had a five-star board chair and we built a partnership and an organization to last.

RECRUITING THE IDEAL BOARD CHAIR

A full 95% of my clients don't recruit board members for leadership abilities, and that is a serious problem.

I sat in on a client's discussion about new prospects. The CEO and the head of development spoke about the personal wealth capacity of each prospect, the perceived willingness each would bring to the fundraising endeavor, and the particular expertise each of them would bring to the board. I couldn't keep quiet a moment longer: "Would any of these six prospects make a strong board chair?" I asked this question for an important reason. In my coaching work with this client, their single biggest challenge was a weak board chair — being too busy, flying the board "plane" at the wrong altitude, and taking no responsibility to actually lead or manage the board. The board "engine" was not functioning, and the chair was the main reason. And yet here they were, talking about new prospects, arguably a perfect opportunity to start to build a leadership pipeline, and they admitted that not a single prospect would have the attributes necessary to partner with my client and lead the board.

Another client worked hard to institute board term limits after six years as CEO. They had the same board chair for six years. Was anyone groomed to succeed the board chair when he "termed off"? Of course not. There was no need. John was great and had it covered. And so, in a case like this, what's an organization to do? Well, in this case, they recruited someone *brand-new* to the organization to join the board as the chair. Yup — that is what they did. Now, to be fair, the organization was clear about the skills and attributes needed, and every indication was that this individual would be a rock star. He is deeply passionate and crystal clear about the importance of his role. He has invested enormous amounts of time in getting to know the organization and getting to know the CEO. But make no mistake. He is a rockstar with no prior experience as a board chair, no prior connection to the organization and no prior giving history to the organization. I am predicting a successful partnership, but in no way was this the ideal strategy for finding just the right copilot.

OK, let's connect the dots here, shall we? I have just said that the chair–ED relationship is the pivotal one that separates the good nonprofits from the great nonprofits. And I have also just said that very few boards recruit with leadership qualities in mind. They may recruit for folks who *run* companies or *manage* large departments of companies, but that's not what I'm talking about. I'm talking about the exact same attributes you are looking for in an executive director.

I was speaking at a conference about the ideal attributes of a staff leader, and I no doubt showed a slide of Kermit and his fellow Muppets. During the Q and A, someone asked me if I would take a minute and offer my thoughts on the profiles of the ideal board chair. I pulled up the slide of the ideal attributes of an executive director and said, "This!"

In Chapter 4, I'll be digging deep into the nonprofit board, its essential role, and the vision of what a high functioning one looks like, but let me just tee up one point.

Nonprofits recruit board members with a scarcity mindset, presuming that it will be challenging to get people to say yes. And so boards take what I call the butts-in-seats approach to recruitment. Perhaps you have some criteria (for example, "We need a CPA"), but the idea of adding a requirement such as "prior leadership role on a nonprofit board"? Well, this person will be harder to find and as the chair of the nominations committee, I might not hit my number of "butts."

You can find more on the systemic problem and how to tackle it in Chapter 4, but for the purposes of this discussion, if recruitment efforts ignore leadership attributes, the organization will suffer — you need two very strong leaders in your "cockpit."

> *Dear Joan,*
>
> *My current board chair is stepping down, and I am bereft. He was terrific. He gave generously and he left me alone to do my thing. I didn't talk to him much, and he protected me from meddlesome board members with crazy ideas. My new board chair has already said she wants weekly meetings — I am sensing a five-star micromanager.*
>
> *Signed,*
> *Just Leave Me Alone*

"Just Leave Me Alone" turned out to be totally wrong. This person traded a well-meaning, dedicated board chair who was a bit of an absentee landlord for a real partner. And there is no question that the growth and success of the organization can be tied back to this partnership. So what did the partner have that made it work?

THE FIVE-STAR BOARD CHAIR CHECKLIST

Here's the board chair you need to go find. Maybe the person is already on your board (wouldn't that be nice?). If not, this search is the number-two priority of the organization (right after finding a five-star staff leader). Here's what it takes to be a five-star board chair:

- **Interest.** It seems like an obvious quality, but a reluctant board chair doesn't work.
- **Passion for the mission.** The board leader has to be crazy about the work of the organization.
- **Time.** Now, most type A board members being considered for leadership positions are so busy that they can barely breathe. That doesn't mean they don't have time to serve. My best board chair was ridiculously busy in her day job, but we planned, and she understood the commitment she was making to work closely with me. She made the time available, and not just on the phone. We met face-to-face to talk, and would allow more time for the less tactical and the more strategic.
- **Schedule autonomy.** Typically, meetings are scheduled. But things come up that require board chair attention. If your boss drags you into meetings with regularity and does so with precious little notice, this can be a problem for an ED with a pressing issue. And frustrating too, because ED schedules are no less challenging.
- **Diplomacy.** Can you hear a really stupid comment or question without rolling your eyes? Board members are a mixed

bag. They are volunteers and don't always have the knowledge to combine with their enthusiasm. Their enthusiasm for
an idea must be honored, but at the same time, a great board
chair must diminish expectations that anything will likely
come of the idea.

- **Asking tough questions well.** Let me put it out there: EDs
  have thinner skin than you think. They get defensive. After
  all, they know their organization backward and forward.
  You? You're just a volunteer. You don't know what it's really
  like. It can be quite unflattering. Board chairs need to, in that
  context, learn how to ask smart, constructive questions that
  lead to productive conversations rather than to a 15-minute
  defense. This could be a separate bullet, but it is this kind
  of attribute that leads to the trust necessary to partner in
  such a way that you talk through what *works and* what
  isn't working.
- **Serving as a fundraising champion.** Board members will follow your lead. If you are out creating connections through
  your sphere of influence, board members will see what that
  looks like. And if they choose not to go that route, it won't be
  because they don't see what it looks like.
- **Motivating volunteers to deliver.** Mentored properly, today's
  committee chairs are tomorrow's board leaders. Have the
  chairs worked with their committees to set annual goals; to
  identify a project they want to work on? Do they meet regularly? How is attendance? What kind of agenda is circulated?
  How is the meeting facilitated? Far too often, the staff liaison
  takes responsibility for the meeting agenda and the forward
  motion at the meeting. Not that person's role.
- **Recognizing the value of appreciation.** When something happens, can you make time to shoot an email to staff ASAP?
  More importantly, can you command the attention of the
  board to encourage them to do the same? I can't tell you how
  demoralizing it is for staff to send out exciting news and get,
  in return, total and complete radio silence from the board. At

first, EDs confirm that the email has gone out. Then they just assume you don't care.
- **Understanding the value of accountability.** The role of the board chair is a delicate one, indeed. With committee chairs and especially your ED, it's true that the buck really does stop with you. But in a world of shared leadership, you need to develop goals and success metrics together and, similarly, evaluate them together. Shared leadership; shared accountability.

THE TELLTALE SIGNS OF WRONG

I get it. Kermit is not in the boardroom. Your board chair is highly flawed. Or are they? How do you know? I'm amazed at how often folks write to me to ask if this is how a board chair should behave when the behavior that's described is outrageous. And so, in the spirit of bringing the "wrong" to light, here are some behaviors that readers have described to me. Each of them represents a big, fat flag on the field. In aggregate, it's a hot mess:

- Your board chair was volun*TOLD* to take the role and constantly complains about how much time the role takes.
- When someone suggests that the board use *Robert's Rules of Order*, the board chair asks casually, "Who's Robert?"
- Your board president announces, "The only people I have ever led are my family."
- As the ED, you have not had a performance evaluation in more than two years.
- The board chair believes that the ED should create the agenda for the board meetings.
- The board chair solicits ideas for the board meeting from the board members rather than design the agenda strategically

(you can only imagine the ideas that get generated with no guidance).

- The board chair checks in for about five minutes every few days and says, "So, what's going on?"
- The board chair is the executive director's best friend.
- You overhear the board chair at an event being asked about the size of the annual budget and the number of full-time employees. The board chair, who is clueless, finally sputters, "I need to introduce you to our executive director."
- The board chair sends the ED flowers on national Secretary's Day and is not being ironic.
- The board chair, in a discussion about trimming costs, asks the ED how old their assistant is.

PLAYING THE HAND YOU'RE DEALT

I was close to my grandmother. Kitty Conlon lived a bike ride away, and I could while away the afternoon with Irish breakfast tea and a few hands of canasta — a warm memory, but a distant one. Kitty taught me (among many other things) that you can win handily (pun intended) with a less-than-ideal hand.

So, let's say that your board chair is good but not great, or is good with great tendencies or is great with vulnerabilities. Let's say that this person was "volun*told*," or, as I like to say, made the unfortunate choice to head to the restroom while the vote took place. How do you play *this* hand to win? Because the truth of the matter is, this scenario is the most likely one you will encounter during your tenure in either role.

Here's what you have going for you: both of you want to do a good job, and you care deeply about the organization. This can take you a long way.

Dear Joan,

I have been on the board for a little over a year and was recently elected board president. I don't believe I'm exactly qualified for this role; however, our board is struggling with leadership and, to be honest, no one has any guts. So I was the only person nominated, and I felt obligated to accept. I'm somewhat happy to take on this role, but I work, I have two small kids, and I'm just one person. I really care about the organization and want to do a good job. Where do I start?

Signed,
Gutsy or Stupid

So here's the deal, Gutsy. Get in line behind thousands of folks who have stood, or who are standing, in your shoes. Take it one step at a time and let your love of your organization lead the way.

GET IT RIGHT FROM THE START

Rosanne Siino, the board chair of the Lindsay Wildlife Experience in California's Bay Area, had served on the board and termed off and was then asked to rejoin as the chair as the organization embarked on a search for a new executive director. Prior to joining Lindsay Wildlife, Rosanne had other board and volunteer experience. When you go looking for a board chair, I suggest that you give her a call and find out when her term with Lindsay expires. Rosanne has the goods.

Rosanne's first order of business was to oversee a search for a new executive director. And wouldn't you know it? They hired a good one. You see, that's how it works. A terrific board chair leads well, and when it comes to landing a top flight ED, you have to get the process right. A terrific board chair oversees a terrific search process. Rosanne worked the board hard to get an agreement to hire a search firm and then built a strong search committee.

Then Carlos de la Rosa was hired. Carlos will tell you that Rosanne understood from day one the critical nature of this partnership. Carlos will also tell you that they spent substantive time together during the first 30 to 60 days. Unstructured time. Getting to know one another. Understanding each other's personal values. As a result, they understand each other and they have developed real trust. Carlos and Rosanne are transforming the board and engaging in hard work. And they are doing it *together*.

Rosanne's strategy mirrors what I have seen work. It is about an investment that a chair must make. It's an investment the chair makes with enthusiasm because folks who stand for board leadership are accustomed to being successful. And, when it comes to an organization they care deeply about, their success as a leader is all the more important.

Prepare to Allocate a *Lot* of Time in the First 30 Days

I mean it. What you do in the first 30 days of *any* new job sets the tone for the work moving forward. It's no different here:

1. **Set up a three-hour meeting.** Just the two of you (or three, if you have co-chairs or a vice chair). This may be the best investment of time you make during your leadership partnership. Here are the basics you should cover:
   a. Review job descriptions — It's easy to find sample descriptions on the Internet and use them as the basis for a conversation about where the roles are separate and where they overlap.

b. Review the list of board members — Talk about their strengths and weaknesses. Talk about how you might rearrange the deck chairs and who is worth investing in for future leadership.

c. Review the list of senior staff — This is where thought partnership comes in. The ED is responsible for the staff, but let the board chair in as a mentor and coach. Let that person partner with you in thinking about moving your staff from good to great.

d. Review board fundraising — Have the ED bring a document that outlines board fundraising, in its aggregate and by person. Talk about needs, opportunities, and the role of the development committee in holding its peers accountable, and then discuss whether tools or trainings are needed.

e. Agree on a weekly meeting — Yes, I said weekly, at least at first. I recommend that the ED prepare a simple agenda and send it the night before the meeting. Get your calendars out and calendar the first six meetings. Lock 'em in and commit to each other that they will happen.

2. **Set up time with the former chair.** Yes, more time. Sorry. But it's another key investment. Learn about the experience. You'll learn about what to do, and what not to do.

3. **Reach out to every board member — 30–45 minutes, tops.**

a. Why did you join the board?

b. How has the experience been for you so far?

c. When you step off the board, what would you like to be able to say you contributed? What would success look like for you?

d. How can I as the chair better support you?

e. Critique our board meetings.

f. Make requests — whatever they may be, based on the three hours with the ED

g. Finish this statement: "In order for us to be successful as a board in the next 12 months, I believe our board needs to _____."

h. Thank the person for their service (even if you hope they resign tomorrow).

4. **Set 2–4 goals for yourself.**

I've been working with a fine board chair. We had lunch just as he was taking on the role of chair. He told me that one of his key goals for the coming year was to take real steps to create a more effective board.

I saw him a few days ago. He has reconfigured the executive committee (with buy-in from all parties); he is reconfiguring board meetings to make them more enriching for the board members and less taxing on the staff. He has even managed to put someone who loves fundraising in the role of development committee chair (he's not just a board chair — he may also be a miracle worker). These are terrific examples of board chair goals. And no, you can't have him.

5. **Run a formal meeting.**

This directive has two key words: *formal* and *run*.

So, I'm working hard here to remind folks that a strong board of directors is a critical element of the success of a nonprofit. The board should be filled with people who understand the role and are motivated by the mission. These folks should be selected with intention, and each and every meeting should be run in a way that respects the investment of time and treasure each person is making. What that means is that if I walk into the boardroom, I should be able to tell who the chair is. If I mistake the executive director for the board chair, the board chair is not running the meeting. I see this all the time. The board serves as a kind of host or emcee to "the ED show."

The board chair has to take responsibility for running the meeting and then needs to run it using some kind of meeting tool that allows for constructive discussion and debate and can then guide a group toward a decision. The most common tool is *Robert's Rules of Order*, but there are many to choose from. You need some kind of parliamentary procedure — you are a group of grown-ups with a big job. Guardrails like *Robert's Rules* will help a board chair manage conversations well, and a board member at a meeting who is following them knows they are at a real meeting, where real things happen. (P.S. The guy's last name, not first name, was Robert.)

As I reflect on the list in this section, I am reminded of the newly recruited board chair I mentioned earlier — the one with no prior experience with the organization. Remember that I said I believed the board chair was going to be effective in spite of that? Here's how I know. I considered the moves they made since saying yes and compared it to my list in this section. This person is making all the right moves.

WHO DECIDES?

High-powered, type A people like making decisions. High-powered, type A people are drawn to leadership. Most EDs are high-powered, type A people. A good board chair is, too. The folks drawn toward leadership are not always wildly comfortable in the gray. In the cockpit of a nonprofit jet, you will find some clear black-and-white, but also some serious gray. Embrace it. Get used to it.

Let's look at the key areas of decision-making in a nonprofit organization, and I will offer my thinking about where the deciding happens — what is black-and-white, and where you should embrace the gray. I consider this to be an important primer on how the copilots share their leadership in a way that benefits the whole organization.

Hiring / Evaluating / Firing the Executive Director

Hiring, evaluating, and firing the executive director lies clearly in the hands of the board. That's an easy one. I take that back — actually, nothing about those tasks is easy. In fact, boards fumble these all the time. I talk a bit in Chapter 10 about the exit of an executive director, and I'll be the first to admit that this task can be very tricky, even for a high-functioning board.

One exception is the evaluation, where I like to see a little gray. The executive director should have a role (not the final say) in the design of the process and should advocate strongly for a formal process that includes a self-evaluation and engages more than just the board chair. It is important that the board develop a process with strong input from the person being evaluated.

Strategic Plan

I like a lot of gray in my organizational planning. While there is no gray in who approves the plan (the board), far too often the staff drives a process, the staff engages the board because it feels an obligation, and ultimately the board votes on a plan it does not feel it owns. Some executive directors might read that sentence and think that suits them just fine. But without shades of gray — without real engagement by a board–staff planning committee, the board will not own the plan. Without ownership, don't count on your board members to be effective ambassadors and champions (read: raise money) for it in the same way they would if they knew they had built it with you. With planning, the gray pays.

Annual Budget

The annual budget reveals the second most important partnership in the organization — the one between the board treasurer and the staff person responsible for finances. To be clear, the board approves the annual budget. Full stop. As for construction of the budget and the process, I like to see this partnership at work — both parties discuss a process that makes sense, is not onerous and provides the board with the information it needs to make an informed vote. I like to see a bit of gray as the process develops and unfolds.

Board Building

The "grayest' part of this work happens up front, when the board and the staff leadership draw a design for the ideal board. What skills, expertise, attributes, and life experiences should be represented on our board — a composition matrix? This design should tie to the goals of your strategic plan. It should be built as a team. It may start in the governance committee, but the copilots' fingerprints need to be all over it.

The voting part (the board) has no gray at all, but there are numerous parts to deciding in this process. Who recruits, who makes it into the prospect pipeline, who interviews — these are three key components. The ED and senior staff should be excellent sources of prospects (if they are not, they are not getting out enough). The board should lead in interviewing and shaping the prospect list, and the ED should be involved. I believe an ED interview is critical — as much for the potential board member as anything else. The question of when in the process and the weight that interview carries — these two pieces can be tricky. There must be good balance here. Under no circumstances should a board give disproportionate power to the

ED in the recruitment-and-selection process — this can lead to "stacking" the board in the extreme and can be quite dangerous. On the other hand, the ED should have a voice in the process — the strength and diversity of that board engine is the key to their success as a leader.

Program Design, Execution, and Evaluation

The board should understand the palette of program offerings and how they align with the strategic plan. As part of approving a budget, a board is approving goals that include how the programs will advance the mission. The design and execution of the programs should be a staff decision, although engaging the board in discussions about how best to deliver programs can create richer ideas and more ownership. The place where boards should be more engaged and active is in monitoring the success of programs. This is one of the ten big responsibilities of nonprofit boards (stay tuned for Chapter 4). The ED should be comfortable in the gray, allowing the board to work with them to build an evaluative mechanism that allows them to meet their obligation and effectively promote the work of the organization to reach new stakeholders and drive more resources.

Staff Supervision

Hiring and firing staff is in the ED's court. Now, at times an ED might choose to ask the board chair to weigh in. This could be because the chair knows the organization well or perhaps the chair has a background in human resources. A new development director, for example, must work with a select group of board members and will be in partnership with the chair of the fundraising committee.

A smart and intuitive board chair can see that the ED has made a bad hire — like, a mile away. There can be a tendency to want to solve for that in the moment: The chair may be inclined to bring it up in the regular meeting and arrive with a heavy hand — "She has to go!"

But it's not the chair's job to decide. It's the chair's job to note the poor hire or the slow hire for the evaluation folder on their desktop.

I know what you are thinking: "What if this train wreck hire is thwarting the ability of the organization to pursue its mission or causing some other problem that is big and important? Joan, you can't be suggesting that the board chair sit on their hands."

No, I'm not. I'm suggesting that in the land of copilots, the conversation happens differently. If you have built the partnership I have described and developed some real trust, here's what you should hear:

ED: "Mary, I'm struggling. I think Sydney might have been a bad hire. I'd love your insights — what do you see? I could use your advice on how to navigate this."

Board chair: "How are things going with Sydney? I ask because I had some recent interactions / observations that I think you may find useful to hear."

I told you. There are some clear ways in which decisions are made, but there is an awful lot of gray — like any good relationship, I suppose. And like any good relationship, one big key is being open to the fact that you may not know the answers — that you are open to learning.

I think that is the key to the success of board chair John Sagos at Third Coast Baroque, a Chicago-based arts organization that shares the aesthetic of Baroque music while unlocking its relevance for today's audiences. Listen to John talk about board service and you'll hear a sense of joy and excitement — he loves the gig. And when you ask why, he tells you that he is a musician and loves the mission. Then you'll hear John say something important: "I have a lot to learn." And in fact you will hear the executive director, Angela Young Smucker, say the same thing. Angela, a founder, sought out John to stand as her board partner. "We both entered this knowing we *both* had a lot to learn." Their exponential growth has created lots of opportunities from which to learn — about their own roles and about what each of them brings to the partnership.

What I hear when I talk to them is a lack of something that thwarts a great partnership: neither has an unflatteringly over-sized ego. Each brings a humble confidence to the work, and Third Coast Baroque is growing in size and impact under their leadership.

I want to highlight one last thing about John before moving on to Chapter 4, where we take a close look at the value and responsibility of the full board. John sees board service as a personal development opportunity and a privilege. He is building new muscles he did not have to use in his day job, and he knows that he is growing as a person, an ambassador, a leader. And John sees his leadership role as a privilege — to be able to take his skills and attributes and invest them in something he cares so deeply about. John knows that the organization needs the best possible leader and is humbled to have been selected.

If you haven't guessed, a sense of opportunity and the privilege of service separate the very good board leaders from the very best.

> A sense of opportunity and the privilege of service separate the very good board leaders from the very best.

I just attended my first meeting - I was just elected to the board of an amazing organization. Do you think anyone will tell me what I am supposed to do?

Chapter 4 Why Boards Matter

If you want a book that provides a clear picture of the roles a board and its members play in an organization, I can point you to some excellent resources. My favorite is Richard Chait's *Governance as Leadership*. The follow up book, *The Practitioner's Guide to Governance as Leadership*, by Cathy Trower, is also swell.

In this chapter, I take a different angle. I tease out the core responsibilities of board service and talk about how board members bring them to life. Assuming they even know the list.

So if you want to see firsthand the havoc a clueless board member can have, if you want to understand the ripple effects of the toxic board member, if you want to see what abuse of power looks like, and if you want to face the truth that boards just don't stay engaged — you have to engage them — then this is the chapter you need to read. And not to worry, the chapter comes complete with proven antidotes.

If I do my job here, you'll finish this chapter and order a copy of this book for every board member.

THE REAL PROBLEM WITH BOARDS

You might have read that and wondered how I can tackle that in a single chapter — or even a section of a chapter.

The real problem with boards? The answer is remarkably simple. The real problem with boards is that board members cannot answer one remarkably simple question: *Why do nonprofit boards matter*?

> The real problem with boards is that board members cannot answer one remarkably simple question: *Why do nonprofit boards matter?*

People who join boards need to know the answer to this question.

Let's talk about why they don't.

First off, have a figurative listen in on the conversations I hear every day. "I have to put up with ill-informed questions and prepare for meetings that don't really help me much and then they don't even do the thing I need them to do — fundraise! I have a do-nothing board."

So that's reason #1. Executive directors have a narrow view of why boards matter: raise money and leave me alone to do my job.

Now travel with me to a board candidate interview. It's all sales. "We have an amazing organization and an outstanding executive director. Great people on our board, not a lot of work. And we have staff that does a great job with fundraising. I feel so honored to be connected to this work and this organization. Would you like to join us?"

There's reason #2. We are so hellbent on persuading a prospect to join that we soft-pedal some of the specifics to get them to yes. We figure the more substantive the job seems, the less likely they will say yes. And so we talk about the great work and the great staff that does it all. And we don't go anywhere near the real "why."

Our last stop is the new board member orientation. If you have one. We provide details, but we don't have conversations that indicate the gravitas of board service, the "big why."

Reason #3: The board members assembled for the orientation don't know the real "why." They weren't told.

THE BIG WHY

Allow me to articulate what we *should* be saying — why nonprofit boards really matter. My brother Steven once asked me how much nonprofit board members get paid. Now my brother is a smart guy and does not live under a rock. When I told him they didn't get paid, he looked puzzled. "Well, why would they do it then?"

You ready, Steven? Here is my take on "the big why" — why a nonprofit board matters so much and why folks should say yes when asked.

A nonprofit board bears little resemblance to a corporate board. A nonprofit board is the legal and governing entity of the organization. Its responsibility is real and substantive. A board is the ultimate steward of the public funds that drive the work. Nonprofit boards are intimately familiar with and passionate about the organization's work and knowledgeable about the sector — its challenges and opportunities. A nonprofit board interviews, hires, selects, and evaluates the executive director. It develops a strategic plan in partnership with staff, and board members stand as the agency's most visible and credible organizational ambassadors, inviting people to know more, do more, and give more to an organization they care deeply about. A nonprofit board partners with the staff to set a vision for the organization and to ensure that every donor can be very, very proud of the contribution she has made to support the work. A nonprofit board does not follow; it leads.

A board member's compensation comes in the gift of service — one that is a substantive contribution of time, treasure, and expertise. It comes in the form of the professional and leadership development secured in running a committee, learning how to engage in fundraising work, and it comes in the form of relationships developed with kindred spirits who share a passion for the organization's work — relationships that can and do last for decades.

So I guarantee you that most board members hear nothing even vaguely like that during any point of their interview process or even during their tenure as board members. Big jobs scare people off. So downplay it, get them to yes, and worry about everything later.

> The bottom line: board members don't know that they have said yes to a very important job.

The bottom line: board members don't know that they have said yes to a very important job.

WE'VE GOT THE "WHY"; NOW ON TO THE "WHAT"

Let's talk about what experts consider to be the primary roles and responsibilities of a nonprofit board. So let's go to the source: BoardSource (https://boardsource.org). Can't get more of an expert than BoardSource. They provide a good list of the 10 basic responsibilities:

THE TEN BASIC RESPONSIBILITIES OF NONPROFIT BOARDS

1. Determine mission and purpose.
2. Select the chief executive.
3. Support and evaluate the chief executive.

4. Ensure effective planning. Boards must actively participate in an overall planning process.
5. Monitor and strengthen programs and services.
6. Ensure adequate financial resources.
7. Protect assets and provide proper financial oversight.
8. Build a competent board.
9. Ensure legal and ethical integrity.
10. Enhance the organization's public standing.

When I show this list to board members, they say that it makes sense. "Yes, this sounds about right. I think that is what I believed I signed up for." They may also be breathing a sigh of relief that the word "Fundraising" doesn't appear on the list, but overall, board members will nod their heads in agreement about these ten.

It's worth noting — but not surprising — how often I walk boards through this list and I can tell right away that they are seeing the list for the first time. First they ask whether I'll be emailing the PowerPoint slides around — that's usually a good clue. But not many clues are needed. We've already established that board members are sold without being educated about board service. After all, if folks really knew just how important the job was, they'd all go screaming in the other direction, right? (Actually, wrong— keep reading.)

HOW A TYPICAL BOARD OPERATES

The 10 responsibilities described by BoardSource are clear and excellent guideposts. But we all know success begins and ends with execution.

One note before we start. I understand that there are boards who execute against many of these guideposts, some of them beautifully. The following reflects an amalgam of hundreds of nonprofit boards. My guess is that you will see yourself or one of your organization's board members in at least some of these descriptions.

1. **Mission and Purpose**

   The board revisits these when the ED feels like the landscape has evolved to warrant a change or when everyone is sick of the blank stares they get when they try to explain what the incomprehensible mission statement actually means.

2. **Select the Chief Executive**

   The Board took three months to write the job description to get it just right when two words were all that was needed — "Messiah Wanted."

3. **Support and Evaluate the Chief Executive**

   The board has to prove that the CEO it has chosen is a rock star and either the board chair decides to let the CEO steer altogether or ignores signs that it may be time to manage more closely. And if things are going well (or the board is ignoring what isn't), who needs a formal evaluation?

4. **Ensure effective planning and actively participate**

   Either the CEO is skeptical that the board will add value or just wants the board focused on raising money, and so the board's role is to hear all about how effective the planning is and their participation feels a lot like a rubber stamp.

5. **Monitor and strengthen programs and services**

   Board asks for program evaluation data and is told that you can't measure the impact. Certain board members may enjoy the idea of generating new program ideas that the organization can't fund.

6. **Ensure adequate financial resources**

   Ah, my least favorite euphemism for fundraising! The "easiest" way to fulfill this responsibility is to micromanage expenses and provide oversight from a place of scarcity.

7. **Protect assets and provide proper financial oversight**

Either the board relies nearly completely on the data provided by staff or is thrilled that a CPA is the board treasurer so they can check their email during the finance report. The board sees its role as ensuring that someone is in charge of knowing the numbers; it is not seen as a shared responsibility.

8. **Build a competent board**

Because board members generally are unfamiliar with their 10 responsibilities and execute against them as I am describing here, it's tough to find the right folks to ask to climb aboard your jet.

9. **Ensure legal and ethical integrity**

The vast majority of boards believe they can effectively deliver on this responsibility when they recruit a lawyer to the board. And you can expect any challenge to the organization's integrity to be met with pure unadulterated fear.

10. **Enhance the organization's public standing**

Here's another responsibility that is painfully downplayed. In fact, its position at #10 illustrates just that. Most board members don't understand what this means. They aren't told that this means that you are part of an army of ambassadors who are responsible to be out in the community, at their place of business, all over their social media, spreading the good word about your amazing work and inviting individuals to know and do more for your organization.

The "typical" board does the best job it can, assuming it does really understand the "big why." This board can exhibit moments of brilliance, but a typical board does not own its power and looks to others to "drive." Board members often believe the executive director should be driving; sometimes they are thrilled that a really strong board chair has everything covered or they have a sense that they are being precluded from doing one of the 10 responsibilities above, and frustration sets in.

THE FOUR DEADLY SINS OF DYSFUNCTIONAL BOARDS

You might be on a board that sounds like this and think things are going pretty well. But without a shared sense of ownership and responsibility, the board described by the preceding section is sliding into dysfunction. I could argue the slide is inevitable.

In my experience, I have seen four key drivers of dysfunction.

The Sin of Fear

Anxiety as a key driver of decision-making by boards will never propel an organization forward in the pursuit of your mission. Fear will eat innovation for lunch. A risk-averse board operates from a place of scarcity and not abundance. Because the board member joined not being 100% clear on the responsibilities and was even less clear on the wonderful opportunities board service presents to them personally and professionally, fear can be an easy default. The following examples are real statements from board members I have heard with my own ears.

- "My colleague will be mad at me if I ask her for a donation."
- "One of our donors called me and is mad that you fired Mary. You need to rehire her"
- "Yes, we selected our new executive director. She was the best of a mediocre lot. We were afraid of being without an ED for too long."

- "I know, we really don't have anyone who would be a great board chair — not a lot of leadership potential on our board — but to be honest, we were afraid we had too few board members. We just had to fill the seats."

The Sin of Penny-Pinching

A corollary to fear, boards are notoriously frugal. Given the chance to try something new and raise money to do it or cut other expenses to make room, boards will vote for the latter far too often. Skeptics will say that this is because board members know that they are responsible for working to raise money, and because they don't want to embrace that role, reducing expenses is their much-preferred route.

- "Ticket sales look dismal and although I have sent out some emails, I'm not getting a lot of traction on filling my own table. Maybe we should look at reducing the expenses for the event?"
- "Nonprofit executives just don't make a lot of money — that's just how it is. But the satisfaction of doing this important work is way more than I get."
- "My year-end bonus wasn't at all what I had hoped — I just don't think we should be looking at cost-of-living increases for the staff this year."
- "I have a number of great prospects to invite to the gala, but I need to offer them comp tickets to get them to come."

The Sin of Cluelessness

Two root causes here. First, as I hope I made clear at the start of this chapter, most board members really and truly just don't know what they don't know. The other cause of this "sin" is a lack of a sense of the "whole." If the board is not a team with a shared sense of purpose, the treasurer only takes care of the numbers, the nominations chair is just responsible for identifying prospects, and so on.

- "Oh, that's a great question. I've been on the board for three years — you'd think I'd know the size of our annual budget."
- "Wow. Over the course of the last two years, the executive director packed the board with friends. I didn't notice that before."
- After a board meeting presentation about layoffs (this really happened): "At our next board meeting, do you think we can do a little better than Subway?"
- Spoken to the long-tenured Development Director: "Oh, I am sorry! I thought your name was Sue."

The Worst Sin of All — Abuse of Power

When either the CEO or a board member loses complete sight of the reason for the work, and their primary motivation is pure self-interest, all hell can break loose. You would think that in a sector that is rooted in altruism, you would not see this at play but it turns out that no organization, public or private, is exempt from this level of toxicity. I have no shortage of examples to choose from:

- A poorly performing CEO worries about board support and begins to aggressively court new board members to the organization. While all share strong credentials for board service, they have something else in common. A stronger loyalty to the CEO than to the organization's mission. Within short order, the CEO has "stacked" the board to protect himself. And so, when the board votes to fire him with ample documentation, the motion does not carry. Three more years go by before there is a change and during that time, the CEO wreaked havoc on the organization's reputation and all but depleted a multi-million-dollar reserve.

- A new board member recently joined a board. She loves the organization, but she is not a fan of the executive director. She has been meeting with staff members working to undermine the reputation and credibility of the staff leader. A weak board chair is reluctant to rein her in. . . Oh, did I mention that this new board member applied for the executive director's job and didn't get it?
- A board member makes sexual advances to a staff member. The executive director learns about it secondhand, because the staff member will not come forward for fear of retribution.
- A board chair's husband filed for divorce, leaving her for a younger woman. Feeling powerless in every aspect of her life, she turns her attention to the CEO. She micromanages, interferes with staff decisions, and criticizes the CEO in front of staff. When the CEO makes a misstep, the board chair sees her opportunity to "lead" and uses her power to build alliances with several board members. A vote to fire the CEO does not carry — it's one vote shy. The board chair resigns, and the CEO is demoralized and humiliated.

HOW DID WE GET HERE?

The patterns shown in these examples are pervasive in the nonprofit sector. To understand how organizations wind up here, we have to go back to the beginning, to the origin story of a nonprofit.

A remarkable person identifies a need in her community and is uniquely suited to fill it. Rather than assume that someone else will take care of it, the founder cannot sit idly by, gets some folks excited about the idea and is encouraged to start a nonprofit.

Julie Lovely didn't know what she didn't know. Here's what she *did* know. Equine therapy had been part of her life since age 11 when she began as a volunteer for a program for kids with disabilities. She went on to become a certified instructor and then the work hit home as she sought out equine therapy as she struggled with PTSD and postpartum depression. She saw there was a need for a formal program and knew she was uniquely qualified to build just such a program. Her program began serving kids and adults with disabilities.

In filing for the 501(c)(3) application for Wild Hearts Therapeutic Equestrian Program, she needed to add names of her board members. Ah, she thought, *I have to have a board!* She added a few friends and family members, and poof! She had herself a board. None of them were very clear about what this whole board thing meant — if you'd asked these new board members at the time, you might have heard sentiments like, "we really want to help Julie out" or "I guess I'm an extra set of hands." Julie was not much clearer — it's possible that someone told her that these folks might fundraise for her, but that's about it.

It took not 5 but 10 years for Julie to realize the whole twin-engine jet thing. Five years into the life of her organization, she nearly called it quits, taking a 3-month sabbatical. When she returned there was still no strategy for board building and, in fact, she was not just the executive director but she was also the board chair (and yes, that is technically legal but oh so problematic on every level). It's only now that Wild Hearts is in its tenth year that Julie stepped aside as board chair and recruited a passionate and dedicated individual to build a board engine that could provide the kind of oversight and thought partnership that Julie needed and her clients deserved.

GET IT RIGHT FROM THE START

It didn't have to be so hard for Julie. If only she had gotten it right from the start. If only she had not seen the board as a necessary evil or something she had to have. This may be the most important lesson I could teach any founder. To get it right from the start, a founder must recognize that she *needs and wants* a board. This mind shift change will make all the difference.

> To get it right from the start, a founder must recognize that she **needs and wants** a board.

Build An Intentional Design

Once you realize that you *need* a board, you begin to approach the task of building with intentionality. The fancy term is a "composition matrix." In the case of an equine therapy program like Julie's, you want someone who works with people with PTSD, such as a psychologist. Now here's a person who may have the means to donate and has lots of connections in the space. Next, Julie and her organization would have benefitted from some prior nonprofit experience, such as a retired ED, maybe even someone who was a strong fundraiser. Legal expertise is always important on a board as is financial management. I'm sure as you read this, other kinds of skills, expertise, and life experience will come to mind.

And don't forget attributes. I believe I made that quite clear in Chapter 3 — every board needs folks with leadership attributes.

Market Board Service

Step two is to create a set of talking points before you begin prospecting. And I offer the most important piece of advice first: *No begging!* If you position recruitment as if board service is an imposition, it will magically feel that way to the prospect.

John Sagos chairs the board of Third Coast Baroque in Chicago. He has a thirst for knowledge and he is passionate about music. He is a musician himself and combined this musicianship with years of management experience. This offers a wonderful complement to Angela Young Smucker, the ED and founder, an artist with a vision. John sees his board services as the professional development opportunity it is. He recognizes that volunteer leadership offers him a greater sense of meaning and purpose. He is learning how to lead in a sector where power is not hierarchical. Last, he knows that his work helps bring baroque music to more people. This makes him joyful and enthusiastic —excellent attributes for fundraising!

Shifting your mindset will be a game changer. If you approach recruitment from a place of scarcity (we really need this person to say yes) and as if service is an imposition (it really won't take any time at all), consider who will join your board and *their mindset*. But if you position board service as a privilege and a learning opportunity, you are very likely to recruit folks who feel this way.

One last thing. Be sure to tell all your prospects that volunteering is actually good for them. You're laughing — I can hear you but it's true. Numerous studies show that it's not just good for your mental health to be of service — it's actually proven that folks who volunteer are physically *healthier!*

Use Diversity as a Lens

Several years back I worked with an organization that offered therapy for families with a focus on parenting skills to lower income folks in the South Bronx. The organization had just gotten its 501(c)(3), having previously been a program of a larger organization. They knew instinctively that the board needed to reflect the community it served.

That said, we never had a conversation that led with "we need a woman" or "we need several people of color." We knew that diversity would bring an essential value to the work of the board as different life experience offers robust debate and richer decisions. But we considered diversity a *lens*.

Here's what I mean. The organization had no strategic plan and no money to hire someone to help. What if we reached out to a NYC-based strategy firm (say, McKinsey)? These firms always have employee resource groups (ERGs) for varying communities — an LGBTQ affinity group, an African American employee resource group, and so on. So the team reached out to McKinsey's African American group and presented the board opportunity and landed on a young man who grew up in the South Bronx who was excited to hear more. The founders nurtured him, educated him about the remarkable work, and within a few short months, he was a board member — one who saw his service as an opportunity and a privilege.

See the difference? In the case of this recruitment effort, we thought about recruiting for someone who had strategic planning experience and then asked ourselves where we might recruit to find that kind of experience in a person of color, a Latina, an LGBTQ person? It is a much more targeted approach and will be infinitely more successful. However, if the board's racial composition is important to you, you will want to set goals for recruitment and retention that are rigorous but reachable. One organization had a board of 15 with just 2 people of color on it. Because the people they served were about 75% of color, they set a goal of having the board be at least 50% the same. By recruiting people who cared deeply about the mission and had skills in finance, management, program strategy and more, while being transparent about their composition goals, they reached 50% within four years.

Invest in Onboarding

You have assembled a good group of folks who are enthusiastic about the mission of your organization. I want you to imagine them having a "mission pilot light" that you can see shining. Their pilot light should be pretty bright. From the moment they arrive for this orientation, your job (and I'm talking to both of you in the cockpit!) is to stoke that flame. An orientation that misses that is simply an organization 411, one that covers the "nuts and bolts."

Now there are plenty of nuts and bolts to cover — from the budget to the by-laws to committee structure — but you have to breathe life into your new board members. Open with the fantastic gala video or give the ED the floor to inspire the new board members by talking about the need and the wait list for services, and tell a story of a life transformed.

An orientation done hastily, over the phone, for a quick 30–45 minutes before the first board meeting is a big fat missed opportunity. One that educates so I can be a valuable contributor from my first day of board service is an extra base hit. An orientation that I leave with a brighter mission pilot light than when I arrived? That's a grand slam.

TRANSFORMING THE BOARD YOU HAVE

Because of the origin story challenge we referenced and because there does not seem to be ample (any?) evidence of an organization that simply fired all its board members and began with a clean slate, it's time to renovate.

Hmm. That word connotes demolition and lots of dust, so let's go with the word *transformation* instead. You'll find five steps in the transformation process.

Diagnose

"My board is useless." I get that a lot. I ask my clients to create a spreadsheet with each person's name, tenure on the board, and professional expertise. Maybe I'll ask about each person's mission passion, degree of influence on the board (positive or negative), leadership potential — maybe a few other questions. Inevitably, we find that we have a handful of folks we can work with. And please remember how we started this chapter: by recognizing most board members don't know what it means to be a useful board member.

My experience has shown that the vast majority of boards have a number of board members who can be central to the transformation.

Different Times Call for Different Board Members

Consider where your organization is in its lifespan as an organization. Maybe you have added a new program, maybe you are going to offer services virtually. Perhaps you know that your ED is going to retire in a few years. These different kinds of inflection points offer you the opportunity to bring in new folks with the specific skills you need.

This is the path that board chair Rosanne travelled before Lindsay Wildlife Experience embarked on its ED search. She knew that a great executive director would need a board with different skills and expertise to partner with in order for the new executive director to actually *be* great. When Rosanne took the helm, some board members had been on the board for

30 years. (Yes, I'm getting to term limits.) Now, a tenure that long doesn't immediately tell us that you need to get off the bus, but Rosanne began talking to each board member about the new ED search, what the expectations and opportunities of board service would look like. Some folks self-selected off, and with others, there were tough conversations. At the end of the process, 10 board members remained, forming the core of the board she and Carlos De La Rosa are now rebuilding together.

Term Limits

I am an unabashed champion for term limits. Let me be a bit clearer. Term limits that are *enforced.* Term limits provide two essential ingredients key to an effective board. First, they introduce urgency into the board recruitment process. There will always need to be prospects in the pipeline because folks don't get a seat and stay in it for THIRTY YEARS! The second reason is even more important. A board with term limits has to be thinking leadership attributes as it recruits. A board with solid and enforced term limits simply has to build a leadership pipeline, both on the board and in the prospect pool.

> A board with term limits has to be thinking leadership attributes as it recruits.

Accountability

To steal from a kid's book, *Yes, Virginia, you can hold a board member accountable to do her job and do it well.* If you have positioned board service as a privilege and an opportunity (and not like a big gulp of Robitussin) and if the board member's mission pilot light is stoked, a board member will want to do a good job and will want to know if you think she is.

When we talk about accountability, we are not just talking about evaluations, which most boards don't do for fear of losing board members. (Most board members who will jump off the board because of an evaluation, by the way, are probably not your very best board members.)

We are talking about committees with clear charges and annual goals. Board members need to know what success looks like so they can be successful. The folks who join boards are generally high performers who pride themselves on being successful. So give them that opportunity! Further, give them ownership of that success. "Mary, I'd like the governance committee to present at our next board meeting. As we start to think about the board, we need to align with our new strategic plan; we'd love for your committee to meet and draft a solid composition matrix and your good thinking about the top 3–5 gaps in skills and experience."

Voila! I'm clear about my role and what success looks like, and I'm being held accountable by allowing me to strut the committee "stuff" at the next meeting. Oh and by the way, the board chair and the executive director will both get a test-drive of my leadership. Wins all around.

Could YOU Be the Problem?

Is your "useless" board *your* fault? I could be talking about a lack of board leadership or an executive director that does not realize that the road runs both ways. A board member who arrives with passion and enthusiasm doesn't just magically stay that way. Is it possible that you weren't really even thinking about what the board members need from you?

Far too often, staff and board leaders focus only on what they need from the board (or what they don't get). "Bob hasn't renewed his own pledge this year." "Daniela didn't even fill a table at the gala." "Luis knows so many people and has not introduced any of them to us."

Did it ever occur to you that Daniela's pilot light went out?

Seriously, did she arrive with enthusiasm and has her board service been a series of gatherings she could have called in for? Is the committee she sits on unclear about its charge? Does the ED constantly nag her to sell tickets to the organization's two big events?

I wish I weren't right, but I bet I am.

IGNITING YOUR BOARD

You have recruited strategically. You haven't begged anyone. You were clear about time and fundraising commitment and equally clear about the opportunity to work with amazing board and staff colleagues on an issue of deep significance to the new board member. You have a new cohort of board members that could shift the overall dynamics of your board.

I hate to break it to you, but your work in creating articulate ambassadors, strategic thought partners, fiscal stewards, and fundraising champions is just beginning. You now must invest in them so that they can deliver.

Board and staff leaders must make and continue to make three core commitments to ensure they are keeping that mission pilot light aflame and to present regular opportunities to stoke it. Trust me. There is a direct correlation between the performance of a board member and that pilot light. Those three core commitments are making board meetings engaging, establishing the right kind of communications, and transforming board members into storytelling ambassadors.

Cue song. *Here's how to take this little light of theirs and let it shine.*

Board Meetings

I have met with more than a few sets of "copilots" and talked about "the case of the disengaged board." I ask to review the last 2–3 board meeting agendas and the accompanying minutes. After the exercise, I ask them point blank: "If you were a board member and attended each of these board members would you be engaged?" You grant their wish of keeping the board meetings short — *WHY????* Board meetings that are painful should be short, but a good board meeting should take the time necessary to "feed" the board with the nutrients they need to fulfill their responsibilities and most importantly, *to enable board members to feel they are contributing in a 3-dimensional way to the organization.*

Board members leave organizations because they feel like they are being used or nagged. "I feel like a human ATM." "I get asked for everything but my opinion about marketing and that is what I *do* for a living."

Board and staff leaders, listen closely: board meetings are not necessary evils. They are major touch points your board members have with your organization. You need to make them count. Here's how (and, again, I'm not gonna lie — it requires planning, partnership, and creativity — oh yes, and time). A quarterly board meeting of four hours should be designed 5–6 weeks in advance so that you can deliver on the following:

- **Put on a show.** If you want your audience to go out and sell "tickets," you put on a helluva good show. Every board meeting must bring the work to life and make every board member feel pride and privilege.
- **Engage them — ALL of what they bring.** Chances are you have board members with vast experience across many industries. You need that, and a board member expects to be asked to have

an opportunity to strut that stuff. I've been working with an Executive Director who likes to present a new idea, as he says, "tied up nicely with a bow so they know he has *got it!*" I suggest a different route that does not diminish the staff leader.

Try this example on. Two scripts.

> *Every board meeting must bring the work to life and make every board member feel pride and privilege.*

Script 1: "We are exploring the acquisition of a smaller HIV / AIDS organization that will add a new program that will make the whole of what we do greater than the sum of its parts. We will add youth programs to our work, three strong staff members, and a cash reserve. We look forward to keeping you posted on this exciting development as our conversations continue."

Script 2: "We are exploring the acquisition of a smaller HIV / AIDS organization that will add a new program that will make the whole of what we do greater than the sum of its parts. There is an opportunity for us to add youth programs to our work, three strong staff members, and a cash reserve. As we continue to explore this new relationship, we would love for you to help us think through the questions we should be asking, the challenges you see, and how we might maximize this acquisition for marketing and fundraising, and enhance the organization's brand."

Many EDs will avoid script #2 for fear that the board will take "ownership" of the strategy. This is not my experience, and a board chair with strong facilitator skills, along with planning each agenda item sent out ahead of time, should in fact result in the board feeling like a million bucks that you care what they think. And if you have the right folks on the board bus, you'll get smart questions and good ideas. And maybe someone will identify a resource they have for PR or something that would add real value.

How much better is that than a disengaged board member who leaves saying "The ED never let us into strategy. I had resources to bring to bear, but I never felt they were valued."?

- **Let them in on the inside scoop.** Board members join to be part of a special club — to get the inside track on the issues in the sector. That's a big perk for board service. Don't forget that. So give the people what they want! A guest speaker? How about an expert in the field, or a foundation program officer who gives you money and knows the sector really well and how your organization fits into it? Be sure board members can ask questions.
- **Share insights from the fearless leader.** When I was a board member, I often felt I didn't get enough of the insights our ED had about the work. There was so much that was transactional on the agenda. In the case of this organization, the ED had a long tenure and insights I felt like others heard but not me. Which felt ironic. And frustrating. How about an interview with the ED to tease this out for folks?
- **Build a cohesive group.** A colleague of mine, a fellow nonprofit leadership consultant and champion, focuses on leadership transitions. Ask her about the recipe for a smooth and effective transition, and she'll offer you a number of key ingredients. One of them surprised me at first.

When an organization is navigating change, the ability of the board to have a shared sense of values and purpose is key. A collection of individuals can engage in fractious conversations and can take their eye off the ball. The moral of this story is that the next time someone turns her nose up at the word *icebreaker,* remind her that a strong board knows and cares about each other and has a good sense of each other's personal values and how those values connect to the work.

And you sure don't get to that place by updating the by-laws or approving the minutes.

And by the way, getting to know each other doesn't have to happen through an icebreaker (and there are many downright awful ones to choose from). Be creative.

A few years back I worked with an LGBTQ family organization. Many board members had young children. I persuaded the ED and the board chair to have a chat over dessert with grown kids of LGBTQ parents — to offer a glimpse into the future. It was inspiring and enriching but to this point, board members started to talk about parenting, the personal stuff that makes people tick. It wasn't just inspiring. It was revealing, and yes, it was a team-building exercise.

Communications — The *Right* Kind

Ask most board members about the emails they receive from the staff and they will tell you "I cannot keep up with all the emails. Every one of them asks me to invite someone to something, sell something, or find a silent auction item. I actually delete some of them without even reading them."

Ask staff leaders and they will tell you "I send the board an email with some great news about a large new gift we got and what do I get in return? Nothing!"

Now you know why. The board member hit Delete without even reading the message.

I joke with my clients that the official insect of the nonprofit board is the cricket because it is the sound of crickets executive directors most often hear when it comes to board communications.

Having been a board member, I can say that all the communication *was* hard to keep up with. I often felt nagged, and the success stories about the work were often long and not easily digestible or shareable. I'm not proud of the cricket sounds I likely made, but as with most everything on our twin-engine jet, we need to assess each engine to ensure that it is high functioning. And in this case, it feels important for the staff leader to take responsibility for what they communicate, how often they communicate, and how they communicate. Attend to this with intention, and the cricket population will decrease dramatically. And the information will stick.

- **Reduce # of emails.** I speak from experience. Emails come from every which way and from board colleagues as well. My favorites are the folks who hit Reply All, resulting in 22 emails in my Inbox that say simply "Great!" Coordinate efforts in some fashion to bundle requests — it's just easier for a board member to look at a single email.
- **Introduce an impact email or video.** You might call it the "goose bump a week" email, but it's a story that you can arm every board member with that they can tell at the gym, the neighborhood barbeque when someone says, "Are you still on XYZ Board? What's going on there?" Give them a story they can tell in under a minute. And if you got a big gift, toss that in for good measure so that board members know they're playing for a winning team that is doing great work and being recognized for it. This email or video, done correctly, is also an antidote for inertia between board meetings. Board members have a tendency to disappear between meetings.

Invest in Their Ability to Be Ambassadors

In Chapter 3, I introduce you to my storytelling equation: "Credible messenger plus compelling story = new stakeholder." Earlier in this chapter, I spoke about marketing board service as a professional development opportunity. Another lesson here: the importance of using board meetings to enrich board members. Building and exercising storytelling muscles enriches board members and will pay dividends for the organization by strengthening its army of ambassadors.

Storytelling Practice

Don't call it *fundraising training* — it is so much more than that. Every leader in the organization, board and senior staff, has to be able to work a room, share their enthusiasm about your organization, and offer a quick story as an illustration. As I said earlier, the only way to get good at it? Practice. Illustrate the value of storytelling by adding 15 minutes to each board meeting agenda, put folks in pairs and role play a scenario. Or ask one or two people to give it a go in front of the whole group, and then ask everyone what they liked about the pitch and what they wish was different. It works like a charm.

Board members feel ill-equipped to talk about your organization; they think they don't know enough to be effective ambassadors. During this kind of exercise, board members realize that they don't need to know *everything*. Far too often, we try to say everything, and what ends up sticking? Nothing.

Support Board Members in Spreading the Word

Board members need to be fed stories to share. These stories need to be current and easy to tell, and they need to be in a format that is a no-brainer for board members to share.

> *Board members need to be fed stories to share.*

I know that executive directors like to do a monthly report and check the box on the board communications for the month. But as with any smart communications strategy, you have to keep your eye on the audience and what it needs. Those long emails have staff info and reminders that there are still fundraiser event tickets to be sold, and maybe somewhere embedded in the lengthy email is an amazing story about the work.

What if you separated the to-dos from the impact stories? You could do something creative that would stick with board members and arrived in a format that allowed board members to share the stories you send with ease.

How about a client video from an iPhone? Something simple, short, and powerful? Along with the video, include a prewritten caption: "So proud to be on the board of XYZ. Take 2 minutes to hear Marco's remarkable story" — no ask but, yes, a link to the site.

Or let's say your ED was interviewed for a written publication, and the story appears today. By the end of the afternoon, a link goes out to all board members asking them to share on social media platforms. Be sure to include a simple headline for board members.

I talk about this in Chapter 8, which deals with small non-profits, but this is a key strategy regardless of size. Board members must get comfortable initiating conversations with people who would benefit from knowing and doing more for your organization.

And staff leadership has to think about what to communicate and really lean in to supporting efforts board members can take to share the work and its impact. In so doing, you educate board members about the work and enrich them in how to get the story succinct and impactful, and make it easy for leadership to get out the good word about their amazing work.

PUT IT ALL TOGETHER AND WHAT DO YOU GET?

Start with the step most organizations miss. Explain what board service really is: a profoundly important job critical to the success of a nonprofit. Build it with intention and provide it with the fuel to fulfill its role.

> Explain what board service really is: a profoundly important job critical to the success of a nonprofit.

The steps I offer here work. If at first the number of steps seems overwhelming, start with a few and work your way toward others. You'll see a big difference quickly.

The right people on the board "bus," clear about their role, and with the tools to hit it out of the park, are just what your organization needs to succeed.

Next up, time to talk strategy.

"You want to triple your capacity without a strategic plan? Don't mind Charlie. My dog often finds things funny."

Chapter 5 The Key Is Not in the Answers. It's in the Questions

Building Successful Strategies with Room for Innovation

THE POWER OF DELETING A WORD

Fingers crossed that the first several chapters have offered you a new perspective on nonprofit leadership. Maybe you even took notes or sent a copy to a friend (this idea I like quite a bit). And then you turned the page, saw the word *strategy* and — fess up — you rolled your eyes a bit, right? Perhaps you're a board chair and you know that the organization you lead lacks the kind of money necessary for the type of strategy work you do in the private sector. Or you have an executive director who balks at the idea — too much work for a process that will unearth nothing new.

I wish more nonprofit leaders felt differently. I get business inquiries frequently: "We have to do a strategic plan," and it is said with all the enthusiasm I feel when I say to my wife, "We really need to do the laundry." Let's focus on the most important word in the sentence (no, not *laundry*): *plan.*

A few years back, I was working with a client that was tracking its progress against its strategic plan, which had been approved by the board about 18 months earlier. The staff found the plan utterly useless. The world of the senior staff revolved around a three-letter acronym: *KPI*, or *key performance indicator*. KPIs are the granular activities that roll up into less granular activities that roll up into even less granular activities, and then if you are *really* lucky (or patient), you find your way to some kind of overriding goal. Allow me to elaborate.

Let's say your overriding goal for the year in your area of the nonprofit is to "run a more effective office to support the program folks so that they can serve more clients." A KPI might be, "Purchase electric pencil sharpener to increase efficiency." OK, I'm exaggerating, but this is how the staff saw it. The staff began to see KPI not as a three-letter word but as a four-letter one. Why? Because all anyone cared about was how many KPIs they could check off in the space between board meetings. It was like a bad game show.

And then, at each board meeting, the board received an update. After all, the board must fulfill its core responsibility to approve and monitor the success of the organization's strategy. In this model, board members were bombarded with a long list of the successfully completed KPIs. Oh, one of the things I just love about this format is that, typically, a percentage completion rate appears next to each KPI. So board members may learn that the office manager is 78% completed with the pencil sharpener KPI. Makes you want to poke someone in the eye with a 78% sharpened pencil, doesn't it?

The point here is that the work became all about the *plan* and that, as a result, every single bit of enthusiasm about where the organization might be headed was lost or

> President Dwight Eisenhower once said, "Plans are useless, but planning is everything."

squashed — or both. My client lost sight of what President Dwight Eisenhower once said, "Plans are useless, but planning is everything."

The folks at Monitor Institute by Deloitte, at www.monitor-institute.com, an arm of Deloitte Consulting, have done a great deal of thinking and writing about how nonprofit organizations should approach strategy work, especially in a world that moves as quickly as ours does. In their article published in the *Stanford Social Innovation Review,* "The Strategic Plan is Dead; Long Live Strategy," they capture it well: "Instead of the old approach of 'making a plan and sticking to it,' . . . we believe in 'setting a direction and testing to it,' treating the whole organization as a team that is experimenting its way to success."

I'm with President Eisenhower and the smart folks at Monitor Institute — it's time to throw the word *plan* overboard and begin to think differently about strategic planning.

It's time to stop engaging in processes that suck the life out of the people involved. The irony is too much for me. A great strategy conversation should breathe life into the organization and its stakeholders.

THE POWER OF INQUIRY

I never rolled my eyes when I was in strategic planning mode as an executive director, and it's not because I am a strategy geek. It's because I am a problem solver. I love to think through knots that need to be untangled, and I love to debate options with smart and diverse folks. During my tenure as an executive director, I had smart senior staff who knew the tough questions to ask, and I believe I created an environment in which it was safe to ask them. I also had a critical mass of smart and committed board members who allowed for the kind of robust conversation that most of them had joined the board to be a part of in the first place.

And I'm not talking about questions that land in the tactical space. You have to ask the *right* question, which is often the question one level underneath your initial questions.

Here's what I mean, for example: "How do we increase the number of students in our upper school and retain them?" This is *a question,* but not *the question. The* question might be, "Given that our best efforts to market and recruit have not succeeded, and we can't get sufficient numbers of students to be profitable, and our attrition numbers are well below average, what radical, innovative decisions could we make to solve this problem? And closing the upper school should be a decision to explore."

Or how about this one, from a nonprofit journalism organization that creates long-form journalism offered to mainstream news outlets for greatest impact and reach: "How do we drive more traffic to our website?" Isn't this the real question instead: " What is our website strategy — what do we need the website to do for us? Our site will never have the reach of *the New York Times,* so if our mission is about reach, about public education, what is our web presence really about?"

The swell thing about strategy work that begins with unearthing the important strategic questions is that you need only *one thing* in order to do it really, really well. Did you think I was going to say "a blank check"? Could you hire someone to help you figure out those questions? Absolutely. Would you wind up with a solid set of questions, and could that same person help you navigate the discussions and provide (or direct you to) the resources that will give you what you need to answer them? Indeed.

So, what is that one thing you need? Guts.

People talk about innovation all the time. It's a key buzzword in our society. And often the focus is on the outcomes of innovation. But where are its origins? The origins of innovation are found in a smart, dedicated staff and board observing the knots in an organization and being bold enough to ask the tough questions.

WE'RE ALL IN THIS TOGETHER

I've known a few EDs in my day who don't exactly respect the board when it comes to designing the future of "their" organization. OK, more than a few. The folks who feel that way end up with a strategy that is exactly what they want — but it

- Lacks the benefit of the good thinking of smart people outside the staff
- Is rubber-stamped by the board, who approved it, but did not have a voice in it, doesn't own it, and is not invested in its success

This approach has another big problem: It's actually not your job. Well, it's not your job alone, anyway. The development and approval of the strategy is a responsibility that ultimately rests with the board. If this statement comes as any kind of surprise to you, you might want to reread Chapter 4!

So how does an ED juggle what they believe is a serious imbalance between board and staff around the knowledge and understanding of the organization and its future challenges and opportunities?

Wait. What? A serious imbalance? Let's start with the problem embedded in that belief. There should not *be* a serious imbalance. Remember:

- The ED is not the lone juggler. That person has a partner in the board chair (is it time to reread Chapter 3?). It can be easy to forget though, right? And it can be *so* much easier to just do it yourself, right? Wrong. At least not in the long run.
- Why *doesn't* your board have the knowledge and understanding? Isn't it the job of the board and staff leaders to ensure that meetings and communications are designed in such a way that board members can engage in rich, robust strategic conversations?
- Simply put, you might not have the right board members. I did mention something in the preceding chapter about how important that is. This is one of the places where a great diverse board really gets to shine.

Let's get real for a minute. Suppose you haven't "fed" your board so that they can truly deliver for the organization on strategic conversations. Maybe you have a weak board chair or a weak executive director. Maybe you have all the wrong board members. Should you move forward with a strategic process or should you delay? My advice? If at least one of your leaders is strong and you have some strong staff and a few good board members, you're good to go. And most organizations have that much. One more suggestion: this is a fantastic opportunity to engage a few smart outside folks — one or two people not on the board can add real value. What about a key donor who isn't interested in board service but happens to work at a strategy consulting firm?

Get your best and brightest to say yes and build the team creatively, if you need to. Then the two leaders of the organization can lead the strongest possible team to create the strongest strategy for the organization you all care deeply about.

START AT THE VERY BEGINNING

The first question to ask as part of a strategy initiative is the same regardless of your nonprofit: "Does our mission statement continue to reflect who we serve, what we do and the intended impact?"

You have to start here because the discussion that follows is the perfect kickoff to any good strategic inquiry. Your mission statement is the essence of your organization. It has to be right, and in a surprising number of cases, it isn't. And, in an equally surprising number of cases, a strategic plan can miss this part of the process altogether.

Your mission statement is the essence of your organization. It has to be right.

For nearly a decade I ran the Gay and Lesbian Alliance Against Defamation (GLAAD). When founded in 1985 by a small group of attorneys, its mission read: "GLAAD works to promote positive portrayals of gay and lesbian people in the media as a means to end homophobia and discrimination based on sexual orientation." In 1985 this statement made all the sense in the world; the organization was founded in reaction to the homophobic coverage of AIDS in national and local news coverage and to films and TV shows that either omitted gays altogether or depicted them in a negative light — as deviant and unhappy and unable to sustain any kind of lasting relationship.

By 1995 the organization's work had expanded and the group of stakeholders — volunteers, donors, and board members — had grown and diversified. The GLAAD family now included men and women affiliated with the media, and so when the group began to update its strategy, the mission statement raised a fundamental strategic question: "Can we legitimately ask the media to cover the gay community only in a *positive* light?" With media executives now at the table, the answer was a resounding no. The job of the media is to be fair, accurate, and objective. While this realization led to many changes in strategy, the lead change was the mission statement: "GLAAD works to promote *fair and accurate* inclusion of the gay and lesbian community in all forms of media as a means to end homophobia and discrimination based on sexual orientation."

It all seems obvious, right? Maybe even straightforward? Maybe not. I was recently asked to help a board become more effective ambassadors for the work of their organization. I did my homework and was inspired and happy to help. The organization was rooted in the Catholic tradition, providing shelter and job training for homeless adults and families in an urban setting. The work is important, and Catholic parishes and schools serve as feeders for both the volunteers and the clients.

But my homework unearthed a fundamental strategic problem with the organization — a core strategic question that flies out at you just by reading the mission statement carefully. Here's the mission statement, see if you see what I did:

"Our organization provides hope for families — keeping them together and supporting their efforts to rebuild independent lives. We serve the Catholic and broader community, offering shelter, mental health services, and workforce development programs addressing each client holistically and offering them hope and a brighter future."

Look closely for the big strategic question screaming out of this mission statement. I summed it up toward the end of the training when I asked the board how long they had worked on the development of this mission statement. I took a guess that it was a protracted, and perhaps even difficult, conversation. They asked me how I knew. Instead of telling them, I asked another question: "How long did it take you to settle on the word *broader*? "Forever," they nearly shouted in unison. Bingo.

This wonderful organization had the need and the opportunity to answer one of its most significant strategic questions when it explored its mission statement in depth. Must you be committed to Catholicism to be eligible for services? Some board members were adamant about this issue; others, not so much. The board clearly had no consensus. The result — a mission statement that does not drive a stake in the ground to answer a key question: "Who do we serve?"

A MISSION SNIFF TEST

You don't have to save the sniff test for the kickoff of the process to develop your organization's new strategy — frankly, I think you should consider it part of an annual "checkup." That said, this is an excellent and easy way for an organization to explore the assets and strategic challenges of its mission statement with substantive context from those who know the organization best.

Feedback from external stakeholders is critical to any strategic inquiry, and when hired to complete a comprehensive strategy for an organization (and an accompanying work plan), I rely heavily on qualitative information from stakeholder interviews. A key question we ask: "What do you understand the mission of XYZ organization to be?" Then we capture their words verbatim. We may learn more from this single question than from any other. A couple years ago, I was retained to work with a client, and we began with 65 interviews. We captured 65 mission statements, including my favorite: "They — um — I give up." After the interviews were completed, we told the board and senior staff that we had captured, essentially, more than 50 *completely different* mission statements. Pun intended here: Mission Control, we have a problem. More on that client in the next section — stay tuned for a happy ending.

> Feedback from external stakeholders is critical to any strategic inquiry.

Many organizations do not have the money (keep reading — I'm getting there) to hire someone to conduct interviews, and so my sniff test can do the trick. Let's assume that you hold a board and/or staff retreat to kick off the process. One month before it begins, you give this assignment to every participant: Identify five people who are connected to the organization in some way — a colleague in the sector, a donor, an elected official, a reporter, a volunteer, or a ticket buyer to an event — and then email those names and their affiliations to Mary, a staff member. Mary makes sure the list is representative and diverse and then sends everyone on their way. Each person reaches out to the five folks with this message:

We are embarking on a process to evaluate our current strategy and make changes as we see fit, and we can't do it without feedback from external folks close to the organization. I have just two simple questions for you:

1. *What do you understand is the mission of our organization?*
2. *Can you describe a tangible success the organization has had in the last year? If yes, what was it? And why was it important?*

Capture their answers verbatim. That's crucial. *Verbatim.*

In a large organization, the info can be compiled and circulated before the retreat. If your organization is small, invest in large sticky notes and have folks walk into the retreat surrounded by the answers — mission statements on one side and successes on the other. That is all the context you need in order to kick off a discussion about the big questions you have to answer to build an effective strategy for your organization, and you will do so with external feedback all around you (literally).

WHAT SUCCESS LOOKS LIKE

Earlier in this chapter I mentioned my client and the 50 different versions of the mission statement I heard during stakeholder interviews. I bet you're wondering how that all turned out. It's been 18 months since I first walked through the door, and it's quite a different organization. It's still quite messy (nonprofits can be like that), but the changes have been dramatic.

The client was in the nonprofit journalism sector and produced content for National Public Radio, content focused on bringing the voices of Latinos to life for listeners. The organization was founded by a charismatic journalist who is fierce, creative, passionate, and persuasive, and who was the first to admit that she knew nothing about running a nonprofit organization. Her vision and passion attracted well-known institutional funders who admired the founder and provided the organization with generous (often restricted) grants for particular kinds of topics and areas of interest they wanted to see covered. When I arrived on the scene, the budget was between $1 million and $2 million, but — because so many dollars were restricted — they often had challenges covering general operating expenses. Yet another common story.

A year before I arrived, the organization moved into television, producing a 10-part series for PBS. Instead of a focus specifically on the Latino community, the series told the stories of the changing American demographic. The organization was ill prepared to enter TV, and being on staff felt more like being a cowpoke trying to hang on to a bucking bronco at a rodeo. The staff clung to the horse and went on to win a coveted Peabody Award for their efforts — worth the ride.

But the staff was badly shaken up. A TV culture and a radio culture. In two different offices in two different NYC boroughs. A different staff culture. The TV folks were largely ridiculously talented documentarians who wanted to tell the great stories. They believed that they worked for a production company and were freelancers. The radio folks were full-time and highly mission driven. Can you say "tension?"

Managing all of this was a small handful of staff. Too small. The executive director (not the founder) had been the organization's director of finance. To save money, she did not replace herself; and the bookkeeping proved challenging. So, in the blink of an eye, the ED was the ED *and* the director of finance *and* the bookkeeper. As this situation continued, the ability to understand the finances became more and more difficult.

Meanwhile, back at the ranch (or rodeo), the founder (like all founders) had new ideas all the time and couldn't quite figure out why the organization couldn't make it happen or couldn't make it happen fast enough. As a journalist, you are hard-wired to run with your story before you are scooped. And, as anyone who has ever dealt with a founder knows, it is hard to say no to the founder.

Let's not forget to talk about product and impact. The product was, and continued to be, of the highest quality, but with distribution only on NPR, its reach was low. And when you are looking for funding, quality alone is not enough. In addition, the organization was at the mercy of NPR, and the show appeared at different times in different markets. For reasons that seemed inexplicable for an entity that claimed to want to increase the diversity of its audience, the show aired at 5:00 A.M. in some markets.

Let's not also forget the board. That shared leadership thing I've been preaching — you know, the core foundation of this book you are reading — well, we had none of that here. We had a *founder board*: four friends of the founder. They met via phone and, while well-meaning and passionate about the work of the founder, failed to understand their role, understood little about the rodeo, and added little value to the organization. To make matters worse (it gets worse?), the chair was deeply committed to the power of public radio and believed that, regardless of reach or impact, the organization's mission was inextricably tied to public radio.

Not a single thing I have written is unusual in an organization run by founders. In fact, in many ways my client was well ahead of the game. The founder had relationships with the heads of some of the most significant institutional funders in the country, and the quality of the product was undeniably first-rate. These two elements put them way ahead of the lion's share of 5-year-old organizations still run by their founders.

My company was hired to answer a question that, on its surface, appears to be quite simple: "Can you help us find a path to sustainability?" If I have learned one thing about clients, it is that the question I am asked to answer is infrequently the question the clients *need* answered. You have to dig around and see just how messy things are, and pretty quickly you can discern the *underlying* question. In the case of the founder, she just wanted us to help her figure out how to raise more money. "Who else can we be asking? Is our development director strong enough? How do we find prospects?" If an organization is having trouble raising money, 99% of the time it's a systemic problem — mission, quality of service, reach, messaging, weak board — the list goes on.

It was clear that this organization needed a new strategy. And so I set off to help them create one.

Whether you hire a big-time firm or a single individual or you have no resources and do it yourself, the steps are all basically the same:

Step 1: Assemble the team. This is the critical first step. Bring together a diverse group of board and staff for whom the work will be intellectually stimulating. The group should not be too large — maybe five to seven people. You can even engage someone who is not on the board who might have some strategic planning experience and who can be asked to participate in this single particular initiative. Despite its not being a decision-making group, it will generate ideas, build a list of external stakeholders to interview, and then work to tease out possible answers to the big questions. Then, as the process continues, generate possible strategy ideas or paths the organization might travel.

Step 2: Check under the hood. In this step, you take a three-dimensional look at the organization. Analysis + interviews. A focus on fundraising strategy, financial statements and cash flow, and the "org chart." A look at the competition and the sector in which the organization lives. Then interviews galore — internal and external. Learn about what's working and what's not. At the end of this step, as in any good physical, the diagnostician sits down with the "patient" (board plus senior staff). They present their findings in the form of key questions.

Clients sometimes wonder: If you spend a month or two asking questions, why do you not have answers? The simple answer is that organizational challenges typically stem from unanswered questions. Remember our friends at the Catholic organization that serves homeless adults and family? If I were hired to go "under the hood" with them, you can bet that one question at the "patient" presentation would be, "Whom do you serve? Catholic people? Or a broader group of clients?" That conflict in audience, "punted" during the mission discussion, will appear throughout the diagnostic phase.

In the case of our nonprofit media client, they had significant questions to answer:

- Should you remain a nonprofit organization or become a production company?
- You began as a nonprofit that focuses on the unheard voices of the Latino community but seem to have shifted to talking about the "new American mainstream." Can you do both?
- Is this organization wed to its commitment to public media (a distribution channel that is limiting in terms of sheer numbers and demographics)?
- Is the public media audience the one you want to reach? Are you working to give visibility to Latino Americans and their stories? Or do you want others to know and hear those stories? If so, who are those others?

See why sustainability is an issue?

Step 3: Attack the big strategic questions. In this next phase, I spent a lot of time with the client and our strategy working group (board and staff are vital). We met often, brainstormed, and, together, figured out what other information we could use that would be helpful in answering the questions.

Actually, let me take that back — we identified information that would be helpful in shaping *possible* answers to the questions. In my world of strategy work, the organization can always travel different paths, and the goal of the process is to explore several options to present. First of all, there is never just one answer, and to present a single strategy gives the board no frame of reference. Second, you own the path when you have to intentionally select it from a short list. Think of it this way: when you shop for something to wear for a big occasion, do you buy the first item you try on?

The other important part of this phase is testing. I like the Monitor Institute philosophy I mentioned earlier in this chapter — treat the whole organization as a team that is experimenting its way to success.

So, when my company works with clients, we brainstorm ideas to test-drive a possible direction. In the case of this client, what if they offered WNYC, the flagship NPR station in New York City, a podcast series in exchange for some undetermined item? Well, to bring the series to life, the client decided to create a sample episode so that the conversation would be real and not abstract. It was well received and helped us shape a particular strategic path for consideration.

During this phase, the working group worked. They had relationships that could get us information and propose ideas more quickly than we could. Also, we worked closely with the staff and built multiple organizational charts — each path demanded something different. And each of those charts had a different price tag.

More than anything, we focused on reach. We probed (and maybe even lobbied) the client to look at the limiting nature of public media and to look at other forms of distribution. We knew that clarity and reach across platforms would drive dollars.

Maybe you are wondering how the client paid its bills during this time (or our bills, for that matter). As for us, our client knew this work was necessary, and so did its lead funder. Money was granted, and my firm was one of several interviewed. As for the daily funding challenges, we worked with the client to build a strategy to return to the funders and ask for the dollars to be unrestricted. We helped message that request from a place of strength and not weakness. We were building something different, more impactful — and we needed the running room to build, to test, and to implement. The unrestricted dollars also enabled us to bring in a nonprofit finance expert who presented a clear picture and became an important part of the team as we built budgets for each path.

Four months of work — inside the organization, talking with media folks and putting the working group to work — paid off. Let me also say that the group was fully engaged and felt a real sense of ownership about the outcome. Folks raised their hands to hold meetings and to spend extra time during the workday to develop ideas to build greater reach for existing products. Being a part of this group was not a burden. The work was exciting — it was not about how would we stay "alive" but rather about how would we "come to life."

Step 4: Drive a stake in the ground. This step takes the form of a detailed board presentation outlining possible paths and the implications of each. But the work is about more than picking a path. It's about picking a path that the board can get behind and that the board leadership believes can attract the cream of the crop — a path with a marketable vision that will enable the organization to build its fundraising capacity.

And we didn't forget to go back to the beginning — to the mission statement. Our new strategy and vision for our client led to a new mission statement for the board to consider:

Our organization creates multimedia content for and about the new American mainstream in the service of empowering people to navigate the complexities of an increasingly diverse and connected world.

Today our client still faces some of the challenges that come with being founder-led — I'm not gonna lie. But the transformation is impressive and gratifying. The organization invested in key program staff to drive multimedia content and marketing. It has paid off and then some. The board, once a group of 4 that played follow-the-leader, is now leading. The group of 12 has even formed committees! And the increased reach and impact have opened many more doors. A major donor program has been created. New institutional funders have been cultivated and have delivered. Donors are cultivated at newsroom events where young and dedicated staff members share stories about how stories come to be. The organization has indeed come to life. And, as icing on the cake, the funder is thrilled, and a significant general operating grant "seemed" likely at the time of publication.

> Their strategy is an ongoing experiment. They are continually trying new things. The picture isn't perfectly rosy, and the nonprofit is still messy. That's how it is with nonprofits.

One last important note: The client's strategy is an ongoing experiment. They are continually trying new things. The picture isn't perfectly rosy, and the nonprofit is still messy. That's how it is with nonprofits.

BIG DREAMS, BIG CHALLENGES, AND SMALL BUDGETS

You may be thinking, "Good for Joan's client. They received a grant from a supportive funder to bring her in. I just asked everyone to empty their pockets, and we came up with $6.27 and a whole lot of lint." Are small nonprofits doomed to suboptimal strategies? Absolutely not.

Before assuming there is no money to be found, read about what some of my clients are doing.

Some strategy consultants will work with you to help secure funding. Try asking a consultant to put together a proposal with a clear situation analysis outlining why the strategy work is needed and why it is needed now. For example, I wrote a strategy proposal for a school for hearing impaired kids that examined strategy and board building (these are intrinsically tied together, of course) and then made the case for urgency around the upcoming retirement of the head of the school. The proposal is being evaluated by a funder who has been continually generous. This strategy work will secure that investment by making sure that the organization has a strong "north star" and that it addresses challenges with its revenue model and has a strong board. These are the elements an organization needs to have in place to recruit the best possible talent to lead the school in the years ahead. The money may or may not come through, but it's a strong, detailed proposal with a sense of urgency behind it.

If you come up short, you have a way to execute a smart and successful process inexpensively: Hire a good consultant on the cheap and build a strategy working group that is prepared to do interesting work — that group essentially becomes the consultant's team, working under their guidance and direction. The consultant guides the efforts and facilitates the in-depth work of the team. Do it in the summer, when things tend to be quieter. Market the participation in the group as an opportunity to have a real hand in building the future of the organization. This format can work with small strategic initiatives and the development of a full organizational strategy.

I worked with a community center that wanted to bring more women through its doors. We pulled together a terrific group of folks who brought with them the kinds of skills we needed on the team — a board member with a marketing background, a staff member who was a CFO, a program person who had recently surveyed visitors, and another staff member with terrific institutional memory that offered critical context. The ED positioned the working group in such a way that it felt like an honor to be asked (in fact, some were miffed that they had not been asked). There was peer accountability about getting work done and the quality of work was very good. Was it as good as the product of a highly paid consultant? Maybe not, but the work product came from a person with some serious skin in the game. I facilitated several sessions of the group and drove them toward the creation of a board presentation outlining several paths the community center could take along with a good development strategy for each.

You could extrapolate this model for a full organizational strategy. In this kind of model, it would be exceedingly helpful to have a board member recruit for participation a friend of the organization who has a strategic planning background. There will be lots to do, and it's possible that a person like that could work in partnership with the strategy consultant to move the process forward.

And — oh, by the way — don't forget to start off the whole process with the mission sniff test. That's how you cover your external stakeholder interviews without spending a ton of money.

10 FINAL WORDS OF ADVICE TO KEEP HANDY

1. Don't start the process until everyone is on exactly the same page about the distinction between a goal, a strategy, and a tactic.
2. Typically, organizations can't afford to have the consultant stick around to create annual goals for each department.

This may seem obvious, but don't forget to complete this step. I have one client that hired a big firm to develop a strategy for determining what the organization will look like in four years. No document could be found that listed the 5 to 10 goals the organization needed to accomplish each year in order to reach its destination.

3. Before you begin to think about the new, think about the current. Are you sufficiently resourced to do all the things you do *today?* At GLAAD, our strategy included increased development horsepower to raise money to rightsize — to make sure we had the financial resources to do what we were doing.

4. A strategy that excludes a meaningful change in the board to complement the strategy is incomplete and likely to fail.

5. The key ambassadors of the organization should be able to summarize the strategy in a few compelling sentences and specify where you are headed, inviting investment in the future. Your strategy should get people at hello (see Chapter 2 for a refresher).

6. I'll take Step 5 one step further: Build a compelling strategy and you can secure multiyear gifts — my favorite kinds of gifts.

7. A plan that leaves the elephant in the middle of the room may succeed in the short run, but the challenge will continue to haunt you (remember the Catholic services organization story?).

8. If you are lucky enough to have a cash reserve, initiate a conversation about innovation and risk. As a donor, I'm all for financial stability, but I also admire an organization that takes a smart risk in the service of greater impact.

9. If your answer to the question "What is your strategy for the next three years?" is similar to this, "We are going to stay the course and grow by 15%," go back to the drawing board. First, the statement is an oxymoron. Staying the course won't generate new revenue. And increased revenue is not a strategy. It's an *outcome* of a strategy.

10. "The main thing is to keep the main thing the main thing." (This isn't the first time, or the last time, I'll quote leadership guru Stephen Covey in this book.) Repeat this mantra as you devise ways to monitor and evaluate the success of your work and as you consider how to provide information to your board. And, I'm thinkin' you may want to avoid KPIs.

"When you ask for donations, you will hear the word 'NO' a lot. I thought this might be helpful."

Chapter 6 You Can Do This

Fundraising is about an invitation to join you in the remarkable work you do. It's about building relationships that last.

Dear Joan:

I'm applying for my dream job. I've always wanted to run my own nonprofit. But there is a flag on the field. I've not done much (any?) fundraising. How can I persuade the board to take a leap of faith? I know I care deeply enough about this organization to ask anyone to do anything for it. But a check would be a new thing for me.

Signed,
Dreaming About My Dream Job

Dear Dreaming:

First, congratulations on getting an interview for the dream gig. *Remember:* the search committee or headhunter must see some skills and attributes in you that have brought you this close. So relax a bit and start thinking about how to message your past experience to fit the situation. In fact, I actually like your line, "I care deeply enough about your organization to do anything for it." As a search committee member, I'd be impressed.

But you'll need to dig deeper and broader. I want you to think about the kind of person you are, your level of commitment and passion for the issues that matter to you, and how you have translated that into action.

I speak from experience. I was one of the final two candidates for an executive director position at GLAAD. I won't bury the lede. The other finalist had many qualities I did not — tons of community experience, significant gravitas, and lots of fundraising experience. As Charlie Brown might have said, I felt like I had "a rock." Not entirely fair. I was a passionate, strong communicator and a relationship builder, and I had experience in the sector in which GLAAD lived — the media.

When the question about my fundraising experience came, I was ready. I thought, "They are going to buy this or laugh me right out of the conference room." First, I told them that I made the pitch for the annual fund at my kids' school. Parents said they came to hear my speeches whether they gave or not (I left that last part out). I had parents weeping and signing contracts in the moment, and, yes, I'm guessing my remarks secured some gifts. But it was the next line I found to be the riskiest.

"In my current role at Showtime, I manage the joint venture between the company and Don King Productions" (Don is a well-known boxing promoter with big hair, big personality, and big questions about his ethics). "Every quarter, I sit with Don and work to extract money from him that he owes Showtime. Don and I have built a relationship that results in my success. So here's what I figure: if I can secure funds from a person not interested in parting with them and who would be happy to walk down the street to HBO, I'm thinking you could put me in front of a donor who's eager to hear how the work of GLAAD is changing hearts and minds and ultimately laws. I should be really good at that."

Did they buy it? Were they impressed at my creativity (or my chutzpah)? I never asked. It didn't matter. I was offered a brand-new, low-paying job and never felt luckier in my life.

Until I sat with the director of finance and realized we had $360 in the bank. And $250,000 in aging (ancient) accounts payable. Oh, and then we had 18 staff members (including myself) expecting paychecks.

And thus, on my first day of work, I realized that it was time to deliver on the promise — to put my hypothesis to the test. The leap of faith that the board took on me paid off for the organization, the gay rights movement, and certainly for me personally. I did it. I raised a great deal of money that made a great deal of difference.

You can do this, too. And I'm not just talking to EDs and development directors. I'm talking to board members. In fact, I *have* to be talking to all of you.

Fundraising is a team sport. Board chairs and staff leaders must lead in partnership to bring together the two most powerful organizational engines to identify resources for the important work of your organization.

> Fundraising is a team sport.

When I talk about fundraising, I need to clarify something: I'm talking about a direct conversation with an individual in which you talk about the organization you care deeply enough about to work for in either a paid (staff) or unpaid (board) capacity and say with clarity, "Would you consider joining me in making a contribution to the organization in the amount of X dollars?" (PS Event tickets do not count — more on this in a bit.)

OK, time to fess up. Some board members have never uttered these specific words. You've persuaded friends to join you at a fabulous event, and maybe you have even sent an email to 10 friends to ask — maybe. And how many of you EDs and development directors have actually made the ask? Something specific. Not like "We'd love for you to get more involved." (I think I see heads hanging low in shame.)

I JUST CAN'T

Why not? You care deeply and you give time or treasure or both. Well, you can choose from many answers that range from "I don't have the information I need from the staff" to "I don't have enough time" to "I don't know any rich people" (more on this later as well).

I hear these all the time, and we'll address some of these as we progress together through this chapter, but I want to dive into the two I hear the most. They just slay me every single time I hear them.

I'm currently educating a newly formed board about fundraising. I ask board members to write down one word that comes to mind when they think about sitting in front of a donor and asking for an outright gift. I shuffle the cards and have board members read each other's cards. The answers are always predictable. I might see *nervous* or *unprepared* and occasionally *willing*. But I always see the word *terrifying*.

The number one reason boards do not ask for individual gifts: they find it terrifying.

Grown men and women, often with big jobs, responsible for large budgets and managing a team of people.

Terrifying. I am kind to them and encourage them to think about putting the word *terrifying* into perspective. I suggest it be reserved for really big things. And then I show them the slide in Figure 6.1 and tell them that this is what *terrifying* looks like to me.

I have the kind of demeanor that leads folks to laugh and not be insulted when this slide appears. They laugh. They get it. It puts the word in context.

FIGURE 6.1   What *terrifying* really looks like.

The number two reason boards do not ask for individual gifts: they are afraid their friends will be mad at them for asking.

This translates into one of two things: 1) it feels awkward and/or 2) they will ask *me* for money in return.

Again, we are talking about grown men and women, afraid their friends will be mad at them or (gasp!) that their friends may also have causes they care about!

Isn't it remarkable, the kind of power money has over people? I try not to let it get me down, but I am confident that if we had a healthier relationship to money, more nonprofits would have great development staff and first-rate board members and all the causes we all care about would move further downfield.

YES, YOU CAN

This leads me to the three most important reasons that you can do it:

Number One Reason You Can Do It: It's Your Job!

For staff, this one is simple. As an executive director or a development director, this is what you were hired to do. If you find yourself at your desk for most of the day and look ahead to next month's calendar and don't see donor meetings (lots of them) — either stewardships or renewals or upgrades — you are not doing your job. Yes, yes — I know there is data to enter/manage/correct and upcoming events and save-the-date cards to get out. But this can't happen at the expense of personal interaction with donors and prospects.

As for board members, I'm letting you slightly off the hook. Many, many organizations are so hungry for your board service that they are not as forthcoming about the fundraising obligation as they should be. We talked about it in Chapter 4. They might "scare you off," right? After all, fundraising can be terrifying. So it *is* possible that the responsibility was not made clear. And, by the way, this is a key reason that board members find fundraising challenging.

Number Two Reason You Can Do It: Money = Programs

A funny thing can happen to a board member when it comes to fundraising. It feels like an uncomfortable (dare I say *icky?*) task, like they are being asked to sell an old, broken chair to their next-door neighbor. Snap out of it!

Remember: You are asking for money to support critical work that you care so much about that you chose to serve on the organization's board.

And the more excited you are about the programs, the more of an ignited ambassador you will be, eager to invite folks to get more involved.

Here's an exercise to incorporate into your next budgeting process. It will help your board understand the program work that the budget covers and the work you *wish* the budget included:

- Let's have the staff build the budget that includes the items they truly needed rather than the items that fit into a flat budget.
- Create the revenue budget you feel is realistic. OK, now, here's where it gets fun.
- Before the numbers go anywhere near the board, prioritize and do the painstaking task of cutting critical and important items because you can't raise enough money. Maybe you decide to increase the revenue numbers slightly but you wind up with a list that we should just call the "*not*-a-wish-list."
- Before the finance committee starts nitpicking the numbers as they should, put this item on the agenda for the board meeting before you approve the budget: Lessons learned during budgeting process. Try to allow for 90 minutes. In this exercise, ED presents the "*not*-a-wish-list." Make it clear and simple and powerful. Maybe just one page. With dollar amounts tied to each big item. And don't forget to total it.

What is the purpose of this exercise? So many executive director clients of mine marvel at how quickly budgets get passed at board meetings. No one seems to ask questions, they tell me. The finance committee can ask good questions, but the budget is neat and tidy by the time it hits them.

This exercise brings to life a reasonable list of program related work, or work critical to doing that program work, that is *not* in the budget at all. It struck me the other day when I was talking to a client who runs a $7 million organization and helping him with time management: "Does your board realize that you don't have an assistant?" Nope, not a clue.

What if these things were on a list and then presented and discussed? I think that if you have a good, solid board, two outcomes are possible. The home run outcome? The board is horrified and establishes its own fundraising goal, commits to it and instructs the finance committee to increase the revenue line by that amount and an important item gets added back in. The other outcome is more fundamental. Your board (and development staff, if you are lucky to have one) will see right there in front of them that Money = Programs. You move from a discussion of, "This is what we can do because this is what we can afford" to a discussion of what is possible with greater resources.

My hypothesis is that if you then follow that up with a discussion / workshop / training on the art and science of fundraising, your board will be exponentially engaged.

Number Three Reason You Can Do It: It Makes People Feel Good to Give to Causes They Care About

> It makes people feel good to give to causes they care about.

There it is. The sentence I was told that turned me from a fundraising "virgin" to a joyful, exuberant, bold, and passionate fundraiser. I cared about the organization with every fiber of my being *and,* by asking for money, I could make someone really happy. Many people drawn to nonprofit work have "pleaser" personalities. And so I realized that fundraising was a twofer — I could give someone the opportunity to feel good and thus set off all my pleaser buttons! Win-win!

YES, YOU WILL SCREW IT UP

So there I was, at my first fundraiser. A major donor event — a room full of $1,000+ prospects, a few board members — my development director has prepped me and, besides, I am just one of those people who comes prepared. I have an index card folded in my breast pocket with handwritten notes like these: "Patrick O'Donnell, lawyer, $2,500 ask" and "Steven and Judy Gluckstern, thank you, major donors for 10 years."

I find Patrick, like the obedient ED I am. He is lovely and seems knowledgeable about the organization. But he is not looking at me. He is staring at my breast pocket. This goes on for an uncomfortably long time. Finally, I can't take it any longer. "Are you reading my pocket?" I ask sheepishly. He smiles. "Sure am." I have figured it out without looking — I have folded the card the wrong way. I try to compose myself. He is still smiling. I ask the obvious question: "So, what does my pocket say?" He reads clearly: "Patrick should be a major donor."

I want to crawl into a dark, black hole, but we are in a fancy apartment overlooking Central Park, so I am kind of out of luck in the dark, black hole department. I can tell that Patrick is kind, and I can also see a mischievous twinkle in his eye. The silence goes on and he says nothing. *I am dying!* He lets it go on just a little bit longer and then he laughs and says that he is impressed that I am so prepared and that I'm well-informed, engaging, and passionate about the work and have expressed interest in him and who he is. "You are absolutely right. Patrick *should* be a major donor." And that night he became one.

I am realizing that I could write an entire chapter on my own fundraising mistakes and while that could be entertaining, I do need to maintain my credibility. With that said, here are a few more, each with a moral.

Don't ever assume that a person with capacity *should* give to your cause. I made that mistake once and the organization paid for it. I had finally secured a meeting with that big donor. What I thought were good sources told me that he hadn't given because he was too busy. He invited me to his glorious home in the Hollywood Hills. We got along well and then I used the word *should* — something like, "Given your credibility in the community, your name should be on our major donor list." All of a sudden, the air turned cold. (This is a figure of speech. The weather was glorious.) The meeting ended soon after, and a few days later I received a letter from this donor with a modest check and an eloquent, handwritten note admonishing me in a pointed fashion. I held on to the letter and referenced it often.

As a postscript regarding this same donor, do not assume that because they have given wildly generously to your organization that they haven't been wildly generous to another organizations (I should have done more homework before the meeting that turned chilly). Turned out, during my college tours with my eldest daughter, we learned that this donor had spent millions to build a campus center at his alma mater. This donor gave to causes he cared deeply about. He was smart and strategic, and I had assumed otherwise. Very bad assumption on my part.

Then there was the time I asked someone for a gift that was much too low. How did I know? I asked for $10,000 and she was a person with significant capacity. We had agreed that this was a great place to start. Her response: "What the hell can you do with only $10,000?"

Hardly the response I expected. I decided to take the direct approach. "Clearly I shot too low, eh?" I had already developed a rapport, and humor was a part of that. She laughed. Then I answered her question — in great detail. But I am not one to leave funds on the table. So I continued. "Now let me tell you what we can do with $25,000." I was not done yet. "I tell you what — 30 days from now, we are having a major donor event at X house. I'd like you to come, and I will consider it my personal challenge between now and then to make the case for you to consider a $25,000 gift. Then you decide at the event the level that feels right for you." The donor liked everything about the idea. I did not hound her, but we worked strategically and, yes, 30 days later, she gave $25,000 as part of an enormously successful fundraiser.

Fundraising is an art and a science. That means you will make mistakes. It also means that people will say no. And to those of us who are competitive, type A folks (those likely to join boards and apply for nonprofit leadership jobs), this can feel like failure — a screw-up.

> Fundraising is an art and a science. That means you will make mistakes. It also means that people will say no.

Note also that fundraising, maybe more than any other aspect of nonprofit life, can raise major questions about race, gender, and class dynamics. Some communities have fewer contacts with wealthy people; some folks will assume there's no money in a particular community and deny them the chance to contribute; asking for money can also trigger feelings of scarcity and humiliation for anyone who has experienced control or abuse through the use of finances. It's good to surface structural and individual barriers and address them collectively rather than expect people to "get over it" without support. Being totally up-front about your fundraising expectations of board members and being creative about how to support folks in meeting those expectations makes a huge difference.

Just do your very best, work from the head and the heart, invite the prospect to join you in the remarkable work of the organization, bring that work to life with facts and stories, and make an ask. Sometimes it will feel like a home run ask, and sometimes you will want to crawl into a big, dark hole. But after you ask, your job is done. You can and should assess and debrief the ask so that your skill improves. But the rest is up to the prospect.

CASE STUDY: GIRL SCOUTS AND THOSE DAMNED THIN MINTS

I selected a provocative title for a reason and not because I have anything against the Girl Scouts (well, maybe just the Weight Watchers membership fees). It's a fine organization that engages and empowers young girls. I probably should know more specifics, given that I invest $100 a year in cookies. Thus, my point.

Every spring they come a-callin'. You salivate over the brochure and place your order. It's usually a very big order. You are delighted. So is the cute little girl in the green outfit with the sash. As I mentioned earlier, it makes people feel good to give money to causes they care about. But as the cute girl with the sash walks away, I realize that what's making me feel good is the idea of Thin Mints in my cupboard. And I know I am not alone in this. Come on, be honest. Unless you have a Girl Scout in your family, *do you have any idea how the Girl Scouts will spend your money?*

I'm gonna go with no on that one. And how about this question: If the Girl Scouts came a-callin' without cookies, would you make a donation? I think I know the answer to that one, too.

You see, for decades, we've all been trained. Make a donation and get a box of cookies. This is unhealthy. And I'm not just talking about the sweets. OK, so we can't blame it all on the Girl Scouts, but you must admit — they are an easy mark. They have trained us all into believing that people won't give to causes unless they receive treats in return.

In my vernacular, *treats* are code. Code for tickets to events. Spend $100 or $250 and sit at my table with my friends — great networking, open bar, sometimes a few good silent auction items and maybe meet a new client or your next boss. Oh, and I heard a rumor that a highly undervalued fabulous celebrity (yes, her show was canceled, but . . .) will be the emcee — I'm waiting for confirmation. Oh, and it's for a great cause — maybe I mentioned that I am on the board?

If you could tell your pal that there will be Thin Mints in the gift bag, it could put her over the top.

That's what I mean by *treats*. Buy a ticket to this great event, have fun and it will feel good because a portion of the profits will go to the worthy cause (that you happen to volunteer for or work for or on whose board you serve). I have even heard folks say, "Don't worry — there won't be a boring program — it's just fun."

Perhaps I am exaggerating. But not much. And, because this kind of fundraising is perceived to be the easiest and least stressful and the kind of fundraising where folks don't feel they are putting themselves out there personally, event fundraising is the go-to for the vast majority of nonprofits. "At least I can get my fellow board members to sell a few tickets, or maybe even a table, to their company."

Anything for that box of Samoas.

Now it's time to look at a different kind of fundraising solicitation. Here's an example of a pitch that I, as a board member of an organization, would make to a member of my community.

To bring it to life, I'll use an organization that has personal relevance to me — the Ronald McDonald House (RMH). Let's imagine I am a new board member and I have a neighbor with some capacity — neither a pauper nor Mark Zuckerberg. My neighbor has kids.

Here goes:

I recently joined the board of our local RMH. In many ways, the people there are extended family. In 1988, my niece Molly was born with serious medical issues. She was airlifted to our five-star hospital, where she stayed for weeks and my brother's family needed more than a place to stay. They needed support, comfort, and a place they could call home. From the staff to the remarkable legion of volunteers there, my brother, his wife, and their eldest daughter were treated like family. The love and kindness they were shown helped them through as much as the first-rate medical care. My brother's family went back and forth to RMH many times during Molly's all-too-short life. And as they become veterans themselves, they were able to provide support and comfort to new members of the RMH family. Since Molly's death, my brother's former wife and his daughter Norah have volunteered regularly, and Norah, now a pediatrician, has been a speaker at numerous Sibling Days, offering hope and the kind of care to siblings that comes with having stood in their shoes.

> RMH has a waiting list and is looking to acquire new space down the road from its current facility. We are looking for support to increase our capacity to help more families. I'm not sure if you know, but the McDonald's Corporation covers only 10% of our costs. And our families stay with us for free. Since my niece passed away in 1994, I have been a donor here — would you consider joining me today with a $500 gift?

Now let's say that the same Ronald McDonald House was having an annual gala and that the child of a celebrity spent time there. It's a great charity, and the room will be filled with elected officials, key business folks — it's a great room to be in. Tickets are $500.

So, riddle me this. Are both $500 gifts equivalent?

Absolutely not. Let's look at the two asks and diagnose:

The Event Ask

- The $500 gift to the gala costs the organization something. A solid special event spends 30 cents on every dollar it raises — without calculating staff time, venue, meals, and other factors. So the gift is really $350 (and less, if you factored in staff time).
- The gala ticket is a transactional gift. I pay $500 and I get stuff. Maybe time with an interesting celebrity, maybe a handful of business cards. Hopefully, I don't talk during the program and I hear something about the good work of the RMH.
- Can a gala ticket lead to something different and more? You bet. I am not suggesting that events not be a part of your

revenue strategy. I'm suggesting that they have to be part of a larger invitation strategy — inviting people to move closer and closer to your organization.

- Revenue from ticket sales to an event is amongst your riskiest dollars. What if my friend is out of town next year? What if something happens and the event is canceled?
- Lastly, an event ticket ask is transactional, and you do not have to put yourself on the line. You are selling attendance at a fun event that will be of benefit to your neighbor. You are not sharing, in some fashion, why this organization is meaningful to you and why you love it so much that you are willing to ask folks to join you in making an annual gift.

The Individual Ask

- As I mentioned earlier, you are talking about money — voluntary charitable giving. Even those of us with lots of experience get anxious. It's so much easier if you are selling those cookies.
- Every single cent of that $500 gift you receive goes right to the bottom line. Unless you paid for the coffee. It is the most efficient way to raise funds
- This is your least vulnerable revenue line. Your neighbor is not buying a ticket to an event; she is investing in the future of RMH and its ability to serve more kids and families like mine.
- You have the opportunity to talk about what the organization means to you and to tell a story about why it is meaningful to you. With an event ask, you are selling the open bar and the B-list celeb.
- This is an easily renewable gift next year, and it is not contingent on an event or its success. I just need to stay in touch with you throughout the year (two or three times when I am not also asking for a renewal). If I can get you to the house to work one night with me as a volunteer, even better. That is the kind of engagement that leads to gift upgrades and greater participation by the checkwriter.

What is the takeaway here? Event fundraising takes fund-raisers off the hook. They believe they are building the road toward sustainability. But it ain't so. I'm not suggesting that they don't play an integral part of your fundraising strategy. But I cannot tell you how many organizations are *all* about events. I had one client with a $1.2 million budget. *All* of it came from events except for a sizable gift from the founder and now board chair (don't get me started on the complexity of this situation).

Or how about the conversations I mediate between staff and board when a board member from Cincinnati says it's time for a gala there? "I can get the mayor there!" she pro-claims. Is there staff in Cincinnati? Uh, no. Is there current program work to point to that can be used for a fundraising opportunity? If yes, is a gala the only way to capitalize on that? Uh, no. How about getting a person of note in that city to host and underwrite an event at her home, invite the mayor as a special guest and make a pitch for individual gifts? Any idea how much easier that is for a small, or even large, organi-zation than a gala?

Here's why I think all this is so important. A thriving non-profit has a strong base of individual giving support — folks who believe deeply in the mission, who believe deeply that your organization is effective and impactful; folks who hear from the organization during varying points of the year so that they know their money is being invested wisely; and people who feel as though they are truly an integral part of the organization and its successes and who feel a deep sense of commitment to and urgency about the work.

You can build this base of support from events if you are intentional. But the most effective organizations focus on individuals — who give at small and large levels and who man-age the purse strings at foundations. They identify folks, invite them in, steward them, demonstrate curiosity about who they are and what they care about and draw them into the organization's family in a strategic and organic way.

And this kind of organization has done two things very effectively:

1. The board enthusiastically accepts its responsibility to raise money and monitor its success.
2. The organization has a strong culture of fundraising — from the person who answers the hotline to the administrative staff and from the program staff to every member of the board.

Yes, I did actually just say those two things, and I mean them. I believe that an organization's board can be enthusiastic about fundraising and that there are strategies to ensure that every member of the organization recognizes that fundraising is, and must be, a team sport.

THE BOARD CAN TAKE THE LEAD ON FUNDRAISING

You are skeptical. I know. That's never how it works, right? Staff nags. Some board members are rock stars, and some board members deliver rocks. But the reason it doesn't work may be because the board recruitment committee never talked about the fundraising obligation (or, more likely, said something highly complimentary about how well the staff fundraises), but something else needs to shift: the board needs to *own* its fundraising obligation. It must *lead* and not follow. It must be *proactive* and not put staff in the position to *nag*.

> The board needs to *own* its fundraising obligation. It must *lead* and not follow.

Think about that for a minute. The staff essentially

works for the board. Of course, in Chapter 2 I made the argument that nonprofits have a unique, diffuse power structure. It is true that the power dynamics between board and staff have an element of hierarchy to them. So, in that context, imagine how difficult and awkward it would be for you to have to nag your boss to do their job. The staff end up resenting the board for not holding up its end of the bargain, and the board members don't appreciate being nagged. Not one little bit.

So we need to change the paradigm. And we start it by rethinking the charge of the board development (fundraising) committee. Quite a few boards don't have them at all — in fact, several of my clients don't believe in them. "If we identify a few folks who are on the development committee, every other board member will feel totally off the hook for fundraising." In fact, this same ED actually vetoed the formation of a development committee for this very reason (yes, I know — the ED can veto the formation of a board committee — another one of those messy situations). Now, I actually get this ED's point, and it could be seen as valid, depending on the charge of the development committee.

Let me pose a few questions about your board development committee:

1. As the lead staff person working with this committee, do you often feel like you work for the chair of the committee?
2. Is the chair of the development committee an enthusiastic fundraiser?
3. Is attendance good and engagement high at committee meetings?
4. Do you spend more than 50% of each meeting talking about the upcoming special event?
5. Does your development committee make any effort to promote board fundraising?

Typical answers:

1. Yes — it seems that they believe their role is to supervise me.
2. No — we did some serious arm-twisting about this role.
3. No — I am asked to report out, people raise concerns about numbers that seem low and quite a few people are unable to stay for the entire meeting.
4. OMG, yes!
5. No — they're too busy nagging me for detailed reports to present at the next board meeting.

If your answers were "typical," it's time for a change. More importantly, you will never develop a group of board members who are even close to enthusiastic about raising money.

The new paradigm for a board development committee is one in which the board takes ownership for its own efforts and the committee works to hold all board members accountable to make its very best efforts to secure new financial resources for the organization.

This is what I believe a board development committee should exist to do:

- **Provide additional reach** The committee should advocate that each board member explore their sphere of influence for folks who either can give or can lead to someone who can. The staff alone has insufficient horsepower to hit its revenue targets without the board engine.
- **Provide peer accountability** this is where the dynamics really change. How different would your organization be if, as part of your board orientation, the chair of the development committee handed out a two-page fundraising plan document and set time for the new board member, one member of the committee, and the staff liaison to review the plan after being given a deadline to turn it in? The group could then help staff

to examine all the plans, create an overriding board goal, and identify places with duplications, for example.

- **Cheerlead and advocate for board success** Change the development reports at the board meetings and give shout outs to board members who have stood out. Advocate for talking points and trainings and whatever else the board needs to fulfill its obligations.
- **Monitor and share the status of efforts** at each board meeting, the development chair should, in concert with the development staff person, share updates and diagnose what is going well, what could be going better, and where the opportunities are going forward.

Let me be clear that this kind of role for a development committee will demand a strong staff liaison. This is another key board–staff partnership in the organization, one that is often imbued with tension and animosity. Not only does it not have to be that way — it can't be that way.

BUILDING A CULTURE OF FUNDRAISING IN YOUR ORGANIZATION

Dear Joan,

I run office admin for a nonprofit, and I'm frustrated that things keep falling through the cracks. One of our programs is to provide rent subsidies, and one person called and was terribly upset. The check had not arrived, and the landlord was threatening eviction. We cut a new check and voided the old one but found the original one just sitting near the copy machine about a week later. Jeanne said it was just an oversight. I get that mistakes happen, but I'm so furious. What should I do?

Signed,
No room for error

Why, you ask, have I included this story in a chapter about fundraising and in a section about building a culture of fundraising? Let me not hold you in suspense.

> To build a culture of fundraising, you have to build a culture of "meaning."

To build a culture of fundraising, you have to build a culture of "meaning." I have a number of clients who work to improve the profound flaws in the criminal justice system. I like to think that my work is excellent with all my clients, but each client has meaning to a close former team member of mine. One of our clients works in the criminal justice sector, and she has a relative who was incarcerated. I think about Tim during the most mundane tasks of my work. Same with our work in the women's movement. I have two daughters. I had a team member with a young daughter who attended many staff meetings. The work we do is for her. And I like to think we go the extra step because of that sense of meaning.

So we brought the group together and, rather than talk about admin procedures, we talked about the clients. We decided to bring the clients to life with pictures around the office, especially by the copy machine. Do you think the administrative tasks were done more efficiently? You bet they were.

When Jeanne goes to copy that check, it is now more than a check. It's a story. It's an apartment. It's a gift. It's an opportunity. With that kind of meaning, it would be mighty hard to misplace the check.

This is what I am talking about. The board chair and the ED must build a culture of meaning in the organization they lead. If the culture becomes about balance sheets and approving minutes and making copies, then your organization will be good but never great, effective but not inspired, and you will never raise the kind of dollars your clients need and deserve.

I suppose I could say that in an organization that has a culture of fundraising, every single person is bursting with pride to be a part of this work and has at least two to three stories they can tell with emotion and conviction. And when I say *everyone*, I mean everyone. Everyone with skin in the game — staff, volunteers, board members, and every one of your donors.

> In an organization that has a culture of fundraising, every single person is bursting with pride to be a part of this work and has at least two to three stories they can tell with emotion and conviction.

A board chair once described it this way: when you decide to become involved in a nonprofit, you must always be wearing your organizational-glasses: always ready to share your enthusiasm about the remarkable staff, about the urgency and the need of your organization, and always talking to and meeting people through your organization's lens. Might this person be a degree or two of separation from the lawyer needed for the board? Oh, my racquetball partner is a videographer for a foundation — how might I engage her? These "glasses" lead to resources of one sort or another. And when you create a culture of meaning, rooted in the fine art of storytelling, folks will be lining up for their own pair.

Think back to Chapter 2, where I talk about storytelling. I believe I may have mentioned that it is the key to fundraising. Here it is: if you can tell a compelling, articulate story (goosebumps are a huge plus) and yours is the voice of a person who cares deeply about the organization, a check is the organic result. Once more, for emphasis: Credible Messenger + Compelling Story = $$$

SAVING THE MOST IMPORTANT LESSON FOR LAST

Perhaps this has been a theme in this chapter, but I felt it needed its own headline. The key that unlocks every door to a thriving organization with stakeholders who stay connected over the long haul is the value the organization places on building, cultivating, and stewarding relationships. And this is the work of every member of your nonprofit. Each and every one of you is not only an ambassador of the work of your organization but also a champion and an advocate for the communities you serve. And in the most effective organizations, organizational ambassadors become a village of people who care about the cause and care about each other. And in the world of fundraising, the moment you start thinking of a donor as a check that hasn't been deposited or get annoyed that no one is returning your calls, you risk falling out of the relationship with them that is necessary to be the best you can be.

The story I am about to tell you is true. When I tell it, I can hardly believe it myself. It is the story of a village of staff and board who worked together to steward a donor. As you read the story, try to forget that the donor was so rich (how rich *was* he?) that his house had its own zip code.

It was the evening before GLAAD's big gala in San Francisco. We were an annual and sizeable client of the hotel, so they treated me nicely. I was in a penthouse suite (courtesy of the hotel). It was beyond lovely. I invited board and staff up to the suite so that we could practice board meeting presentations (board meeting in the morning, fundraiser in the evening). We were working and enjoying each other's company. The hotel had wine and cheese sent up (they liked us — they really liked us). We worked, we laughed.

And then the phone rang. It was one of our biggest donors. He had not RSVP'd to the event but had just landed on the tarmac at the airport and was soon to head to the local hotel we were staying in. Now, when you have your own zip code, you are accustomed to the finest accommodations. And he expressed disappointment that the penthouse suite was occupied. That would be the penthouse suite we were all sitting in. I told him that I would call the front desk and see what I could do and promised to call him back.

There were no other penthouse suites. There was only one option. We had to get out of Dodge — and fast. And we knew something else: We knew this donor well — we had a longstanding relationship with him. He would want his penthouse suite, but under no circumstances would he ever want to impose on his friends at GLAAD who worked so hard for a cause he cared so deeply about. So it was clear that, not only did we have to get out in 15 minutes, but he could also never know.

There was no time for housekeeping. We all became the housekeeping staff. My board chair folded towels, my staff threw leftover cheese into their briefcases. And my favorite: my board member went through all three bathrooms, tidied up and folded all the ends of the toilet paper rolls into those lovely triangles. I packed my roller board and we raced from the suite, down the hall and to the elevator. The suite was ready. Oh, did I mention it was nearly midnight?

We exited the elevator and somehow the donor missed seeing us as he and his small entourage entered the elevator. We had done it! I settled into my decidedly smaller room and crawled under the covers, so happy that we had taken care of our committed donor.

I was nearly asleep when the phone rang. It was the donor: "You gave me your suite, didn't you?" I could not read his voice and was dumbstruck. I tried to play dumb, but he wasn't having it. "When I called the hotel looking for you, they put me through to extension 248. When I checked in, I ordered something to be sent up and noted the extension, 248."

I had been found out. And I still could not read him. Then he asked me to meet him in the lobby bar in 30 minutes. Did I have a choice? I figured that PJs were not quite the right attire for a 1:00 A.M. rendezvous in the hotel bar, so I made a quick change and headed down.

And there he was. Still hard to read. I sat down. I definitely ordered a drink. I had not a clue what to expect. And then:

"I have been a donor to dozens and dozens of organizations since I was fortunate enough to come into wealth. And no one — I mean, no one — has ever been so kind to me before. I am treated like a human ATM. Organizations know nothing about me. I am just a rich guy with a checkbook. Not only were you kind, but you didn't attempt to exploit that kindness to reap some benefit from me — to "use" it as a chit that would help you the next time you approached me for a donation."

He went on. As if this weren't good enough.

"I am so moved by the kindness of your team and so impressed with the integrity you bring to this work. I'd like to make a one-time pledge of $3 million as my way of expressing my deep gratitude for what you do for our community and how you treat the people who matter to the organization."

OK, the story is true and the $3 million was real and the funds enabled us to be a first-class advocacy organization — one that my $3 million man was proud of.

A quick quiz to end this chapter. What is the takeaway from this story?

a. This is a story about how to raise millions of dollars.
b. I hate you. Why do you have a donor with his own zip code and I don't?

c. You were just plain lucky and you know it.

d. It takes a village of dedicated board and staff and an understanding that people come in three dimensions in order to be a successful fundraiser.

Not the toughest quiz you will ever take.

We were all in sync — never any question. Mr. Zip Code could never know. We just needed to do a nice thing, the right thing for a man who was generous, year after year, in supporting our work. That's it.

We were all in sync. One senior staffer threw melted Brie in her briefcase. My board chair made my bed. Another board member folded toilet paper. We had a sense of urgency but also a sense of joy. We raced through that suite, laughing the entire time.

Another important note: Mr. Zip Code had already given us a generous gift for the year. This was not a means to an end. We just worked together on what turned out to be a pretty remarkable donor stewardship effort.

It's a crazy story, right? Actually, it's not at all. Maybe it is because of the magnitude of the gift he made. But as I said, the gift is not the point. The gift was emblematic of a donor who felt like the organization cared about him. The process of getting out of "Dodge" was illustrative of the board and staff's shared leadership and ownership of the relationship.

It's not terribly likely that you will encounter a situation quite like this one. But the recipe of the success is an easy one to follow. Here are two simple things you can do to create a sustaining connection between your organization and the individuals who support your work.

1. Write and mail good old-fashioned, paper thank you notes — no emails. Send a notecard with an envelope and a stamp that goes out the *very same day* as your meeting.

No kidding. Have the envelope addressed before the meeting. Everything will be fresh in your mind and you can wish them well with their bunion surgery or include a picture of your dog (if they showed you theirs!). A handwritten note that arrives fast is gold because it says you cared. Just like the Hallmark people say.

2. Assign Board members to donors for ongoing stewardship. My wife and I give to many organizations. And we often receive either standard direct mail updates or a quarterly newsletter before we are asked to renew. What if every board member received a bimonthly draft of an email to send to 10 assigned donors? The email was simple and included a powerful story — not a list, but rather a story of an event that would not have happened without your organization. It was *not* an invitation to anything — just simply a story that ends like this: "When you read this story, please take a great deal of pride. Your fingerprints are all over this and all the other great work we do every day."

   The email cannot appear to be canned in any way. It must be in the voice of the author. Make a personal reference so that it cannot be mistaken for an email blast. I promise you that a few folks will respond and say thank you! A few will say how much they appreciated the personal touch. And not a single one of them will feel ignored, come renewal time.

As the chapter title indicates, *you can do this!* And you can because you are surrounded by teammates, because your love for the organization is greater than your anxiety about asking for money, and because, if you were not a person who believed in the power of relationships, you'd be one of those people sitting on the sidelines.

I have been a proud major donor and a corporate sponsor. I have been a board member and an ED In each of these situations, it was a joy and a privilege to be "on the field" — meeting and talking with folks who cared enough about the world around them to engage at some level with the organization I represented.

> Fundraising is, in its simplest form, an invitation to "come off the bench" and join a remarkable team on the field doing the most remarkable work.

Fundraising is, in its simplest form, an invitation to "come off the bench" and join a remarkable team on the field doing the most remarkable work.

"You say you think of your staff as family. Have you ever tried to fire your own kid?"

Chapter 7 Managing the Paid and the Unpaid

or

I Came to Change the World, not Conduct Evaluations

I imagine the board deliberations about my hire at GLAAD: "She has *never fundraised!* We have no money!" And then the other folks around the table: "But she came from corporate America and has a reputation as a stellar manager of people and businesses. She can *manage* us out of this situation."

Clearly the management side of the board won the day. And frankly, they were not wrong. The organization had just completed a major "renovation," merging numerous chapters into one national organization. It was a management challenge, to say the least, and a particular challenge because I was a nonprofit management "virgin."

Day 1. I was told that my first order of business was to fire a young man named Jason Burlingame. Exhibit A was all I would need, I was told. Jason had written a letter to the deputy director that bordered on offensive. He was arrogant and bold, and by all accounts a most entitled young man in his first job out of college. In the land I had come from, his level of insubordination would not be tolerated. The hubris of this letter was stunning.

And, before I could reach any decision, my phone rang. It was his immediate supervisor, Julie. You might remember Julie from the Introduction — "Heart Monitor Julie." That call (yet another item to put on the list of gifts Julie has given me through the years) introduced me to the world of nonprofit management. There was something different about it.

"Promise me you will talk to him before you fire him," Julie said. "Jason's frustration is most decidedly poorly expressed, but it is rooted in passion. It is rooted in believing that in a nonprofit, you trade a big, fat payoff for a voice — a stake in the game — the opportunity to change some part of the world for the better. He had great ideas, and no one was hearing him out. He took matters into his own hands, never showed me the letter, and let loose. Just talk to him."

I did what Julie suggested, and after my first meeting with Jason, I knew I was no longer in Kansas. He was passionate beyond measure about the organization and deeply committed to the sector, and I realized, in that minute, that this would have to be the most important attribute in any hire I made. You can teach the basics of management, but it is way harder to light a fire in someone's belly. Managing passion would be the biggest challenge and the real opportunity of management in this new land.

> You can teach the basics of management, but it is way harder to light a fire in someone's belly.

I didn't fire Jason. I'm not sure who learned more in that first meeting. Jason had his "diva moments" in our eight years together and we were quick to call him out on them. But he delivered. His work was of the highest possible quality because his passion for our work led him to hold a high standard for himself and his team.

After my meeting, I knew in my heart that when it came to managing people in the nonprofit sector, I should get myself ready. I was going to get as much as I gave, if not more than I gave.

Fast-forward to years later, and I was offering strategic counsel to a nonprofit ED. He too had come from corporate America in a most noble effort to run a research organization desperately seeking a cure for a catastrophic illness. I asked him about his senior team, not as workers, but as people. I had a hunch and asked about their families. He knew nothing about them — not even their spouses' names. Not only did he not know their kids' names — he wasn't sure they had them. In that moment I knew he was not cut out to run a nonprofit. He talked a lot about how much more money there was to raise (sales) and his cash reserve, but when nudged to talk about the progress the researchers were making, there was data but no goosebumps. It seemed like he could manage the organization well — financially sound and even a cash reserve. But he missed what I consider to be the key element in successful nonprofit management, whether you are managing a staff or board members.

MANAGING IN 3D

I guarantee you that if you evaluate staff or board members who did not work out in your organization, you can find a pattern. Sure, there will be people who did not have the skills to do the job, but that's not the pattern you will find. The majority of folks who don't work out have come for the wrong reason. Author Simon Sinek has a single lesson: it's all about the "why." And in recruiting board members and staff members, understanding their Why is your biggest and most important job. And I'm not talking about this kind of Why — *I want to build my skills as a CPA*. That doesn't count. The Why must be clear, articulate, and passionate. Why this organization? Why this sector? Do you have skin in the game?

This is the first management lesson corporate America can take from the nonprofit sector — hiring folks with a real investment in the outcome. Far too often, folks in the private sector focus on the What and the How, and as Simon Sinek so eloquently puts it, you have to "start with Why."

> The first management lesson corporate America can take from the non-profit sector — hiring folks with a real investment in the outcome.

Here's another element to 3D management, and you heard it in the story of the CEO who knew nothing about his leadership team members' families — building quality relationships. I learned early on in my tenure that asking about someone's weekend was nonnegotiable and that nonprofit staff at all levels look for compassion and empathy in their leaders in a way that I know I never did in corporate America.

Never was this clearer than during the early months of the COVID-19 pandemic. Organizations were on overdrive with overburdened staff attempting to work remotely, some with kids "in school" and everyone contending with real and present danger. Leaders who focused on the tasks getting done or leaders who sent emails instead of picking up the phone were missing the spirit of management in three dimensions.

I coached dozens of leaders during those days and talked about the importance of nurturing their teams. Tina Luongo at The Legal Aid Society introduced two optional gatherings via Zoom videoconferencing each week for her team of over 1,000 in the Criminal Justice Practice. No agenda, just gathering — one over coffee and one late in the day, no doubt BYOB.

My favorite gathering was at Fenway Health in Boston. You'd imagine that a federally qualified health center would be attentive to the whole person and you'd be right. Two members of the senior team cooked up a similar idea — optional gatherings twice a week. One of the engineers of the gathering is a social worker and the other is a minister. Each gathering opens with a reading and ends with a reflection. Thirty minutes is all it takes. Attendance varies and it actually doesn't matter — I'm sure the buzz carries to the team of hundreds, especially because of what they call the gathering. It is called (wait for it) "A Priest and a Therapist Walk into a Bar." The absolute best. That's what I call nurturing.

And the last element to three-dimensional management can be the hardest to get right. For nonprofit staff, it's not about a year-end bonus check, because there isn't one. It's the lesson Jason taught me in that first week: There *is* a bonus. It's not money. I know what you are thinking — it's about changing the world, right? Yes, it's that, but it's something else.

It's having a voice.

This is the management gift that the nonprofit sector gave to me, and it may be the biggest gift that the nonprofit sector has to offer corporate America. When you are in a position to manage folks and their success is measured in dollars, it's straightforward. I'm hardly suggesting that all managers are of the command-and-control variety — "Reach these specific goals that we have set for you and you'll get a 20% bonus. Reach most and you'll get a 10% bonus." But surely it is safe to say that much of corporate America operates from the top down in this way.

If reasonable increases and bonuses were off the table, corporate America would need a new model. And they would, could, and should turn to the nonprofit sector for such a model. But it requires a greater degree of investment in your board and staff. It may be more time-consuming, more complex, and, frankly, messier. But you can't beat the payoff.

HAVING A VOICE: DECISION-MAKING

Here's what a nonprofit staffer and a board member want to feel: "Decisions are not being handed down to me. I believe my thoughts, insights, and opinions have real value in shaping decisions."

The reason this can be scary territory for managers is that it is fuzzy. If you ask for a point of view, what is the expectation the employee should have about what will happen to that point of view? How much weight will it carry? Will the employee feel valued as a result? Or is there a risk that the employee will feel devalued? How do you clearly distinguish voice from vote?

Read on.

> *Dear Joan,*
> *So my boss talks the talk and at senior team meetings always describes his management style as collaborative. He tells us that our voices matter in the decision-making process of the organization. It sounds good in concept until*

he asks you to give a certain issue some thought — that he wants your best thinking on how the organization should tackle it. I go away and give it my best thinking and return to tell him I think we should do X.

I provide all of my good thinking and then he says, "Why don't you go back and give it some more thought?"

I get it. X was not the correct answer. My job now is to go away and come back with Z — the answer my boss was looking for me to affirm.

Why is he bothering? Just tell me that we are doing Z — won't it just save a boatload of time? And besides, I won't feel like my voice is worthless.

Signed,
Feeling Voiceless

Dear Voiceless,

There are three possibilities here. One is that your boss doesn't really care what you think and has already made up his mind. I so hope this isn't true — and frankly, if this is the case, he should not have even engaged in the sham of asking. Time to freshen up your résumé? Another possibility is that your boss doesn't trust you and asked either to affirm his belief or to be surprised. Time to take a deep breath and ask some real questions, hoping for candor. The third option is that he doesn't really understand how to ensure that voices are heard in a way that makes a staff member feel valued — win, lose, or draw.

Let's see if we can eliminate lack of understanding as an option. If a nonprofit manager can get this right, it can turn a group into a team. It can make decision-making better, smarter, and richer.

Before walking through a few core elements, let's answer a key question: is there ever a time when asking for input is *not* appropriate? My sense is that in nearly all cases, if you are surrounded by the right people, there is only upside in giving folks a voice. I'd say there may be two exceptions and really only one. First, if the issue is inconsequential, you can create a sense that you are indecisive if you ask for input about every little thing. Surely the selection of a new copier is not something everyone needs to weigh in on. And remember, every minute you spend talking about getting input is one less minute you spend serving your community.

The second circumstance is when you have already made up your mind. With the exception of terminating an employee, I believe that if you find yourself in this circumstance, you have missed a step, a valuable step to engage the voices of key players on your team. But how do you get it right?

Let's say that you are the ED and you are hiring a new development director who will be a member of your senior staff. It falls under nonprofit best practices to hear the voices of two groups — the folks who will report to the development director and their new colleagues on the senior staff. It can be difficult. Ask yourself these two questions to ensure you hear the correct voices during the interview process:

1. Did you get input before the interview process started? This is a smart tactic, for a host of reasons. You may have some idea of who you are looking for, but your smart colleagues will offer you more perspective, and they have a view you do not. Together, you can draw a fuller picture of the ideal candidate. Add this to an agenda of a senior staff meeting, call a meeting of the development team (or talk to each one-on-one), and don't forget the board! Most senior positions will have interaction with the board, and you might find it quite valuable to hear what your executive committee has to say — perhaps a debrief of the prior staff member in the job — and anything they believe you might want to look for.

2. Be wildly clear about where the final decision rests and what you are asking for. So often, folks are given the opportunity to meet-and-greet possible final candidates. I think we should eliminate that phrase from the nonprofit glossary. It means nothing. As an ED candidate, I had an "interview" with a preselected group of staff. This group spoke with both final candidates. They had no idea what their authority was. Because they were not told anything other than "We'd like to have a representative group of staff interview our final two candidates," they *assumed* it was an interview and that the collective vote carried weight as a *vote*. This group was aware of the financial straits of the organization, and upon hearing that I had no fundraising experience, unanimously voted for the other candidate.

Just a few days later, the staff learned that I had been hired. Well, that went well, huh? They were furious and thought the board was out of its mind. The process of including them backfired completely. Here's what they should have told this group explicitly: "This is not an interview. The word *interview* presumes authority, and in the case of the hiring of an executive director, this decision rests with the board. That said, we believe that it is important to take your input into consideration as we make our final decision. After the process is complete, we'll circle back and, to the best of our ability, share our decision rationale, especially if it is different from any input you have provided."

The same would hold true in the example of an ED hiring a development director. I generally recommend soliciting input up front from those who will report to the new hire rather than have a conversation for input late in the game. It can be hard to offer objective feedback about which of two candidates should be your new boss. Colleagues are another story. I believe that a meeting with final candidates with clear expectations set can offer you the view you do not have that could shape your final decision.

HAVING A VOICE: OWNERSHIP

Author Daniel Pink, in his book *Drive,* writes that when it comes to being motivated at work, only three things truly matter. Money is not one of them:

1. Autonomy
2. Mastery
3. Purpose

I agree with Pink, but I believe that the list is missing #4. Stay with me.

In the nonprofit sector, we have #3 covered, and as I mentioned earlier, if a staff or board member is not dripping with a sense of purpose, that person should not be allowed on the bus — or should be escorted off at the next stop.

Let's talk about Pink's #1 and #2 before I share my friendly amendment. Autonomy and mastery are the core elements of ownership, a key part of this idea of having a voice. This is not about having a role in decision-making, but rather about the staff or board member's ability to develop a sense of confidence about their skills to do the job and being given the autonomy (what I would characterize as a good length of rope) to use this mastery to move their work forward.

Here's how I see it: a staff member or committee chair becomes great when given clear expectations and just enough autonomy to feel a sense of ownership and when managed by someone who stays close but not too close, acting as mentor/boss.

Makes all the sense in the world, right? Yup. But when you unpack the theory I just mentioned, you have a couple of obstacles, unique to nonprofits, that can really muck things up:

- Everything matters. A *lot*. How can I possibly delegate when there is *no margin for error?* Here's another phrase that needs to be yanked out of the nonprofit glossary. There is no learning without error, and there is no innovation without error. There is no sense of mastery without it. And if you don't delegate, there is no sense of ownership of the impact of the organization, and that is what your staff and board signed up for. Otherwise, your board members can just buy a rubber stamp, and your staff members can probably get paid more to work in another sector with an equal amount of autonomy (read: not much).
- Many board and staff leaders have control issues. Not everyone! Let me be clear. Not every leader has control issues, but I have seen hundreds of board and staff leaders who do. They didn't get to the top by being nonchalant. They are drivers. Often intense. I have one client who delegated a project to a staff member. It was a total success, and she later admitted she was furious at her staffer. As the compassionate truth teller that I consider myself to be, I put my response in the form of a question: "Do you think this might indicate some control issues?"

Do you have a tendency to tell your staff the answer? Come on. Be truthful. You are smart and driven and you feel a sense of urgency. Why beat around the bush? Tell them the answer and then have them go do it, right?

Wrong. This runs counter to the culture of mastery and autonomy you need to foster in order to motivate your staff to go above and beyond the call of duty.

Try these two techniques and I'd bet they will help:

1. Test the power of *might*.

   Rather than directly lead someone to an answer, begin a sentence directed to a staff member or a board colleague with this phrase: "You might want to think about . . ." I also think of it as helping someone "try something on" in response to a problem they are trying to solve. It offers a sense of ownership. It can even lead to a conversation about why someone might *not*.

2. Another good trick is to build mastery and allow *you* to offer a longer rope.

One day, Glennda, my lead programming person (today an executive director in her own right) came into my office with a knotty problem she was struggling with. She asked for my help. I asked her a simple question:

What would you do if I weren't here — if the decision were entirely yours?

With that question posed, Glennda spoke for maybe five minutes, outlining the pros and cons of each different option. Without my saying a word, she reached a conclusion about how to resolve it. And then I spoke two more words: "Sounds good." And, with that, Glennda left the office with her problem resolved.

How did Glennda feel leaving the office? She felt affirmed that she was gaining needed mastery and a sense of ownership. I did not tell Glennda what to do. I just listened and thought her path was spot-on. The conversation built trust, which led to a longer rope.

THE MISSING PIECE: CLEARLY DEFINED ROLES AND GOALS

Roles

It's possible that when Daniel Pink identified autonomy, mastery, and purpose as the three things that matter in being motivated at work, he might have taken defining roles and goals for granted. But in the nonprofit space, where many senior staff members wonder if they ever even *had* a job description, a clearly defined role is mission critical. Literally. The key to the motivation you have for your work is mastery and autonomy. Mastery of what? Ownership of what?

I encourage newly hired executive directors I work with to meet one-on-one with all staff within the first two weeks. Before the meeting, I suggest that staff be given a homework assignment to pull out their job descriptions and review them. They are to assess what is on the job description that they actually don't do — maybe someone else does that task now or it's been so long since the staff member did it that they forgot it was ever on the list — and then write down what they are responsible for that is not on the list. This becomes the central agenda item in this one-on-one meeting (after getting to know the staff member and their motivation, sense of job satisfaction, and the names of any pets they may have).

This excellent exercise can be revelatory for both parties. People can't develop mastery in their work without a sense of clarity about the specific work that rests in their purview.

I mentioned earlier that the nonprofit world has lessons to offer the for-profit sector (three-dimensional management). The reverse is true as well. The discipline of developing clear job descriptions arrived with me from corporate America and has held me in good stead ever since.

Goals

Here's another tool in my corporate toolbox: annual goals — and a shared understanding of what success looks like. To make it a livelier exercise for staff, I call it the New Year's Eve List. It should be developed as part of a staff member's annual performance review. And for board committee chairs, it's a great way to start the calendar year. It's simple. Here's all there is to it.

Ask everyone — every employee, every board member, every department head or board committee chair — to imagine themselves sitting in front of a fire on New Year's Eve. Ask them to imagine turning to a spouse, a kid, a pet, or an imaginary friend. Reflect on the past year. You have a glass of something bubbly in one hand and a document (or laptop) in the other. You'll need the document you created in January as part of this exercise. It should be only one page and should outline specific successes you want to be able to point to while staring into that fire. I call this document 5 to 10 Big Things — the things you keep your eye on all year that guide how you spend your time.

And yes, these big things should be the annual big things that should surface from that strategic planning process we spoke about earlier. These 5 to 10 things each year from all parties, if achieved, keep your feet firmly planted on the road to the strategic plan destination.

When I talk about "big things," here are the kinds of things I mean:

- Create a strategy for board recruitment, beginning with an ideal board matrix. Use this to add three to five new board members this calendar year.
- Work with the board chair to develop a new model for board orientation, meetings, and communications to heighten board engagement and enthusiasm in the work of the organization.

- Manage out two poorly performing staff members, and by Q4, hire a best-of-breed replacement for both positions.
- Increase the number of clients served by 15%.

Get the idea? Now you can see that there are "hows" and "whats" that fall under each of these goals — though I believe that all board and staff should have a New Year's Eve List and it should rest near your computer or on your desk or wherever else it remains in your view. As you careen through your day, peek at the list. Or, perhaps every Friday, take 10 minutes with your morning coffee and look back at the week that was. How did you spend your time? There are only 52 weeks in the year, so I'm hoping that you will feel you kept your eye on the most important balls. If not, it's time to start thinking differently about how you are looking at the upcoming week. No lie: 52 weeks goes by *fast*.

And of course, board chairs should have a similar list. You don't want to spend a year as board chair and then not be able to point to 5 or 10 accomplishments that you can be proud of — that moved the organization forward. And ones that had a clear intersection with the ED's New Year's Eve List.

OK, let's recap. Here's what I believe I just said. You need to manage in 3D. You need to motivate folks by stirring their emotional connection to the work. Then you need to give them a voice and allow them to have a strong sense of autonomy, and you need for them to do all this through the lens of clear roles and clear goals.

WHAT ABOUT THE UNPAIDS?

The core question here is, do the same basic management techniques apply to a volunteer? Is there a different set of rules?

I have been known to say that nonprofits are messy. For oh-so-many reasons. It's because the answers aren't simple. The answer here is "Yes, but . . ."

Why is there a "but?" Remember the type A control freak I keep bringing up? The nonprofit space has a disproportionate percentage of them. Changing the world, or even some small part of it, requires some of that type A juice. No doubt.

Here's the "but." Far too often, nonprofit leaders are biased against volunteers. Seems crazy, right? Folks who raised their hands to serve on your board or a fundraising committee, to chair an event, to work check-in at a conference — you would never be able to afford that person-power in any of those organizational spheres. And yet, I hear many leaders besmirch the very people they cannot do without. Why?

The three most common complaints I hear:

1. "Volunteers are too much work. I have to figure out what the heck they can do that is finite and requires little supervision. I am too busy — this is just more work."
2. "Volunteers are just not reliable. I just can't count on 'em. I don't pay them, so who knows if they will even show up when I need them? Can't take the chance."
3. "My work needs to be perfect. I cannot afford to let any balls drop — there's just too much at stake."

And I'm not talking only about folks handling the coat check at your spring gala. Leaders often express these exact same concerns about the most important volunteers they have — their board members. I know an executive director who won't *let* board members fundraise on behalf of the organization. She says it's because she is concerned that it won't get done, but I don't buy it. She wants control of those relationships.

Yes, it can get this bad. And yes, I cover burnout and retention, so keep reading.

Nonprofits need volunteers. I'm not dismissing the concerns staff leaders raise about volunteers — they can be real. And as a staff leader, you need to be conscious of managing risk. The fact that they are not beholden to you through payroll makes things a bit different. Volunteers can flake out. True.

But does this lead us to a conclusion that different management techniques apply? Absolutely not. In fact, I think the challenges with volunteers come from treating them *differently*. With or without a paycheck, a manager or a board chair must place faith in the people at the table, create meaningful opportunities for them, and appreciate the hell out of them. Each of these cohorts made intentional decisions to join your organization. They raised their hands and said, "I want in." So, no kvetching. Make it work.

"Wait," you say. "Maybe I get this with the board, but other volunteers? Really? Who are you kidding, Joan? Working registration at your annual gala isn't meaningful." I beg to differ. It sure is, if your most significant donor's name is missing from the list or is treated poorly.

It is *your* job as a board or staff leader to inject meaning into each activity — to place it in context. In my days at GLAAD, we were totally dependent on volunteers for our annual GLAAD Media Awards — for several years, the LA event was held at the Dolby Theatre in Hollywood. Our volunteer manager would always gather all the volunteers together before the event, and I would join for a few minutes — not just to mention how much money the event would raise but also how this money would be invested by the organization. And then I would thank the volunteers endlessly. Our first-rate volunteer manager loved his volunteers — Ruben's eyes twinkled 24 hours a day. Volunteers felt appreciated. Actually, more than that. They felt lucky to be a part of the event, whether they were a celebrity escort or worked at the registration desk.

THE CLASH OF THE TYPE A'S

As I noted earlier, three-dimensional management is core to success in a nonprofit. So, as you consider how a board should best be managed, let's look at those folks three-dimensionally as well. And when you do, you'll see that staff leaders and board members are dispositional kindred spirits.

Board members arrive on the scene because they too are of the type A variety. Otherwise, they would be on the sidelines, in the dugout, or at home watching the game on TV. In nearly all cases, board members are successful and ambitious at their jobs. They are accustomed to getting A's on their book reports. They have either worked ridiculously hard to get to where they are, or they are working ridiculously hard to get to where they want to go next. Folks who raise their hand for board service are accustomed to environments in which there is a clear path to success and they are driven to follow it. They will do what it takes — nights, weekends — you name it. And success brings money or stature or some combination of both. Board members, for the most part, arrive as winners, accustomed to winning and doing what it takes to win.

And then they arrive to their first board meeting. The path to success is not always clear. And, more importantly, the path to an A-level board member feels overwhelming; after all, these folks have day jobs in which they are very successful (a core reason you recruited them to begin with). It is unrealistic for either the board member, the board chair, or the staff leader to think that these board members will be able to give 140% to board service when they are often well above 100% in their day jobs.

"OK," you might think, "I get that. Who's asking for 140%? I'd be happy with, like, 85% from my most promising board members. Isn't that OK?"

My friend, colleague, and former board member Dan taught me that the answer to this question is "not always." Dan was one of my highest-performing board members. He was strategic and asked good questions at meetings. He identified corporate sponsorship dollars. He loved the work of our organization and was an eloquent ambassador. He gave generously. And then one day, he resigned. I was flabbergasted.

Our conversation has stayed with me: "I just never feel like I am doing enough." Enough for whom? As an ED, I thought he was doing plenty. In *my* mind, he was an outstanding board member. But not in *his* mind. As a type A high performer accustomed to earning A's, he felt unsuccessful with his B+ as a board member — and his grade was higher than 85% of my board. But that was not his frame of reference. He gauged his own performance in the context of what he was capable of doing if he dedicated more time (which he couldn't). He applied day-job standards to a high-level volunteer gig.

I can think of no more important context for managing high-level volunteers than this. How you set up the role makes all the difference, shaping the responsibilities, the committee leadership — all of it — in such a way that a board member feels success as they define it. Not how *you* do.

Dan left my board because he was basically beating himself up about what he was not doing. I felt this exact same experience when I sat on a board. I spent so much time kicking myself for the calls I said I would make that I just didn't — I had no bandwidth. There was so much more I *could* have done. And yet, I do know in my heart that I was a valuable board member and one of the higher-level performers.

So, I have seen it and I have felt it myself. What are the implications? Being a type A and managing type A's requires finesse. It requires, in my mind, a high level of clarity, clear management of expectations, and, with board members, an extra helping of appreciation. I still feel that if I had been more appreciative of what Dan felt was a B+ performance, he would have *felt* that it was closer to the high standard he set for himself.

> Being a type A and managing type A's requires finesse. It requires, in my mind, a high level of clarity, clear management of expectations, and, with board members, an extra helping of appreciation.

I believe it requires a few other components that tie right into managing the "paid" folks as well. The meaning and purpose of your work should always be front and center. This is why I argue so vigorously for board meetings that give board members goosebumps. *Goosebump* is code for me — code for that visceral emotional connection that makes people feel good to their core that they are involved and that motivates them to do more.

One last piece is vital to the management of nonprofit personnel resources: *esprit de corps* — a sense that everyone is in the work together. The work isn't easy. Sometimes, the work is painful when you have real opposition. Sometimes, when the work is rooted in tragedy, it's heartbreaking. You must feel a sense of team. And I'm not talking about two teams — the paid team and the unpaid team. I'm talking about a team of one — one in that everyone is working collectively in pursuit of your mission.

Before reaching this desired end state that offers everyone a piece of joy and privilege, we have to define one word:

Team.

GROUP, TEAM, OR FAMILY?

Dear Joan,

I am the COO of a $4 million organization and the ED likes to say we are like a family. I think it sets up the wrong dynamic — the ED is a charismatic leader and people want to follow him. The staff looks up to him because of it. And when he reinforces the idea of "family," he presents himself like a father figure. People won't say no to him, and as a "pleaser," he doesn't say no to new ideas we can't implement or afford. I think "family" is a problematic metaphor for a workplace, especially a nonprofit. Frankly, we don't all get along very well (like a family) which is kind of ironic. So we are not even a good team. What should we be striving for?

PS I have a real-life dysfunctional family of my very own, so it doesn't actually paint the most positive picture for me.

Signed,
"We are not fam-uh-lee (1979 song by Sister Sledge — I just googled it)

Dear fam,

You are, in my opinion, spot-on. Words matter. I have worked with organizations that use the word *family* regularly. "We work together and we have a shared sense of where we want to go — we are family." All you really have to do is think about the distinction between a boss and a parent and you get it. Some nonprofit leaders take pleasure in being thought of as parental figures, but it's not healthy. I could write another page or two on this topic, but let's just cut to the chase: a parent can't really fire their own kid. A nonprofit is a workplace, and you can create a culture that is nurturing, but a family it is not.

The other word that gets tossed around *all the time* with no consideration of its true meeting is *team*. I see this word used most often to describe the collection of individuals who report to the executive director: the management *team* or the leadership *team*. And then I see them in action. If they were a group of kids in the sandbox, the sand would be flying, they would be crying, and let's not even think about sharing. I see some of the singularly most uncivilized behavior in groups that call themselves teams.

For staff leaders who just start calling their direct reports a team, it's time to hit the Pause button and determine whether you have done the work necessary to foster a team environment. Have you talked about what it means to be on a team? Or your expectations of individual and team behavior? In my experience, *team* is assumed. Ask any professional coach or general manager of a sports team how often they talk about team culture. I'm guessing often. Because you don't win without one.

And then there are boards. Often, they don't even aspire to be teams — they are lucky if they even know each other's names. Or what they do for a living. Or why they are on the board. The list goes on.

You don't get to call yourself a team if you don't do the work, if you don't understand what the word implies, and if you don't see the value in those implications. That said, if you build a team and the board or staff leaders hold folks accountable to the norms that come with being on a team, guess what? People feel supported, the impact of burnout is decreased, and retention skyrockets. Now, if that isn't motivation to actually walk the walk when it comes to team building, I'm not sure what is.

Time for another messy topic. The most effective nonprofit organization has a few key teams, and they intersect:

- The entire staff must feel like a team (especially true if you run a small organization).

- The individuals who report to the staff leader are a team, and they model it for the rest of the organization.
- The board is a team.
- The senior leadership of the staff (ideally, a true team) relates to the board (ideally, a true team) in a partnership that feels team-like. (This last one is important.)

Can I be honest? The interchangeable usage of the words *group* and *team* bugs me. Big-time. So now that you know that my soapbox is out and I'm standing firmly on top of it, allow me to continue.

Let's dissect the two words with the simple grid shown in Table 7.1.

TABLE 7.1 Working group versus team comparison

Working Group	Team
Strong, clearly focused leader	Shared leadership roles
Individual accountability	Individual and mutual accountability
Same purpose as the broader organizational purpose	Specific team purpose that the team itself delivers
Individual work products	Collective work products
Runs efficient meetings	Encourages open-ended discussion and active problem-solving meetings
Measures its effectiveness indirectly by its influence on others	Measures performance directly by accessing collective work products
Discusses, decides, and delegates	Discusses, decides, and does real work together

If you want to be a team (and I'm here to tell you that your clients and the community you serve *need* for you to be one), those hats must be left at the door and everyone must enter the room wearing an organizational hat. Decisions are made collaboratively, with open communication. Diverse perspective is welcome; so too is healthy conflict, because the team knows that it can lead to creative problem-solving. The end decision is what's best for the organization and the organization is richer for the discussion and the debate.

This is what you are going for. Senior staff, full staff, and board: did you look at that grid, read the preceding paragraph and say, "We are *so* not a team"? Join the club.

Here's what needs to happen in order to even hope to turn your group into a team:

- Every single person needs to understand the difference between a group and a team and must aspire to move in the direction of the team.
- The leader (board chair, staff leader, or department) has to articulate the need — the charge for this group. Why do we need to come together?
- The leader has to establish expectations of the values and behaviors expected of all team members.
- An investment must be made by all parties to welcome and introduce each new staff and board member so that they arrive knowing and understanding the responsibility that comes with being a new member of the team.
- You need to make time to talk through all of this; it's not a minor agenda item in a standing tactical meeting that is already packed.
- Because of the third bullet in this list, the leaders of wannabe-teams have to carve out time for retreats.
- And yes, those retreats must include icebreakers (sorry to break it to you).

RETREATS ARE NONNEGOTIABLE

An effective nonprofit needs to work as a team. Building a team takes time. There is never time. You have to make time. Thus, retreats are nonnegotiable and can be, if designed well, invaluable.

> An effective nonprofit needs to work as a team. Building a team takes time. There is never time. You have to make time.

Back in my corporate days, retreats *could be* valuable — we'd cover annual goals or another topic that would take a good amount of time — but truthfully, it was in corporate America that I learned the word *boondoggle*. This is a word for an activity that costs time and money with an outcome that calls into question the time and money invested. That was diplomatic, huh? This one corporate retreat involved night golf. Glow-in-the-dark balls and headlamps, and a bar and food just behind each green. I will never forget it. Actually, I take that back. There is quite a lot about that evening that I don't remember. But I digress. Here's where I'm going: If we opened the dictionary and searched for *boondoggle,* we might see this: "*i.e.,* night golf at corporate retreat."

So now that we've talked about what your retreat should *not* be, let's talk about an annual retreat for high-functioning teams or collections of direct reports that need to work like a team. What should happen? What should it feel like?

MY RETREAT RECIPE

Retreats take participants on a journey. At the most effective retreats, participants leave more engaged, more inspired, and reenergized about the mission and the road ahead. And this requires a great deal of work up front. I tell people that you need six weeks of preparation for the best offsite events. The ones who believe me see the payoff. Here are 8 things you need to include:

1. **Team building / icebreaker.** Stop! I saw you roll your eyes. If you believe, as I do, that it is important to manage in 3D, then we need to offer opportunities for folks to share their full selves. Do not — I repeat — do not take this item off the agenda because of moaning and groaning. The groaning comes from the poor execution that participants have experienced in the past.

   Please don't let lousy ideas keep you from this critical piece of work at a retreat.

   Here are two ideas that have never failed me.

   The Foolproof Bio Book.

   I mean it — foolproof. Folks will groan about having to do homework, and later they will thank you. It's a 2-page bio. The bio contains anything you want folks to know about you. It must include at least one picture that isn't a formal headshot, and you must also add some type of reference to why your organization is meaningful. No format is off limits. A CFO once submitted hers in Excel, and a graphics person submitted hers in cartoon form — whatever works for staff members and allows them to express who they are.

   I like to start with a funny pop quiz to get the group warmed up at the start of the retreat. Then I begin a discussion of the "ties that bind," followed by a chance to ask colleagues questions about the bios. The range of issues that comes up is stunning. In one group, the common thread was about nannies. A few had been raised by nannies, one woman resented the family her mom worked for as a nanny, and one board member was, in fact, a nanny.

It was one of the most powerful (and riskiest) conversations I have had to navigate. It was about class and race and there were strong feelings in the room. Combining the generous spirit of the participants with a strong facilitative hand, the conversation brought a diverse room together in the most remarkable way.

<u>Bring a Thing.</u>
Ask every participant to bring *something* that reminds them of why they are committed to the work of the organization. Give each person two minutes to describe the item and its significance. After everyone is done, place all items in a central location so that they can be appreciated throughout the retreat. I will never forget the social justice attorney who brought a pretty, solid-clay sculpture of what appeared to be a man behind a desk. The lawyer said (yes, with tears) that her son had made the sculpture for her. It was Attticus Finch from the movie *To Kill a Mockingbird*. Her son wanted her to know that this is how he thought of her. (I can't even type that sentence without tearing up.)

2. **Shared vision.** Board meetings and staff meetings are too tactical to be inspirational. Bring the work to life with a picture of the road ahead. In spite of challenges, it should be a journey that no one wants to miss. I'm working with a head of school who is planning an offsite with her "team" because, based on meetings and conversations, they have no shared vision of the education provided at this school. In our next session, we will talk about language. Until you reach a shared sense of vision, you are a group and not a team.

3. **Bringing the work to life.** A few years back I worked with a board of an organization that delivered produce to food pantries and shelters. It was so cold that I wore gloves over my gloves. But I wanted to be able to lead the group with

authenticity. At the board meeting, I was in the minority of folks who had touched the impact of the work by riding the truck to deliver that food.

If you are clever, you can combine #1 and #3 in this list. Here's a great example: One organization I worked with offered a Friday night dinner to its clients — it had been going on for years. At the opening of the retreat, rather than a fancy social dinner, board members were asked to come to the dining hall. Their job: talk to one client over dinner and capture their story. We began on Saturday morning by going around the room and having each person introduce themselves to the group as the client they had met the night before — 18 board members and 18 different characters, each touched by the organization in different ways. Then we put the names of each client on large sticky notes on the wall and referenced them all through the day: "What would Maria think about that long-term goal for the organization? Would it help *her*?" It was crazy powerful.

4. **A few words from the leader.** Here I want the leader to articulate their leadership style, to set out the charge for the group so that it can evolve into a team. "What do I need from this group of senior staff?" Is it simply a vehicle for sharing information, or is the leader looking for creativity, dissent, or pushback?

5. **Assessment of how the group works.** You have gotten some dimension from folks, the ED has shared the road ahead, and the work has come to life in a way that inspires you. Goosebump stuff. Now the question is posed: Are we, as the direct reports to the ED or as board members, working together as best as we possibly can to serve those clients? Are we a team or are we really a group? Do we appreciate what each of us brings to the table? Are we (or am I personally) coming to these meetings to advocate for the interests of our own areas, or are we thinking of what's in the best interest

of the clients, the community, the shelters, the food pantries? What's working? What could be working better? What do we need from each other to make this a stronger group — to maybe actually *deserve* to be called a team? What would need to change to get there?

6. **Time to exhale.** Do whatever you can to find a spot that enables the group to take a walk and breathe in some fresh air. If you can't do this, please do not overschedule the day so that it feels breathless.

7. **Appreciation.** Every participant should feel valued for every dimension they bring to the work. I'm a big fan of a leader bestowing something unique and meaningful on each person there. It works well at the end. The simplest recommendation I make involves flowers, and each flower is different. The leader bestows an individual flower on each person and, when doing so, says something appreciative about the person. Then all the flowers are placed in a vase in the center of the room. The whole is greater than the sum of the parts.

8. **Clear actions and follow-up.** Retreats are measured by what happens after they conclude. Can a group volunteer to make sure that the action items really happen?

What is all this in the service of? Ensuring the expectation that the collection of individuals must move in the direction of team behavior? Yup. Having a shared vision of where the organization is headed? Check.

One more important outcome of this kind of attention: retention.

KEEPING THE KEEPERS ON THE BUS

I had the privilege of interviewing Caroline Samponaro in a recent podcast (www.joangarry.com/ep-12-community-organizing-caroline-samponaro-podcast). She has been with the same organization, Transportation Alternatives, for a decade. It feels almost unheard of these days (in a land where, if I had a dime for every time I heard the word *burnout* . . .), but Caroline was not burned out — not even close. And she could be. Every day, she works with families who have experienced unimaginable loss. But nope — Caroline loves her job. She loves the people she works with, she feels a deep sense of purpose, and her role in the organization has evolved over time, so she feels she is given regular opportunities to take on new challenges.

Daniel Pink has it right: It all starts with *purpose*. Harvard Business School and the Energy Project (a company that assesses workplace productivity) joined forces on a study. They found that the single most important influencer in job satisfaction and retention is purpose: "Employees who derive meaning and significance from their work were more than three times as likely to stay with their organizations — the highest single impact of any variable."

And why have I dedicated an entire chapter to what it takes to be a good manager in the nonprofit sector? Because really good managers build great teams and retain great people. A great nonprofit staff leader gives their staff member a clear picture of success, a voice and new opportunities, and appreciates the hell out of them — financially when possible, and creatively when not.

> A great nonprofit staff leader gives their staff member a clear picture of success, a voice and new opportunities, and appreciates the hell out of them.

We need to talk about one other "managerial" relationship. It's the trickiest of them all: the board and the executive director.

SUPERVISING AND EVALUATING
THE EXECUTIVE DIRECTOR

I know, I know. I said it was a partnership. And yet, the staff leader is accountable to the board. One of the board's core responsibilities is to hire and evaluate the executive director. Now, I'm not taking back anything I said. I see a highly effective nonprofit as a twin-engine jet — two excellent engines that work in tandem. However, the ultimate buck stops with the board. If something bad happens (stay tuned for Chapter 9!), you can fire the staff leader, but it is the board that is ultimately responsible.

What makes this tricky is that it's odd to have a boss who is a volunteer, and a volunteer who is, by design, only your boss for a finite portion of your entire tenure. And your boss isn't in the office next-door. Actually, your boss might be halfway across the country and have another full-time job.

I have found that you must do a few things to set up this tricky relationship to succeed. These things tie back to everything we've been talking about throughout this chapter:

- **Regular meetings.** I don't mean "we talk all the time" meetings. I mean biweekly meetings with an agenda set out ahead of time and approved by both parties.
- **Annual goals.** Both parties *must* have a clear picture of success.
- **An annual evaluation.** It must be complete on or before the executive director's anniversary date. The top-line information must be shared with the full board. It cannot be done simply by the board chair, and I recommend engaging in some kind of 360-degree evaluation in which the executive director is evaluated by supervisors, colleagues, and staff. They are helpful and, given that the board has only a single perspective, I argue that the information is more than just helpful — it's critical.

- **A contract or a detailed letter of employment.** You should
  have this for retention, for succession planning, for risk management on the part of the organization should the relationship terminate, for smooth transitions, and for good,
  old-fashioned clarity.

Your executive director deserves to be treated professionally,
and the items on this list enable you to do that. Anything short
of that is not only unprofessional — it's risky.

If only organizations followed these clear and simple steps. If
only executive directors were not defensive because they have
a bias against volunteer bosses who don't quite know what
they do or appreciate how hard they work. If only board chairs
remembered that this process (of managing the executive director) is the most important and best opportunity to build that
partnership I talk about — to offer good solid feedback, to set
clear goals and to appreciate the hell out of the passion and
commitment to the mission of the organization. And when it
comes to compensation, to be thoughtful, generous when appli-
cable, and creative about how to ensure that a five-star executive director is incentivized to stay.

Take it from me: I have heard every story at least twice. There
was the executive director who was fired by the board while he
was on vacation. I have worked with executive director clients
who have been in their jobs for years and *never* had a performance review. I've seen reviews completed so late that it was as
if the board were getting an early jump on the review for the
following year. I've heard a board member say that he didn't
write exactly what he thought about the executive director's
performance, because he was sure the executive director would
figure out it was his comment. I have seen executive directors
spend hours trying to figure out who-said-what. I have heard
blow-by-blow defenses against every piece of constructive

feedback. I have seen boards create evaluation instruments with absolutely no input from the executive director. I have heard a board try to include a noncompete clause. Yes, you heard that right: "If you leave our organization where you are an expert in the field of autism, you can't work for another autism organization for 12 months."

I am not making any of this up.

I just spent a chapter offering my insights on managing the paid and the unpaid. Please know that the best-managed organizations are well-run from the top.

TWO THINGS EVERYONE IN YOUR ORGANIZATION WANTS

These are the only two things that anyone in your organization needs in order to be productive, to be a good team player, to manage generously and to give it their all:

1. People in your organization want very badly to be successful.
2. People in your organization want to be treated like human beings.

Every single idea, suggestion, and insight included in this chapter is a no-brainer if viewed through the lens of these very simple needs.

I get it. You are small and mighty. Let's gently put my chair down now."

Chapter 8 The Small and the Mighty

I began writing my blog in 2012, and as I mentioned earlier in the book, in pretty short order, it seemed that folks saw me as the nonprofit "Dear Abby." As readership increased, so too did the emails and phone calls.

Some of the emails were funny.

Do you know any funders in Santa Clara that might fund our organization's work?

My board chair never returns my call. What do I do?

The phone calls increased as folks tracked down my cell phone number: "Hi, I'm calling from Hawaii and I'd like to start a nonprofit and need your advice."

In the early days, I tried to answer all emails and all phone calls, but soon it became too much. As we tried to consider what to do to help them and manage expectations about my ability to do so, we started to look at the real underlying need.

These leaders needed resources and support they could not afford. After doing some research, we realized that the vast majority of nonprofit leaders run very small organizations, and coaching and consulting are just not options.

One more discovery — these small organizations? They are not small in terms of impact. These organizations often are the backbone of small communities. They are small nonprofits with vastly greater needs than they can fill. They are small nonprofits filling important gaps, but they are just getting started.

Small. And mighty.

And all these emails, calls, and revelations led me to build a membership site with content and community for board and staff leaders of small nonprofits — called *The Nonprofit Leadership Lab* —and thus began the kind of love affair I have with these small organizations and the superheroes who lead them.

In the early days, I learned that our work has provided the resources, support, a shot in the arm, and the occasional kick in the pants that these hungry folks need to see their messy nonprofits turn a corner.

The nonprofit leaders I meet teach me and inspire me every day. You want to see determination? Passion? Grit? See these leaders in action. They offer me such hope.

WHAT I BET YOU DON'T KNOW

The 2019 nonprofit employment report shows that nonprofits are responsible for 12.3 million jobs, over 10% of the US employment. Nonprofits represent the third largest workforce behind retail and food and just above American manufacturing.

You might want to read that paragraph again. Non-profits are responsible for more jobs than American manufacturing. In addition

> Nonprofits are responsible for more jobs than American manufacturing.

to all the good nonprofits do to fix our broken world, this sector is a key driver of our economy.

A *big* driver: $985B to the US economy; 5.4% of the Gross Domestic Product (GDP). So when we say nonprofits matter, we are not kidding around.

Let's dig deeper. Most of these organizations are small. We're not talking St. Jude's here. We're talking about your local animal shelter, a state organization advocating for gun control, a faith-based food pantry. Small. Sixty-seven percent of the nonprofits we rely on, that we count on to lead in our communities, have budgets of less than $500,000.

I call these nonprofits small and mighty because they have outsized impact. But the organizations themselves? Not so mighty. Here are some statistics that should worry all of us:

- 50% of nonprofits have less than a one-month cash reserve.
- 8% are technically insolvent with liabilities exceeding assets.
- According to *Forbes*, over 50% of all nonprofits are gone within 10 years of securing their 501(c)(3) status.
- Over half are destined to fail within just a few years due to a lack of leadership and planning.

We can look at some of the key reasons that cause these small nonprofits to fail. Leaders are passionate but may lack management and financial experience. These organizations do not prioritize board building and engagement. Then, related to the first comment, developing diverse revenue streams can present an existential threat.

But let's talk about the organizations that live in this 75% or this 67% of US nonprofits. Let's talk about how bedly we need them, the gaps they fill, particularly in the places we call home. Consider your own community or county. Nonprofits, especially these smaller ones, provide a backbone, a moral center to our ability to understand what it means to be a good neighbor.

Consider that, for over 100 years, The Essex County Legal Aid Association has given free and immediate legal help to poor folks facing legal crises. On a budget less than $200,000. Or how about Threshold Choir, an organization that supports 200 chapters around the world who sing at the bedsides of the dying? On a budget of $285,000.

So the moral of this story is pretty damned simple. Our society relies on our small nonprofits to fight for equality, feed the homeless, and ensure that everyone has an equal shot at the American dream. Our society relies on our nonprofits to ensure a healthy economy. And we rely on the leaders of small nonprofits as role models whose leadership offers us hope.

In this chapter, I dig more deeply into what makes these organizations special. I describe their unique challenges. And, because I can't help myself, I offer practical advice on how these leaders can have outsized impact and drive toward stability and sustainability.

NOT ALL THE SAME RULES APPLY

While writing the first edition of this book, I offered frameworks for readers to help them think about the structure of a nonprofit differently — less hierarchical and more like a partnership between board and staff. When you chat with Carlos De La Rosa, who runs a wildlife hospital, refuge, and visitor's center, and has also served on other nonprofit boards, he will tell you (as he told me) that this reframing was game changing. "In my last roles, I felt like I had a whole posse of bosses — the chair, of course, but every board member felt like a supervisor. It was stressful and overwhelming. . . To shift my thinking to consider Rosanne Siino not as my boss but as my board chair and my 'copilot' allowed me to redefine my relationship. I now have a thought partner, and I feel comfortable sharing my challenges and then talking them through."

How great for Carlos and Rosanne, but I have found that in this unique and important niche, not all the same rules apply.

What say you, Joan? This twin-engine jet philosophy of yours — it's core to a thriving nonprofit — you told me so!

I am not walking that back. Consider this a very friendly amendment. When we think about this subset of the non-profit sector, we have to consider brand-new nonprofits. And when we enter that land, we meet the most remarkable of creatures — the founder.

NONPROFIT FOUNDERS

When I entered the land of the small nonprofit, I found myself surrounded by founders. What remarkable people. I have learned that nonprofit founders have a kind of X-ray vision. They see a gap, a problem — something the rest of us don't see. Or maybe we see it and assume it just needs to stay the way it is. Or in the worst scenario, we figure someone else will tackle it.

Founders have no ability to sit idly by. They shout about the issue from the rooftops and don't rest until they get the attention of someone ready to join the cause. If you ever want a deep dive into the genius, the vision, the determination, and the grit of a founder, grab a copy of *Just Mercy: A Story of Justice and Redemption,* the story of Bryan Stevenson and his work to found the Equal Justice Initiative. Stevenson could simply not sit idly by thinking of innocent people behind bars.

My point? Founders are the lead players in the land of the small and mighty nonprofits. And their organizations are literally *their* organizations. They drive, they lead, and everyone else follows. They are, to a person, extraordinary.

Kayla Abramowitz was 11 when she saw the gap. Kayla battles a chronic illness that lands her in hospitals regularly. Dissatisfied with the video libraries in hospitals, remarkable young Kayla and her remarkable mom Andrea started Kayla Cares 4 Kids, securing donations of entertainment and educational materials and getting them to kids who need them. Today nearly every major US hospital and every Ronald McDonald House in the US has been the beneficiary of Kayla's work. All this on an annual budget of $30,000.

Todd Crawford likely wishes he never had to file for a 501(c)(3). One morning his wife was reporting on ABC News in NY and the next day he and his sons lost her to a brain aneurysm. He threw himself into being a single parent and into understanding the warning signs of aneurysms and realized there was a gap. No one was talking about the warning signs. And those warning signs might have saved Lisa and since his organization, The Lisa Colagrossi Foundation was started in 2018, it has indeed saved lives — on a budget of just under $300,000.

And in the world of founders, it's hard to top Robin Steinberg. I call her a "serial founder." She began in the South Bronx as a champion for holistic defense, a team that includes social workers as well as lawyers, and follows a client through the tangled web of the court system. During this experience at Bronx Defenders, she saw the staggering number of people who were behind bars simply because they could not make bail. She could not sit idly by, left Bronx Defenders, and founded

The Bail Project. As if those two organizations were not enough, in 2019, Robin founded Still She Rises out of North Tulsa, OK. Oklahoma incarcerates a higher percentage of women than any other state in the US.

Julie Lovely is another remarkable person with superpowers she didn't know she had. As a lifelong horsewoman, she volunteered as a kid for an equine therapy program. Then she experienced the magic of horses personally when fighting PTSD and Post-Partum Depression. She understood the power of the work and the growing need, and in her own backyard south of Boston, she founded Wild Hearts Therapeutic Equestrian Program in 2009.

Julie and many other founders like her wear many hats (yes, Julie wears a cowboy hat, but that's not what I mean). I have a nickname for the multiple hats — I call it the *trifecta*. Just as it sounds, this superhero wears three hats: she is the founder, the executive director, and the board chair.

Hard to imagine right? Sounds problematic on nearly every level.

But if you think about how organizations are founded, the need for founders to wear multiple hats makes sense. A brand-new organization is founded by a remarkable individual (more on founders to follow). This founder *has* to run the show — no question. She is the person who saw the gap and identified that an organization focused on closing that gap could make a world of difference. And so run it she should. When it was time to put the list of board members on the 501(c)(3) application, the founder went to close friends and relatives. And do you think anyone of them was willing to *lead?* Of course not. Founder boards *follow*, at least at first. You can imagine a conversation like this: "I believe in you Marge, and I really love what you are doing. I want to support you. But I've never been on a board before, no less run one." Bottom line: Marge can't find a board leader and so Voila! Founder, Executive Director, and Board chair all wrapped in one person — Marge.

Now, while having a founder serve three leadership roles may make sense when an organization is just starting out, clearly having a "three-headed leader" presents an array of challenges and ultimately thwarts the best-practice governance model. Later in this chapter, I offer some thoughts on how to move from this model but the point here is that early stage nonprofit organizations are not always on sound financial footing nor are they set up to succeed from a governance standpoint.

For years, not months, for *years*, Julie wore every hat. In fact, do you know what Julie got for the twentieth anniversary of Wild Hearts? A board chair.

Julie rode solo for five years. "I didn't know what I didn't know." The work began as a labor of love and then it took its toll. Five years in, Julie might have called it quits, adding Wild Hearts to the statistics above. Instead, she took a summer off, regrouped, and entered a new phase. And as a testament to her determination and passion (the superpowers of founders), she is building a board, growing the reach of her organization and has a new energy about her work that is palpable.

THE SUPERPOWERS OF THE SMALL NONPROFITS

I fear I have presented small nonprofits as weak and vulnerable. And the statistics may point you there. But we'd all be naive to think that the strength of a nonprofit is best measured by the number of zeroes in the annual budget. Large nonprofits don't have the same kind of need to be scrappy, to consider how a service might be donated, or to spend time developing a creative plan that might cost a bit less.

Small nonprofits live in this world. The scrappy world. While many small nonprofits are financially vulnerable, there is no shortage of small nonprofits that make big things happen.

> While many small non-profits are financially vulnerable, there is no shortage of small non-profits that make big things happen.

Dawn Kemper runs Young At Heart Senior Pet Rescue, a $500,000 rescue and haven for senior dogs and cats. She sums it up. "My superpower is the ability to be scrappy, creative, tenacious, laser focused, passionate, and ultra personal." Her ability as a founder to ignite a fire in the belly of others is central to the success of the organization, including its ability to be nimble and seize opportunities. Heather Bland who is the CEO of My Refuge House, a $400,000 organization that offers safety and a path of restoration for girls who have been rescued from commercial sexual exploitation, human trafficking, and sexual abuse, puts it this way, "I like to say that we are big enough to see patterns and small enough to pivot and this allows us to innovate and develop cutting edge programs."

Becky Brett Caldwell runs Virginia Highlands Festival, a $280,000 organization that hosts an annual festival to preserve and showcase the arts, crafts, and skills that developed in Southwest Virginia. Ask her about her superpowers, and she's quick to talk about how she feels she can make "much from little or nothing." And unlike many nonprofit leaders who would prefer to see their boards stay at arms' length and just raise money, Becky has a different take. " Our board is very close to mission driven activity, which is very energizing for all of us."

Remember Todd Crawford? The mission of his organization is deeply personal. For him, the upside of his small organization? "I am agile, willing to experiment and to take risks to put it all on the line." For a founder like Todd, he and his sons will never ever lose sight of what's at stake. Todd is quite literally the heart of the Lisa Colagrossi Foundation.

Sometimes a lack of resources can lead to the discovery of superpowers you didn't know you possessed. A lack of resources often inspires a more creative, higher touch. Many leaders of small nonprofits tell me so, and this rings true from my own experience.

Early in my tenure at GLAAD, when we were just barely out of our financial crisis, we began a conversation about holiday gifts for our higher end donors. Many of our colleague organizations were bigger at the time, and we knew there would be money in their coffers for gifts. Not so at our house.

Besides, I just simply cannot bear the idea of donor dollars being spent on coffee mugs. And so we chose a different route — lovely holiday cards that we designed in-house. We decided that I would write a note in each card. Our development director liked the idea so much that she extended the list to our mid-level donors. So 300 cards landed on my desk. The list of names included any personal information I might not know or remember.

And then my family and I went on a family ski trip. I didn't ski, but the kids did. Off they went, and I found a comfy chair by the fire and went to work.

Our notes arrived at the same time the branded coffee mugs arrived from our sister organization. Do you know how many thank you notes I received? Many. Some were about the high touch gesture and how meaningful it was. Others seemed downright relieved that we didn't send mugs.

Other superpowers come up when you talk to those who lead small nonprofits, include autonomy and adaptability. These leaders don't have large boards that question their every move and can pivot and change when necessary. They will tell you that they know all our clients by name, and that donors feel a greater sense of transparency.

Sounds appealing, right? But as we know, every superhero has her kryptonite.

THE KRYPTONITE OF THE SMALL NONPROFITS

Julie Lovely will tell you. As a one-woman show who threw her heart and soul into her equine therapy program, not knowing what she didn't know, she came face-to-face with the kryptonite of exhaustion, arriving at the intersection of big dreams and no resources.

And so it goes for so many of these small organizations. I remember early on at GLAAD telling a board member who asked me to tell her about our long-term vision on an admittedly bad day. My thought balloon read (and aren't we so glad these are not visible to the naked eye?): *It's a bit hard to look down the road when you have your nose in the cash flow statement.*

But that's it, isn't it? Leaders of small nonprofits need time to plan, to get out and educate the community, to engage folks as volunteers and board members, to explore new revenue opportunities. Oh, and while they are at it, many of them are paying the bills (if they can), running the programs, and working to engage their board in some fashion.

No wonder there are so many small nonprofits. It is true that running a nonprofit is an endeavor that folks are often ill-equipped to run. But there's another reason.

They get stuck. They don't know what to do or how to do it to get from a small messy organization to one that is growing or healthy.

Their superpowers weaken because they cannot sustain the pace for the work they care so deeply about. Add either a need for control or a lack of tools, and the footprint of the organization is just too small.

GETTING UNSTUCK AND SCALING UP

So you find yourself in Julie Lovely's shoes. You know the work matters. The clients who ride with you talk about impact and transformation, and the work is rewarding beyond measure, but it's just Julie. And Julie's organization is one of the nearly 1 million nonprofits that get stuck.

Kathleen Kelly Janus, my friend and colleague in this land of nonprofit leadership, interviewed hundreds of these organizations and looked at others who had successfully scaled up, gotten over the hump, added that first staff person, and begun to grow the impact and reach of their organizations.

Janus advocates for a number of strategies and you just simply need to buy her book *Social Startup Success: How the Best Nonprofits Launch, Scale Up, and Make a Difference,* but I want to highlight a few of them that feel important and quite connected to the philosophies you'll find throughout the chapters of this book.

First off, Kathleen and I are kindred spirits around storytelling. The organizations that scale are filled with first-rate storytellers who develop creative ways to tell stories. Amen to that. She also has seen that organizations that scale lead collaboratively. This is something we tackled in the leadership chapter, recognizing that the power in a nonprofit comes from all around the leader. Engaging the voices of your stakeholders creates ownership, alignment, and a kind of energy that propels an organization forward.

In addition, Janus makes a compelling argument for funding experimentation and experimentation in general — test-driving a new idea to create a real *proof of concept.* I love this idea because having a proof of concept opens doors to funding in a way that a description of a good idea simply doesn't.

Janus's fifth strategy aligns beautifully with how I think about how a nonprofit can move from the vicious cycle of a small founder-led organization and how an organization can move from messy to thriving. She calls it *measuring impact,* but I'd like to reframe a bit.

What if the organization was laser focused on defining success? Janus says it this way: "We need to spend less energy keeping organizations alive and more energy in spreading positive impact."

This is it! It's that simple.

Do you know how often I talk with CEOs of organizations large and small who ask for advice about an upcoming board meeting or a leadership team offsite they might be having with a prospective partner, and I'm asked to help craft the agenda or talking points? The first question I ask is, "What will success look like — for the participants and for you?" Once we answer this question, we can get to the business of designing an agenda that drives to that definition of success.

This is the big missing piece for small nonprofits. It creates mess and causes them to get stuck.

What if Julie Lovely took time to focus on this question. Perhaps she would say:

- I have capacity for more clients and there is a need, so I'd like to *increase clients by 15%* over the next 12 months.
- There is so much research that illustrates that horses work magic for PTSD. I'd love for us to reach out to veterans and maybe over 12 months, *5% of our client base could be veterans.*
- We need to know that our program is helping people. We only have stories. We need a strategy for *measuring impact.* It's all well and good to increase the number of clients and broaden our reach to veterans, but are we really helping?

So let's say achieving these objectives defines success for Julie for 12 months. Can you imagine what a game changer it would be if she could measure that success? In a very, very simple way from the very, very beginning? It could be as simple as a client survey before lessons began. Or some kind of preassessment from the professional working with the client. Simply repeat those two assessments at the end of a period of time, and there you have it. Add in some anecdotes and you have exactly what you need for a case statement for funding. You have defined success metrics and measured that success.

Let's look more closely at these successes. What other decisions do these successes help you to make? A key one would be the composition of your board. You might be looking for:

- Someone who can help get the word out about your program.
- A person deeply connected to the veterans in your community.
- A former nonprofit ED who can help you think about how to take your success metrics and turn them into a case statement for support with individuals and funders.
- A person with expertise in autism or PTSD who can be an advocate, a voice, and who can help shape the impact measurement work.

You're getting the idea, right? Start at the "end." What does success look like in 12 months? How might you illustrate impact? Then design the path to get there. And build the "village" you need to accompany you on the journey.

I know you like what you are reading and yet. . . You are a one-woman show. Maybe you get paid *something*. Your board is weak and often MIA. And if only you could hire a development director.

But my pal Janus is on to something. The path to high impact (even if you are small) starts with defining success.

And just for the record "I really love horses and I know they would really help veterans with PTSD" is not a definition of success. That is the origin story of your organization. For founders, it is the result of the X-ray vision they have that I spoke about earlier.

At the root of these insights Janus learned as she met and appreciated the hundreds of small nonprofits, often "stuck" and "messy," is the muscle every nonprofit leader must learn to exercise. But for a small nonprofit, it is key not just to scaling but to surviving.

It's not a four-letter word but it sure can seem like it to the aspirational world changing nonprofit leader.

Prioritize.

THREE BIG MOVES (NOT PRIORITIES)

In these last three years getting to really know the folks who run the small but mighty nonprofits in our sector, I've learned a lot about their motivations, their determination, their control issues, their sense of overwhelm, their tendency to be drawn to bright shiny objects.

And when absolutely everything feels critically important, the notion of identifying one thing as more important than another is just plain hard. It goes against the grain.

Time to adjust the grain.

Kathleen Kelly Janus speaks to how an organization can get over the hurdle and move over the $500,000, but you and your organization have to actually survive to even get *that* far.

In my work, I have found that there are three big moves a leader of a small nonprofit must make to move away from "messy" and set their organization on a path toward a thriving nonprofit that can create an outsized impact.

Move #1: Invest in Yourself

I know nonprofit leaders. These are the people that cackle maniacally when the flight attendant suggests you put your own mask on before helping others. I have found that a leader of a small nonprofit will have often have

> I know nonprofit leaders. These are the people that cackle maniacally when the flight attendant suggests you put your own mask on before helping others.

this mindset because from their perspective, if it is going to get done, you better do it yourself.

These leaders will say there is no money for staff, the board is disengaged, and you just can't always rely on volunteers.

Welcome aboard the express train to burnout. And the express train to burnout will drop you off by the side of the road, bruised and battered, and far short of your destination.

So every single nonprofit leader must invest in themselves, but this is especially true for those who run small nonprofits because the pressure on the leader is in fact greater when the organization is smaller.

And while I could be talking about yoga classes, I hope you'll give me just a bit more credit. One antidote to the chronic imposter syndrome leaders of small nonprofits face is coaching. Asking for coaching is a sign of strength and not weakness, and it is something you deserve. Actually, your clients deserve it. And as for the investment, it pays dividends. More and more funders are receptive to providing funding for professional development. My client Drew Dyson runs the Princeton Senior Resource Center and sought funding from the community foundation there. It's been a win for Drew, and the foundation is further investing in the future of the Center.

Another strategy is to consider your growth areas: time management, delegation, or volunteer management. The learning opportunities both in person and online are out there. You can find courses, great books, and podcasts. You just have to see them as "musts" and not feel in any way "indulgent."

You know how much I love a good twin-engine jet metaphor. Wouldn't you be happy to know that your pilot invests in her own professional development and is a person always striving to be better in the cockpit? And can't you see how building strength in an area like time management might allow you to focus on external outreach or fundraising?

> Wouldn't you be happy to know that your pilot invests in her own professional development and is a person always striving to be better in the cockpit?

I worked with Nina Meehan, Founder and CEO of the Bay Area Children's Theatre in California. Her goal was to get to yoga (yes, yoga) three times a week. And in a month, she was back once a week and in six months, back to three times a week.

The adrenaline a leader has driving an early stage nonprofit can feel like a sprint. You're not in the sprint business. Great nonprofit leaders of thriving organizations get it. It's a marathon.

Move #2: Invest in Your Partnership

I suppose I could just simply say, "Reread Chapter 3." OK, I will. Reread Chapter 3. But let me add a few thoughts.

Remember our friends Carlos De La Rosa and Rosanne Siino, the ED and the board chair of Lindsay Wildlife Experience? Carlos is nine months into his job, and we all know that year 1 can be really tough. How much easier do you think it is if you have a board chair as a thought partner and "copilot"?

In this context, it is of course very clear that the founder who also serves as the board chair simply doesn't work. If I could gather every nonprofit founder together after they receive their 501(c)(3) certification, I'd give them a single piece of advice. Go find a person you are not related to, someone who did not go to high school with you, someone who is deeply passionate about the mission you have set, and someone you could hear the word *no* from. Ask them to partner with you for just one year to get the organization off the ground, to define success, to build a board aligned with that definition, and to set the organization as a nonprofit built to last.

Our friend Julie from Wild Hearts Therapeutic Equestrian Program will tell you. For nearly 20 years, Julie has struggled. She has been the founder, the ED, the only staff member, and the Board Chair.

When her husband had a health crisis in the fall, Julie realized something needed to change. She had to learn how to do this well, she needed to invest in herself. She chose our learning community, The Nonprofit Leadership Lab, and it has made a big difference for her. She wishes she had invested in this kind of professional development sooner.

That was step 1. Her second step was to dig into her contacts. She reviewed the list, all folks who had been touched by her program, with an eye toward a person who could lead with her, who was passionate about the work, and not someone who would simply follow her lead. She found just such a person and she now has a thought partner to really talk about the kind of impact the organization should be having and will then build the board that will have the horsepower (no pun intended) to scale, to move from away from "messy," and to build a plan for high impact.

Julie has made two of the three big moves. And those two moves will allow her to make the third one. This last move has the biggest ripple effects of them all.

Move #3: Build Your Army

We've talked about defining and measuring success, we've talked about storytelling, we've talked about professional development and partnering with your board. I saved the best for last.

Let's go back to our friend Nina who runs the Bay Area Children's Theatre. For the first few years after she founded the organization, she kept a death grip on the steering wheel, the finances, and just about everything. She pulled a board together of friends who shared a love of theatre and were excited to follow Nina's lead. They didn't have much of a plan or strategy. And success was defined quite simply: can we put on a show with limited funds and will people come?

Today Nina is in a different place. Yes, she is in a yoga studio three times a week, but wait! There's more. Her original board chair was wonderful, filled with passion for the work. As the organization grew, it required a different kind of board with members who had different skillsets, attributes, and experience. She began to identify a few new board members and one was just what she needed in a board chair. Fortunately for the organization, he was also interested.

OK, so what's with the army?

Your impact is directly correlated to the number of folks who know and care about the work, folks who *need* to know about your work, and people whose lives will be enriched by knowing about your work. Who am I talking about? Clients, donors, potential volunteers, the next great staff person, a prospective board member, a journalist, a foundation program officer.

So you have got to build an army. Even if you are the lone staff member at your organization. You and your copilot need to get to work.

It's time to think about growing your sphere of influence. Have a look at Figure 8.1. When Nina began, you can see that

FIGURE 8.1   A good organization's sphere of influence.

the first ring, her original board members, were what I call
FoFs, Friends of the Founders. To grow the reach of an organization, you add rings. You add the obvious ones first. In Nina's
case, she looked for folks who could say with enthusiasm: "I
love theatre," and then, "I love kids." This is how she expanded
her reach in order to sell tickets and secure funding.

The difference between a good organization and a great
one — one that truly thrives — is the creativity with which a
leader approaches what happens next.

Leaders of small nonprofits (or even large ones for that matter) tell me things like:

• *I can't find any board members;*
• *My individual donor base is really small;*

- *No one knows about the work we do;*
- *We don't get much engagement on our social media;*
- *We didn't sell many tickets to our event;*

The problem? Their spheres of influence are limited and obvious.

Allow me to explain. To begin, look at Figure 8.2.

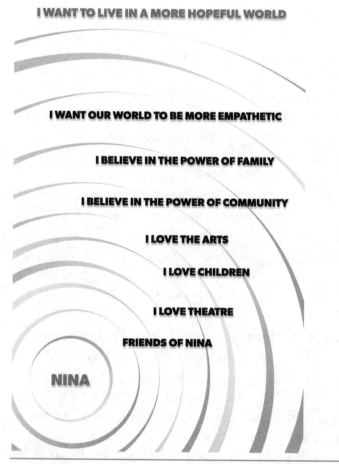

I WANT TO LIVE IN A MORE HOPEFUL WORLD

I WANT OUR WORLD TO BE MORE EMPATHETIC

I BELIEVE IN THE POWER OF FAMILY

I BELIEVE IN THE POWER OF COMMUNITY

I LOVE THE ARTS

I LOVE CHILDREN

I LOVE THEATRE

FRIENDS OF NINA

NINA

FIGURE 8.2   A great organization's sphere of influence.

This is exactly the kind of work Nina did. She expanded the spheres. She thought creatively about the different ways that

Bay Area Children's Theatre touched the lives of people in the Bay Area. So we added

- **I Love The Arts** A board member terming off of another arts organization in the Bay Area might have kids or grandkids. Could be a donor or board prospect.
- **I Believe in the Power of Community** One of the theatre's programs reaches low income kids and brings theatre to them in their school districts. Nina's work can absolutely speak to those who appreciate and embrace the diversity of the Bay Area and understand it to be at the core of what makes a community strong.
- **I Believe in the Power of Family** This new ring led Nina to write for a local mommy blog. It might lead Nina to seek out a psychotherapist for the board who works with families.
- **I Want Our World To Be More Empathetic** This ring was a game changer. A study conducted by Theatre for Young Audiences illustrated a real correlation between the introduction of the arts to kids and the development of empathy. A kid introduced to the arts in a real way before age 10 builds empathy. After age 10, the impact drops. Do you see the power in that? Children's theatre, based on this alone, can be legitimately seen and positioned as good for what ails our society.
- **I Want to Live in a More Hopeful World** This last ring took Nina beyond the Bay Area. Many of the Bay Area Children's Theatre productions were original, written by Nina. She began to see that other theatres may be interested. And so she began to commission the work outside of San Francisco, garnering visibility for the organization around the country. And then she joined the national board of Theatre for Young Audiences. New income source from the commissions, increased credibility for her work and for the theatre has led to board prospecting outside of the Bay Area. And her first national grant from the Shubert Foundation.

Nina's organization began in 2004 with a bank balance of $250. She was hitting a wall. The wall that my colleague Kathleen Kelly Janus saw with hundreds of small nonprofits.

And she made three big moves that made all the difference. She invested in her own professional development, she built a true partnership with her board, and she creatively built an army by expanding her organization's sphere of influence.

Today, she still struggles (what nonprofit leader doesn't). But today her organization has a budget of $5 million, has national funding, receives earned income from commissioning original work, and collaborated with Chelsea Clinton to turn her book into a musical. Today Nina is the chair of the board of Theatre for Young Audiences and has a profile well beyond the Bay Area as a leader in this sector.

She made three big moves.

She made her own professional development a *priority*.

She made building a partnership with her board a *priority*.

And she made it a *priority* to think creatively about how to reach more people, to invite them to know and do more for the theatre.

I know that everything feels important. It's hard for nonprofit leaders to say no. But if you say yes to everything, it just won't be possible to do much well.

> She made three big moves. She made her own professional development a *priority*. She made building a partnership with her board a *priority*. And she made it a *priority* to think creatively about how to reach more people.

IMAGINE

Let me be really clear. I am not suggesting that all nonprofits should strive to be bigger. Small nonprofits — the ones you see every day driving your kids to school — these are the backbone of our communities. The food pantry, the animal shelter, and yes maybe even your local children's theatre.

I'm suggesting that the size of your *impact* matters, and you owe it to those you serve and to those who support your work with time or treasure to strive for an *outsized impact*.

I'm suggesting that there is a strategy for turning the statistics around — those stats I referenced at the beginning of the chapter about the percentage of organizations that fail.

It doesn't have to be like that. I see it every day in my learning community. Nonprofit leaders, founders, board leaders — they are investing in learning, working to take better care of themselves. They are reframing how they understand the value of their board and seeking out strong leaders to stand with them as partners. They are setting goals and trying awfully hard to measure success. And those that are overly dependent on a gala for annual revenue see the vulnerability in that strategy and are exploring new ways to raise money (using the same approach Nina used as she built her army).

Our small nonprofits don't need to be big. They just need to be mighty. The clients they serve, the causes they advocate for, the audiences who are given the gift of art — they need these organizations to be mighty. They need for these non-profit founders' mighty visions, the ones that led to the 501(c)(3) paperwork, to come to life through an organization that is built to last.

It can be done. We see it every day.

You can do this. It does not have to be so hard. In fact, the harder it feels, the more quickly you will burn out. And it doesn't have to be like that.

The world needs what you do. We are counting on you.

"OK, remember. You are the leader. You're going to need to pull yourself together."

Chapter 9 When It Hits the Fan

This is one of those chapters you might feel compelled to skip. I, on the other hand, wouldn't consider writing a book on nonprofit leadership without addressing it head-on. In fact, I was stunned to see how many books on leadership don't tackle crisis management head-on. When I suggest to nonprofit leaders that they prepare for a crisis, they tell me, "I have enough trouble managing the challenges of the small and medium variety" or "If we focus on what we do well, we can avoid the big, bad crises."

Neither is this a topic that readers raise with me; thus, you will not see a *Dear Joan* included in this chapter. No one ever asks me how to manage a crisis before it happens. But I am *regularly besieged* by emails about big, hot messes and how organizations can dig out of them. And, as I read the emails, I know the organizations are often making things worse because they didn't have a plan.

You see, nonprofit leaders are by disposition an optimistic lot. They believe that with time, energy, smarts, strategy, and sheer will, they can improve society in ways large and small through their organizations. It's one of the things I love about the people I work with. So fierce. So determined. So clear that "If not them, then who?" And "If not now, then when?" I spend my days with folks like this, and this attitude leads me to work harder for them.

So, advocating that these nonprofit leaders take the time to consider the worst possible thing that could happen to their organization, their sector, or their client? This kind of request can fall on deaf ears. These fiercely determined, optimistic change agents don't want to go there.

But go there you must, for two reasons: first, leaders are expected to take the reins in times of crisis. The great leader gives their community a sense of comfort that the crisis will be handled well, that folks will be cared for, and that everyone is working together. Now, the second reason: leaders are wrong when they say that if they focus on doing good work, they can avert crisis. It would be lovely if this were true, but it simply isn't.

In October 2013, a severely autistic 14-year-old boy named Avonte Oquendo walked out of his school in Queens, New York. He was in special education classes there and somehow eluded adult supervision and ran out of the building. His mom had told the school: "He likes to run." School officials were unprepared for what followed. There was such confusion that they believed Avonte was in the building and a lockdown was ordered. More than an hour passed before anyone realized that young Avonte was on the streets of New York City. City police pulled out all the stops to hunt for him. His parents grieved for him, hired a lawyer, and sued the city and the school. Nearly a year later, Avonte's remains were found in the East River. So terribly tragic.

In June 2014, Greenpeace International lost $5.2 million based on a poorly timed, reckless investment. According to

Greenpeace, the CFO acted beyond his authority and was terminated. Based on how the story played out in the media — *five million dollars!* — it was clear that a crisis management plan was not in place. Do you really think that announcing the termination of the CFO qualifies as a crisis management plan? Might it have been smart and transparent for the treasurer of the board of Greenpeace International to come forward and take responsibility for being asleep at the switch? And that would be one of many decisions, messages, and actions Greenpeace should have been prepared to take.

On November 18, 1999, 12 students at Texas A&M University were killed and 26 others injured when the bonfire students were building in advance of their annual contest with rival University of Texas collapsed. This bonfire was an annual tradition for 100 years. Had Texas A&M taken precautions? Had it ever considered that it was simply too dangerous to continue the tradition? And how did university leaders handle the tragedy and its aftermath? Yes, yes, and very well. More on that in a bit.

What about the sex abuse crisis at Penn State in 2012? The crisis, and the public relations nightmare associated with assistant football coach Jerry Sandusky's criminal behavior, became a story of international proportion. In deconstructing how the University handled the crisis, it's difficult to find a single thing the institution did right.

Lastly, Orlando, June 2016. The LGBTQ community and the world were rocked by the largest mass shooting in US history at a gay bar. The shooting was by a man claiming allegiance to an Islamic terrorist organization and, at the same time, clearly struggling with his own sexual identity. Hate crimes are not new to the LGBTQ community. It would hardly be a surprise to anyone that LGBTQ people are targets. Were the organizations that were advocating for LGBTQ equality ready for a crisis of this magnitude? Had strategy sessions with movement leaders ever been held to discuss how organizations might work together to spring into action on all fronts should a hate crime occur? I can speak from my own experience and say that, while I was at the helm of a gay rights organization, we had no plan, nor was there a movement strategy. I do not say that with pride. It's just a fact.

> If you haven't had a crisis yet in your nonprofit, the reason probably isn't that you are good. It's more likely that you are lucky.

These are just a few examples of crises. A report by the Institute of Crisis Management reported over 600,000 crisis stories in the news in 2016. While this number includes both corporate and public sector organizations, it is vital for nonprofit leaders to understand that if you haven't had a crisis yet in your nonprofit, the reason probably isn't that you are good. It's more likely that you are lucky.

You could make the argument that the nonprofit sector is in fact disproportionately impacted by crisis. Why?

- Often nonprofits are in the business of advocating for issues that are controversial — nay, *polarizing*. Oh, I don't know — gun control, for example. Debates can get ugly and go in very difficult directions.
- If you are working for a marginalized community, you know full well that they have been climbing uphill for a long time. When communities like this get really tired, they can get vocal, they can impede your ability to move your organization forward and, if they feel your organization isn't doing absolutely everything to fix things, the anger can turn on *you*.
- You may make a decision that your stakeholders disagree with — to close a program or to accept corporate sponsorship dollars from a company your stakeholders feel works against you.

- You simply can't control for all possible problems. A student suicide at a college or a university can happen suddenly. It can wreak havoc on the entire university community and present a real quandary for the institution about how to handle it with respect for the family and maintain the integrity of the institution.
- Money. You have to manage it well and ensure that your revenue streams are diverse enough to sustain a precipitous drop in revenue. A corporate sponsor with a change in leadership can lead to layoffs. Layoffs, reductions in services — these are crises. You can build and steward relationships with the best of them, but you are not the decision maker. And all the good work in the world may not change that funder's mind.
- The issue may be internal. Like the Penn State scandal, something may be profoundly wrong inside the organization — with a staff member, for example. It could be the ED, a board member, or a beloved staff member.

HOW ARE WE DEFINING CRISIS?

We need to have a common understanding of what we mean when we use the word. How do we distinguish from the crisis that falls under the category of "the one who cried wolf?" Every one of us has encountered staff and board members who are what I like to call "fire alarm pullers." They become frantic before even counting to 10 to determine if what they have is a crisis.

My mother was like this. I loved her dearly, but her anxiety led her to push her internal panic button. A few years ago, she thought her pacemaker alarm was going off, so she called 911. Paramedics don't mess around with 89-year-olds and arrived on the scene within minutes, only to find that her smoke alarm battery needed to be changed. My mom assumed a crisis and also created one where a crisis did not exist. It certainly wasn't the first time — my mom was a fire alarm puller. Literally.

So how do you know a crisis is real?

Well, sometimes it couldn't be clearer. Sadly. You learn that an autistic kid at your school is missing — clear, simple, and heart-wrenching. And it's a crisis, without a doubt. You learn that a finance staff member is embezzling money and the proof is in a report on your desk — another kind of crisis. You terminate an employee and maybe you have crossed all your *t*'s and dotted all your *i*'s and still you wake up to a prominent piece in the local paper besmirching you and your organization — a crisis, for sure.

According to Kathleen Fearn-Banks, author of *Crisis Communications: A Casebook Approach*, a crisis must have one or more of the following four key elements:

1. The incident damages the reputation and public opinion of the management or the organization.
2. The incident is so all-consuming that it interferes with the ability to get normal business done.
3. The incident leads to government or media scrutiny.
4. The situation leads to a substantive loss of funding.

WHEN THE LIGHT AT THE END OF THE TUNNEL IS AN ONCOMING TRAIN

Here is the conversation that your standard do-gooder can't bear to have. And not only do they need to have the conversation, but the board should also hold the staff accountable to present a crisis management plan that is updated annually based on new information and context. This conversation, and the plan that evolves from it, could save your organization's reputation, the sustainability of your work and, literally, lives. Reread that last sentence if you had been previously unconvinced.

And if you are still unconvinced:

- Ask anyone who has been in the eye of the storm the degree to which they were consumed by the crisis.
- Ask anyone who has been in the eye of the storm how demoralizing it was.
- Ask anyone who has been in the eye of the storm how little time the storm left them to do the other 99% of their job.

As you consider what I call the "oncoming trains," you cannot be timid. You have to say the things no one really wants to say out loud.

> You have to say the things no one really wants to say out loud.

As a leader, you must be a model for your staff and the rest of the board. You must create an environment in which staff and board feel empowered enough to share bad news and potentially bad news. You must be sure they understand that it is their job to speak up and that this is a sign of strength, not weakness.

"Two-thirds of all crises should never make it to the level of 'crisis.' From the top of the management chain to the bottom of the organization food chain, everyone should always be on the lookout for those little problems or issues that, ignored or underestimated, can grow into a full-blown public nightmare."

—*Larry Smith, senior consultant, Institute for Crisis Management*

BUILDING A CRISIS MANAGEMENT PLAN

Please do not be daunted by the hard conversations around creating a crisis management plan. This plan, incorporating some of the wisdom of Kathy Bonk and Emily Tynes from their book *Strategic Communications for Nonprofits,* can be developed in less than a day by a core group of folks. It would be great to include the board chair. That person will be in the hot seat, and it will create ownership and buy-in.

Only a day, you say? Or less? Yes. Because the real truth is that, if you peek under your pillow, you can find a small bag of worry dolls, each representing the things that keep you up at night — the really big things that will serve as the list for Phase I.

Phase I: Listing the Worst Things That Could Happen

Begin by developing a list that includes situations I would consider to be blazes of the five-alarm variety. I really don't like even having to type these:

- A missing child who was in your care
- A teacher accused of abusing a student
- A hate crime against the community you represent
- A shooting in the office of your organization
- A college student suicide
- A change in your programs that will enrage your clients
- A decision by a single source that provides 85% of your revenue to pull funding
- A charge of commission of a crime by your staff or board leader
- The issuance of a credible, widely distributed report that makes a strong case for misuse of funds
- A staff termination that leads to a lawsuit, staff unrest, negative publicity, and key funders walking away

Have you broken out in a cold sweat yet? OK, hang on. I'll get you there with this next exercise.

Phase II: Imagining the Worst Headline About Your Organization on the Front Page of *the New York Times*

You may think this is the same exercise as in Phase 1, but please stay with me. We'll come back to headlines later in the chapter. So I want you to create these as a benchmark. As you do this, I also think you should visualize the photo that will accompany the headline. The photos often stay with folks much longer than the words.

One last word of advice here: don't get *too* carried away. Just pick three or four scenarios and flesh them out. Make sure that one is about an internal decision the organization makes and that three others are potential crises. You don't need a long list, as the plans will have common threads.

Phase III: Making Assumptions

Here you are trying, in each of your nightmarish scenarios, to put yourself in the shoes of the press, the board, the public, staff, and donors. What will they think and feel when they find out? I'll give you a big, fat hint here. People will always assume that you didn't do enough right away. And what kind of actions can you take or messages can you deliver (and how quickly) to get out in front before assumptions are made? Make a list of assumptions for each scenario, and then list actions or messages that may preempt those assumptions.

Phase IV: Outlining a Process

The process should have several important elements:

1. **Create an organization crisis management team.** Clearly, it needs to include the ED and the board chair. But there will

be lots to do because "it" will be flying. Here's who you need to include:

a. Start with a point person for the media. Typically, it's the leader. Should the leader be at the heart of the crisis — legal or criminal — a backup should be identified.

b. If you have a communications staffer, clearly they get pegged.

c. It can be *very* helpful to have someone who is not part of the day-to-day work — a volunteer or donor you ask to be a part of this in the event of a 911 situation. Perhaps someone who works at a PR agency in your community? Having an outside perspective can help you avoid a bunker mentality — feeling like this is all you talk about and think about and believing that the entire universe is talking about it and thinking about it.

d. Choose someone who will monitor the media (this might be a volunteer role), set Google Alerts and stay on top of the buzz and how it is playing out. Things move quickly, and the team needs to have its finger on the pulse.

2. **Write the antidote headline you most want to see in the newspaper.** Time to compare and contrast the "worst" scenario from Phase I. Create the headline for each of your two to four crisis scenarios and then back into core messages from the headlines.

3. **Train spokespeople for the world of 911.** Is there any way that anyone in your community can, after the development of the plan, offer a two- or three-hour crisis management team training, pro bono? Or what about the communications person at another, larger organization in town who has completed their training? This is a specialized kind of training — high stress and high intensity.

4. **Build ally relationships before you need them badly.** When you have developed relationships with elected officials, business leaders, and other nonprofit leaders in your community,

your organization is richer for it. You are more informed about the goings-on, you have the opportunity to be of help to one another and, in a crisis situation, you will be there for them and *they will be there for you.* You will need external validators who know about your good work and your integrity — who can publicly support you and privately offer you guidance. This may be the last item on the list, but don't think for one second that it's the least important. It takes a village to manage through a crisis.

NOW YOU ARE SET FOR WHEN IT HITS THE FAN, RIGHT?

Time for three little secrets:

1. **Even with a plan, you are never really ready.** You are *prepared,* but not really ready. When you are in the eye of the storm, one ingredient blurs and causes short-term memory loss of all this planning. It's called emotion. It manifests itself in everything from self-doubt to defensiveness to panic. And that, my friends, is why planning is so important — because you have a road map you can focus on and know that you have done your best to be prepared.

   True story: a direct service organization has to move out of its current space. The new space that is identified has many plusses that will enable the organization to offer better services but is outside the core neighborhood of the community it serves. That neighborhood is now prohibitively expensive. Clients are in an uproar and, more importantly, the figurehead founder has gone to the press to condemn the decision *and* the quote is mean-spirited toward the current ED and board. This founder is a well-known personality in the community and in the organization's history of more than 20 years. He has been a go-to person for the press — often more than the current organizational leadership.

Not to sound like a shrink, but how do you think that ED feels? Hurt? Angry that he was not sought out? Defensive about the decision? Upset that the clients are upset because these are the folks whose lives he is there to improve? Now, *that* is a lot of emotion. Having a plan helps keep emotion in check.

> Having a plan helps keep emotion in check.

2. **Nonprofit leaders tend to be pleasers who look for middle ground.** (Is that a common theme in this book? I'm thinking yes). That is frequently *not* the answer to a crisis. More often than not, crisis management is about bold leadership, clear decision-making, and sticking to your guns on what might be unpopular decisions.

I'm remembering a situation a community center found itself in. The center was in a major urban setting, and one of its offerings was space rental for meetings. An Israeli organization reserved space, much to the chagrin of a Palestinian organization. The center's leader focused on trying to make both sides happy and met with each group often — not a bad strategy, but solving the Israeli–Palestinian conflict was well above this leader's pay grade.

The issue wasn't about solving the conflict. Instead, the issue was developing a clear policy about who could and who could not rent space in the center. Did all organizations interested in renting space need to share the core values of the community served by the center? And don't think for a minute that every member of the community was like-minded. An assessment of the rental policy needed to be made. The organization's leadership — board and staff — needed to own and buy into any changes. The policy needed to be presented, a stake placed in the ground, and all had to live with the consequences. Bottom line: someone is likely to be very unhappy. Leadership is not about making people happy — it's about making decisions that are in clear alignment with the mission and values of your organization.

> Leadership is not about making people happy — it's about making decisions that are in clear alignment with the mission and values of your organization.

3. **In a crisis, you don't want to make the wrong decision, and being deliberate can result in moving too slowly.** You want all the facts before you move. You won't have them. Trust me. But those who learn about the crisis want information faster — way faster than you are comfortable providing it. And if you don't provide it, someone other than you will fill the void — likely inaccurately or not in your favor.

Figure out what you can say ASAP that 1) is totally authentic, 2) honors the need for information, 3) makes a commitment to frequent communications and continued updates, and 4) reiterates the integrity of your organization as a core value and your commitment to doing what it takes to be true to that core value throughout the crisis and its resolution.

THE DOGNAPPING THAT WASN'T

The three little secrets were not secrets at all to Emily Klehm. You may remember Emily from Chapter 2. She is the executive director of the South Suburban Humane Society, and you may remember that I shared with you the exciting vision she has for the future of her organization. Emily is an impressive leader, and so it won't surprise you to learn that when a crisis arrived at SSHS, she was ready even though she wasn't ready at all — because she knew the ingredients.

It began with a 6:00 A.M. call alerting her that a dog had been stolen from a transport vehicle — the staff member said he had been held up at gunpoint. After Emily ensured the safety of the staff member and sent him home, the hunt for Polly the dog began. By 9:00 A.M., 10,000 people had viewed a Facebook post, and because of Emily's deep media contacts, an NBC reporter was on their way to cover the dognapping. Note that Emily began her career as a community organizer and thus Polly was in the best of hands wherever she was, with Emily's ability to engage and mobilize folks driving the hunt.

With a number of media interviews under her belt, Emily received a call from the chief of police alerting her that the whole thing had been a hoax. The staff member had given Polly to a friend. Turns out that SSHS had mobilized a community around a dognapping that wasn't.

Emily was deeply concerned about the impact of the incident on the reputation and credibility of the organization. She made a number of very smart calls in the moment, and it will not surprise you to know that this bowl of lemons turned into a big ol' pitcher of lemonade.

Emily's first call was to Barbara, her board chair — the one she had built a real copilot relationship with. Barbara asked the right question: "What do you need me to do?" Emily knew: "We don't want board members to find out on the news — please call each of them ASAP." Check. Next, Emily went out to the reporters still gathered. She knew them because she had cultivated a relationship with them during her tenure. Smart. Then, time to develop three key messages. It didn't take her much time; previous media training came in handy. Her messages: 1) SSHS never intended to deceive the community; 2) Polly was safe and back at the shelter; and 3) The organization took action and everyone at SSHS was very sorry.

The last choice was the smartest. "Let's go live on Facebook ASAP. This is where the story is most alive — let's get the word out." That alone would have been smart, but Emily went on with no notes — authentic and emotional. Her 4-minute video went viral, and comments like "So glad Polly is safe" and "We love you as a leader" appeared in the thread.

I don't know if Emily Klehm actually had developed a plan, but she sure made all the right moves. She was a clear, compelling, and articulate spokesperson. She moved quickly. She had cultivated relationships with journalists and avoided any risk of an exposé piece. And Emily was a lucky ED who came to her role having had media training.

What I love about this story is that the crisis is not catastrophic. And so the crisis itself does not overshadow just how adept Emily was in navigating it. The lessons really sing out. Brava, Emily!

IS A CRISIS PREVENTABLE?

Don't you just hate it when a good question gets asked and the answer is "It depends?" But it does depend on the nature of the crisis. That said, you often have clues.

Could the LGBTQ community have prevented the attack at the Pulse nightclub? No. Were there clues that Omar Mateen had a plan? Yes. When a student takes their own life on a college campus, were there missed clues that the student was deeply troubled? Yes. The assistant head football coach at Penn State was accused of sexual abuse — were there clues? Yes. At Texas A&M, had there ever been injuries to students while building a massive bonfire? Yes. If a staff member were embezzling, wouldn't there be some oddity in the financial statement? Yes.

But do we see the clues? And if we do, as I mentioned earlier, is the culture of the organization such that its members are receptive to sharing those clues and is there a proactive culture that leads to exploration of those clues?

Crisis management expert Kathleen Fearn-Banks talks about the four phases of an organizational crisis:

1. **Prodromal:** "Look closely and you'll see it coming."
2. **Acute:** "Eye of the storm."
3. **Chronic:** "Please let this stop!"
4. **Resolution:** "There were actually a few minutes today when I didn't think about this."

The "clues" I've noted here are what Fearn-Banks calls prodromes.

Prodromes are often right there — clear for the right people to see. I remember thinking during the Penn State crisis: "With a crisis of this magnitude, *someone* had to know." And of course, someone did know.

Eleven years before the scandal became public, the *president* of Penn State was alerted by two key staff members: the VP of administration and campus police and the athletic director. These staffers reported that assistant football coach Jerry Sandusky had been seen in the showers "horsing around" with a naked minor boy. The president of Penn State asked two simple questions. "Are you sure that was how it was described — 'horsing around?'" The second question he asked the men: "Are you sure that was all that was reported?" He received affirmative responses to both of his questions. And nothing was done — *for 11 years*.

WHAT CRISIS MANAGEMENT SHOULD LOOK LIKE

Penn State made too many mistakes to count. And frankly, it is easier to find examples of missteps than it is to find strong leadership in crisis.

A few minutes spent deconstructing the Texas A&M bonfire crisis is instructive. Led by the executive director of university relations, the University was on its game from start to finish.

Only five months into her job at the time of the tragedy, Cynthia Lawson was not a stranger to crisis — but her experience was in the private sector. Fifteen years earlier she was an executive at a large utility company building a nuclear power plant. You can bet they had a crisis plan and even practiced it annually. She had no idea how ideal that experience was for what she encountered at Texas A&M.

During Lawson's first five months, she invested a good deal of time in developing relationships with folks inside and outside the university — from media to elected officials and from business owners to colleagues at other institutions of higher education.

As I mentioned earlier, in the 100-year history of the bonfire, there had been no casualties as a result of the collapse of the bonfire. Rigorous instructions were given and close attention was paid by students to ensure that the utmost care was taken. So, in her first five months on the job, Lawson was unaware of any prodromes or clues.

The moment of the collapse began the acute phase of the crisis. It was the middle of the night. Lawson was the point person and shouldered a good deal of the work until the morning. She held four or five news conferences the first *day*, ensuring that the media had what it needed in the most efficient way. She also used journalists (the ones she had built relationships with) to put out the word about what was needed — food, cell phones, batteries, blankets. The media became a mouthpiece to promote a hotline parents could call. It became a community effort and not a blame game. Everyone stuck to the key messages, including students who wanted to be of help. One of them was, of course, care and concern for injured and deceased students and their parents. Another one included facts about the bonfire tradition that put into context what seemed to be an irresponsible activity. Last was a message about how special the Texas A&M community was and that, together, the community would get through the crisis and be there to support each other.

The hotline and the website that were set up especially for this situation fed the media everything they needed. The university's internal communications fed information to student government, residence hall staff, university trustees, and other stakeholder groups so that no one felt out of the loop. Everyone had the key messages ingrained, and everyone had specific ways in which they could help. The entire process was proactive and transparent.

The chronic phase of this crisis — when the story was still front-page news — lasted two weeks with plenty of coverage continuing for months. During this time, an outside person was appointed to lead a commission to investigate the incident. Again, Lawson was supportive and proactive.

Also during this time, negative stories emerged and Lawson's approach was simple and clear: the University would make no comments that could interfere with the commission's work.

The resolution phase began with the report from the commission. The commission found that a safe bonfire would have been possible had the school taken the right measures before and during its construction. Lawsuits were filed and ultimately the bonfire tradition was moved off campus and was ultimately discontinued.

Even though Lawson survived this crisis in stellar fashion without a plan, she likely was poised and prepared because of her prior experience in the private sector.

FINANCIAL CRISIS AND LAYOFFS

I am often called upon to help a nonprofit executive director pull an organization out of a fiscal crisis, and I'd be remiss to write a chapter titled "When It Hits the Fan" without talking about the most common crisis, and often the most chronic one, that nonprofits face.

What can it look like? Several common scenarios come to mind — each of them, frankly, way too common.

A brand-new ED arrives on the scene and learns that the organization is in the depths of a fiscal crisis. Did the board mention this during the interview process? Yes. Maybe they even showed you some numbers. But it isn't until you open those books and sit down with the staff member responsible for keeping them that the reality of it hits.

Why didn't the board tell you the truth? They might have told you the truth as they knew it. Or as it was told to them by the predecessor. They might not have known. Please do not get me started on board members who shirk their responsibility to understand the basic finances of the organization. It is not *solely* the job of the treasurer. And sometimes, to be honest, the treasurer is asleep at the switch too. Then, of course, we have "pleaser" executive directors who are fearful of sharing bad news. A whole lot of intersecting dysfunction is at play in this kind of scenario.

Another is what I call the accident waiting to happen. One of the single biggest illustrations of the impact of the COVID-19 pandemic was the resulting canceled fundraising galas for nonprofits. And for many smaller nonprofits, the annual gala could represent over half (or more!) of the total revenue.

Many nonprofits' revenue streams are simply not diverse. Most of the organization's eggs are in a single basket — in many cases it's the gala, but it can be one big donor, one significant special event, or one very large government grant. All kinds of things can go awry — it doesn't have to be a catastrophic health crisis. Your biggest donor may have a falling out with a senior member of your organization or realize that the organization is too dependent on you (duh) and then decide to take a year or so off. New leadership with a corporate sponsor means new priorities or a request for impact metrics you can't deliver on time.

One or more of these happens and — poof! — you are sweating payroll. You are making decisions about which vendors to pay and which calls should go to voicemail. Paid staff is anxious, wants assurances, and knows assurances are not forthcoming. You meet with your board chair, who wants an expense reduction plan. You want a board that will step up and fill the gap.

How do you manage *this* kind of crisis? You follow the same basic recipe. You are authentic, transparent, and proactive. I have worked with clients where we used the crisis as an opportunity for everyone to understand Nonprofit Finance 101 using a simple dashboard that could be easily explained to *everyone* around the table. (See Figure 9.1.) What works about this is that it is not a page filled with numbers. It is a page filled with *the most important* numbers. The second helpful aspect is that the numbers are put in the context of the *healthy* numbers you want. This just drives me crazy about finance presentations — *no frame of reference!* It would be like your doctor reporting that your LDL cholesterol is 215. And that is *all* they tell you. *Board and staff need to know what the numbers mean and what they* ought *to be!*

Speaking of high cholesterol and personal health, I used a personal medical metaphor when keeping staff apprised of our financial situation. At my first meeting, GLAAD was on a fiscal respirator. We moved to breathing on our own, and then to a step-down unit, and so on. It brought the challenges to life for folks, and they felt very much a part of what was happening. And just like a doctor, I answered the questions I could and was honest about what I couldn't. "Will there be layoffs?" In that first week, I was clear and adamant that I was working with the board and doing everything in my power to avoid them

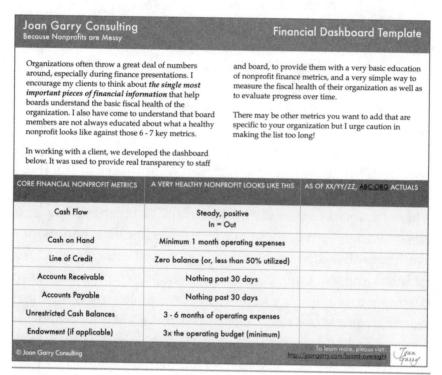

Joan Garry Consulting
Because Nonprofits are Messy

Financial Dashboard Template

Organizations often throw a great deal of numbers around, especially during finance presentations. I encourage my clients to think about *the single most important pieces of financial information* that help boards understand the basic fiscal health of the organization. I also have come to understand that board members are not always educated about what a healthy nonprofit looks like against those 6 - 7 key metrics.

In working with a client, we developed the dashboard below. It was used to provide real transparency to staff

and board, to provide them with a very basic education of nonprofit finance metrics, and a very simple way to measure the fiscal health of their organization as well as to evaluate progress over time.

There may be other metrics you want to add that are specific to your organization but I urge caution in making the list too long!

CORE FINANCIAL NONPROFIT METRICS	A VERY HEALTHY NONPROFIT LOOKS LIKE THIS	AS OF XX/YY/ZZ, ABC.ORG ACTUALS
Cash Flow	Steady, positive In = Out	
Cash on Hand	Minimum 1 month operating expenses	
Line of Credit	Zero balance (or, less than 50% utilized)	
Accounts Receivable	Nothing past 30 days	
Accounts Payable	Nothing past 30 days	
Unrestricted Cash Balances	3 - 6 months of operating expenses	
Endowment (if applicable)	3x the operating budget (minimum)	

© Joan Garry Consulting

To learn more, please visit:
http://joangarry.com/board-oversight

FIGURE 9.1

but could make no promises. As we moved from dire straits, I was still unable to make promises, but the staff could see the improved health for themselves and understand that things were getting better.

In tough situations, I wish more organizations would focus on driving revenue rather than on reducing expenses. I am working with one client whose biggest source of revenue was a single corporate sponsor who dropped out. This client identified some foundation money for capacity building to bring us in to identify other corporate sponsors and to build an individual giving program. The organization is now steady with a diverse revenue portfolio.

And, as for the rapid-fire fundraising that you may need to do, be aggressive without being desperate. Be honest and transparent and remember to paint a solid picture of what the organization will be capable of doing when it overcomes this hurdle. The funding you need now is a bridge to a stronger organization with greater impact.

I have been there. I was fundraising for payroll early in my tenure, and I was right in the eye of the cash flow storm. A donor suggested an expensive restaurant. I'll admit it: I was sweating. Dinner was lovely and the donor was engaged. I was new and shared my vision and she got it — she understood where I wanted to take the organization and that funding now was a bridge to that new place. I talked around the money challenges, but I must have made the need clear. I asked for $25,000 and she said yes. But she went one step further: "I'm hearing a bit of urgency here — would it be helpful if my business manager wired the funds tomorrow?" My development director and I nearly wept. We said yes as calmly as we could. And yes, the donor took care of dinner. We knew we could meet payroll. That was the first time I ever danced a jig in a parking garage.

If your senior-level conversation turns to expense reductions and possible layoffs, many of the lessons of this chapter will be of value. The choices you make must be smart, strategic, and equitable. If money really is a challenge, take the time to examine your programs. Is anything *not* mission critical? If so, your messaging can be about a strategic assessment of your programs that led to this elimination (rather than simply to save money). I also hope that if you are in a tough financial situation, your board will be vocal, messaging its own commitment to invite more people to be engaged in the work of the organization in an effort to drive fundraising revenue.

And if, after all this, your plan must include layoffs, I encourage you to read the communications plan outlined for the departure of the rock star staff leader in Chapter 10. I beg you to be equally methodical about how the information is communicated and to whom and in what order. The methodology should also include a look at the racial, gender, sexuality, disablity, or other markers of the staff you plan to lay off, to make sure that the impact is not disproportionate on a particular group. If you see such impact and decide to go ahead, be prepared to speak to the implications of the cuts.

And don't forget an important step. Layoffs are not just about those who have lost their jobs. In my experience, staff and board leaders neglect the folks still in the house. They are relieved yet deeply saddened about their colleagues. Maybe they are angry because they disagree with the choices. They know that they are about to have more work added to an already overflowing plate. And of course, the question "Am I next?" pulses through their veins.

> Layoffs are not just about those who have lost their jobs.

Oh — and when you do sit with those who remain on the job, I ask you to avoid this single statement: "Well, I guess we all have to do more with less now." If this is your mindset, don't sit with those folks until you have had an attitude adjustment. In many situations, staff is *always* under-resourced, and it is a source of frustration, anger, and burnout. Please don't make it worse.

Then there is *external* messaging. All of it should reinforce the importance of your work. Always remember to focus on why the work of your organization matters. And please engage your board in the public comments. Often the board sits on the sideline and leaves the staff leader to carry the water in these situations. Your organization is always perceived to be stronger when the public sees that strong partnership — in good times and in times when your organization is in the financial ICU.

THE MAIN THING

The moral of this chapter lies in a statement by Stephen Covey, the author of *The 7 Habits of Highly Effective People: Powerful Lessons in Personal Change:* "The main thing is to keep the main thing the main thing." At some point in your leadership, you will experience a crisis. It will be one that comes out of nowhere or one that could have been nipped in the bud (more likely the latter). How you handle it will be a key component of your identity as a leader.

Before I spell out the moral, compare and contrast the crises at Texas A&M and the one at Penn State. What was the "main thing" at each institution?

I would argue that the main thing at Penn State was to protect the reputation of the institution at all costs, even if that meant a cover-up of nearly heinous proportions. Penn State had a terminal case of institutional arrogance. At Texas A&M, the main thing was, first and foremost, to do whatever it took to take care of students and their parents. Texas A&M leaders were a central element in a caring community, and their objective throughout was simply to do the right thing.

So let's go back to talking about the moral to be gleaned from these anecdotes. You could say that the moral is to "be ready for that crisis when it hits" and you would not be wrong. But that's not the only answer. I believe that another answer is that you have to create a culture in which good news *and* difficult news are received well.

> You have to create a culture in which good news *and* difficult news are received well.

What is the most important answer? Covey nails it: It's about understanding your organization's *main thing* and keeping that main thing the main thing throughout your leadership tenure.

Let's say that you run a homeless shelter and a minor is abused by a staff member (I hate even writing that sentence) and that the "main thing" is tied directly to your mission. Your organization is about the care of kids who need homes and caring environments. *Be that* if something heinous happens. Communicate as quickly as possible with whatever you know. And go ahead and be clear that you will be outraged if you find out that there is truth to the accusation and that *you* will lead the charge to get to the bottom of it. If it's true, you will make the changes necessary — not just with that individual but also with recruitment, background checks, hiring, and evaluation. You are an advocate for these kids. Just because one person engaged in heinous activity does not diminish your passion and commitment to care for these kids. Keep that main thing the main thing.

Remember the direct service organization that relocated and then the founder used the media as a bullhorn to mobilize clients to protest and wreaked havoc on the image of the organization in the media (and to some funders)?

First off, the behavior of the founder, through the years, offered plain clues that she would potentially make an effort to undermine the organization should it make a strategic move that she felt was the wrong one. She was a walking prodrome. With lots of media access.

Perhaps relationships were not cultivated and called upon — folks who could have been credible external spokespeople about the opportunities the move presented. Was the founder brought in and honored early enough in the process? And what kind of communications plan was in place so that the clients understood what was happening, when the dramatic improvements in service would occur, and what the new space would afford?

I don't know, but a strong answer to those questions would make a big difference. The organization did not control the messaging — the founder did. As a result, the acute phase lasted for a painfully long time.

Did the organization lose clients, as the founder predicted? No. The organization was able to retain current clients and grow its base with added space and services. Other accusations did not come to pass. But because the founder controlled the messaging, the crisis was prolonged, and the organization's reputation took a hit.

I read a while back that Cynthia Lawson has retired after a distinguished career in higher education and as a national expert on crisis management, so you can't hire her to consult with you as you proactively build a plan of your own — although that would be mighty nice.

Instead, you have the kick in the pants I just spent most of this chapter giving you. Please take it to heart. Invest a day. And start the day by agreeing on one thing as a group: What is your organization's main thing? Write it in a big font on a flip chart and keep it front and center throughout your discussion about how you would handle a crisis. It will be your north star.

If you can build a plan that enables you to keep the main thing the main thing, you will be a leader admired and respected by everyone who touches, and is touched by, the work.

That may not be the *main* thing, but that is a good thing. A very good thing.

"At a two-hour executive session, they mentioned something about me getting hit by a bus. Is this about succession planning or should I be paranoid?"

Chapter 10 Hello, I Must Be Going

or

Navigating Leadership Transitions

I hope I have been making a strong case for the joy and privilege of joining a nonprofit organization as a leader, either paid or unpaid. My "conversion" in 1997 at the age of 39 was personally and professionally transformative and I could not recommend nonprofit work highly enough. I'm nearly evangelical about it (thus, this book!).

I also hope it's clear that it takes a special kind of leader to lead and manage a nonprofit and that, in fact, it takes *two special people* — an executive director and a board chair, each responsible to lead and manage a high-functioning "engine" and together responsible for ensuring a smooth ride to a vitally important destination.

This kind of unique leadership makes transitions very, very tricky. In fact, this unique kind of leadership often leads an organization to avoid making transitions it should make. And *not* making a transition you know should be made can create as much mess as the transition itself.

OK, I'm going to go there. The nonprofit sector has many challenges that drive organizational instability. The COVID-19 crisis revealed many of them in heartbreaking ways from organizations crippled because a gala was cancelled to challenges of meeting payroll without a cash reserve. All in the face of exponential need for the service you provide.

That said, I believe that our sector severely underestimates the kind of toll a leadership transition takes on an organization. I would argue that regardless of circumstances, the transition of an executive director puts a nonprofit in its most vulnerable state. Further, I would argue that a group of volunteer board members recruited without a very clear understanding of their roles individually or collectively (refresh your memory with a skim of Chapter 4) operates from a place of anxiety (fear) during ED transitions. When it comes to ED transitions, weak boards will generally make poor decisions during a transition and even the best boards often do.

> I believe that our sector severely underestimates the kind of toll a leadership transition takes on an organization.

And what about the other copilot? I've talked you through the issues that thwart strong board recruitment and offered strategies to overcome those obstacles and create a high-functioning board. I've also made the case for recruitment with a strong eye toward leadership capabilities because far too often the board chair stood for election reluctantly, or the board chair is so capable and strong that no one ever wants her to leave — either because there is no one on deck or no one wants to be on deck because the board chair has made the job look so daunting.

Does all this sound like a recipe for vulnerability? You bet. But wait, there's more!

This is a sector that has disproportionately high turnover at the top, well above the national average. A study from Concord Leadership Group, a top flight consulting firm in the nonprofit space, tells us that 67% of senior leaders plan to leave their positions in the next 5 years. So, if you haven't just experienced a leadership transition or are not currently in one, you probably have one right around the corner. Think about this: sometime during the average tenure of a board member, that member will need to help navigate a significant change in leadership.

> If you haven't just experienced a leadership transition or are not currently in one, you probably have one right around the corner.

The New Jersey Family Planning League has wisely sought outside support to navigate these turbulent waters and difficult circumstances. The ED is retiring after 40 years as its staff leader. The long-tenured board chair's term is expiring at the end of the year. My sleeves are rolled up, and I'm excited to work with board and staff members to address these challenges, providing my experience and expertise for what lies ahead for this organization. Two leaders. Lots of reasons for transitions. I'll tease them out, and I'll offer advice specific to different situations and universal strategies that have proven helpful.

To help you navigate, we need to look at each copilot and the different transition scenarios.

Why an ED leaves:

- They retire.
- They experience burnout (these jobs are really hard and only getting harder) from the work.
- They call it quits because of a board chair or board that abuses its power.
- They move on to an even better gig.
- They move on to a better paying gig.
- They are terminated for cause.

Why a board chair leaves:

- Their term expires.
- They're toast — they have just had enough.
- They have a change in situation — board chair has a family or professional change that doesn't allow for the investment of time necessary.
- What's the point? The ED does not want a copilot and does not invest in building the capacity of the board with them.

ARE THESE FOLKS GOOD AT THEIR JOBS?

So we're flying this plane, we're onboard, passionate about the mission, and excited about the journey and then we realize that we have taken no real responsibility for a formal evaluation of either copilot.

Formal Evaluations

Let's start with board chairs. Raise your hand if you are a board chair who has had a formal evaluation. Oh look — *no hands!* Because we recruit from fear and the role of board chair is seen as daunting and not as a privilege, what would be the point? I mean, can you imagine if you determined your board chair had to go and then you had to find someone else? So we know that isn't happening.

I have now worked with hundreds of clients across many sectors with annual budgets from $500,000 to $300 million. And do you know how many EDs I encounter who receive formal, written, annual reviews from the board that are the result of a thoughtful and inclusive process? I guess "hardly any" isn't really a number, is it?

Do you know how many EDs I encounter who receive formal, written, annual reviews from the board that are the result of a thoughtful and inclusive process? I guess "hardly any" isn't really a number, is it?

But that is the correct answer. Really? Really. Why not? I wish I better understood the answer to this. It is one of three fundamental responsibilities of a nonprofit board: *Hire, evaluate, and fire (if necessary) the chief executive.*

Do boards not know? Hard to believe, right? Board members are typically employees who expect and receive annual performance reviews. Why would an ED be different? Are boards lazy? I don't think so. People who join boards are infrequently lazy people — in fact they are usually high performers and type A personalities. Does it just fall off the to-do list? And does the ED not remind them because she thinks the board can't effectively evaluate because they are not engaged? I don't know the answers — I suppose each circumstance is different.

Here's what I do know: an annual performance review that evaluates the executive on the accomplishment of goals that have been approved by the board as part of the *last* annual review process is a nonnegotiable activity. And here's a concrete suggestion for ensuring that it gets done, gets done fairly, and gets done on time: Recruit an HR professional to your board.

HR Professionals

Every board should have an HR professional. Give that person the responsibility to develop a process and to hold board leadership accountable to execute it. No one in sight for board recruitment? Ask someone to serve as your pro bono Human Resources (HR) consultant — a few hours a month for leadership evaluation and some consulting time on high level staff hiring and firing decisions. In exchange, offer your pro bono HR consultant visibility for their company on the website or fundraiser invites. People like to be asked to volunteer to do very targeted things that are seen as valuable.

You can do this. You should do this. To be a professional, grown-up board, you need to do professional, grown-up things. And it needs to be multidimensional (a 360) — I spoke about this in Chapter 7. As board members, you do not and cannot have the full picture. And it is the only avenue staff may have to raise big concerns without fear of repercussions.

Unlike Executive Director evaluations, which actually do happen, albeit infrequently, I cannot think of a single client that has conducted some kind of evaluation of the board leader for the reasons I mentioned above. Let's talk about why this is such a big problem.

You see, this is a dirty little secret in the nonprofit space (now that it is in my book, maybe not quite so secret). Do you know how many Executive Directors either jump ship to another gig or burn out because the board chair is weak, unavailable, micromanaging, or unethical? Me neither, but it is way more than you think and way more than most people know. Because EDs don't tell. Executive Directors are not quick to raise serious concerns about their board chairs. First, while I refer to it as a partnership (and I believe that), the buck stops with the board chair. The ED sees that hierarchy — the board chair is my boss. Second, who will they tell?

Here's a hypothetical. The board chair takes the job as chair for the wrong reason. It's presented as altruistic and downright noble. But she raises her hand because she needs power in her life. I cover this in Chapter 4 — a board member who takes the role of chair for the wrong reasons can cause a whole lot of trouble, abusing her power and pushing the ED toward the door. I don't need to repeat those real-life examples; they were hard enough to write in Chapter 4.

It's hard to see these problems from a chair around the boardroom table. As a fellow board member, maybe you feel some tension but are not totally sure what that is about. And then some other board issue comes up and it flies out of your head. ED has no formal avenue to raise concerns — no one asks him. Another two years under her thumb? No thank you says the ED And you wonder why the ED jumps ship.

It happens *all the time*. I work with clients, strategizing about how to find allies on the board to talk to about concerns. It's not easy. I talk about building leadership capacity and a pipeline on the board so that everyone (board and ED) can see board members in action as chairs of committees and be evaluated by all to see if board leadership is right for them. This work takes time and intention, and is worth every second of that investment.

Again, I point to HR support from outside. A facilitated conversation by the HR person (or even a certified mediator) to talk through what's working and what's not working. Perhaps a memo from that person to the Governance Committee of the Board. Another route is the co-chair model. This can work nicely because it can be a thought partnership of three, offering differing perspectives. In addition, if one chair is weak, the other sees it as well so the ED has someone else in his corner. The strong co-chair and the ED can strategize or work around the more challenging co-chair.

No doubt other strategies may work — perhaps you have come up with even better ones in your organization. Regardless, boards *must* evaluate Executive Directors, and the board *must* provide checks and balances on the performance of the board chair as the supervisor of the executive. I ask you to do this on behalf of the hundreds of staff leaders who leave their jobs and/ or the sector and never tell anyone in a position of authority the real reason.

BOARD CHAIR RED FLAGS AND ACCOUNTABILITY

I'd like to believe that we can shift the dynamics around board leadership and evaluations tomorrow. But I know better, and boards need to do *something*. Let's take a look at a few different board chair profiles, the challenges these types of leaders present and some advice on how to introduce some level of accountability.

The Autocrat

Symptoms

This board chair has appeal to board members who are on the board just so they can say they are. This board chair gets it done and tells people what to do. Power is a significant perk of this gig for the Autocrat. Board meetings are ridiculously efficient, so much so that board members wondered why they had to show up at all. Then there is the Executive Director. They feel micromanaged. Board meeting agendas are set by the board chair with little input from anyone. The Autocrat will have definite opinions about staff performance and won't hesitate to tell you so, sometimes directing you to take action. At raise time, the Autocrat may be the board chair who believes that nonprofit folks somehow deserve to be paid less. And they might not be a big champion of overhead expenses. Oh, and they will want to review many things that get sent out to stakeholders. They will also be the first to find typos in your annual report before saying a single good word about the extraordinary work.

Challenges

- Strong board members who came to have a voice, add value to strategic discussions, and ask tough questions will feel stifled. They will be serious flight risks. Weak board members will just like that stuff is being taken care of.
- Miserable staff leader. The Autocrat is tough and intimidating, so there is no release valve for sharing feedback with anyone about the challenges the Autocrat is creating. Staff leader is disempowered and feels a lack of trust. Staff leader becomes a flight risk.

Antidote

Change rests in the hands of those strong and disgruntled board members. If you see yourself in this scenario, please know two things. First if *you* are disgruntled, you can bet your ED is feeling even worse. And disgruntled, unmotivated EDs don't typically do their best work.

Please do not jump ship. You came to be a strong and engaged board member, so here's your chance. The strength and engagement required just isn't the kind of strength and engagement you may have anticipated. Find one or two other board members who feel similarly, and do three things:

1. Take the ED out to lunch. Share some of the challenges you see at the board level with the Autocrat's leadership and see if you can get them to talk about their own concerns. Just that outreach alone will give the ED hope. Strategize together on how things can be different. And ask the ED to be patient. Change may not happen quickly, but together, perhaps you can develop a plan. You will all have ideas.

2. Perhaps you as a board member are not chairing a committee, and maybe you should. What about joining the executive committee where you can start to ask questions in a smaller setting with the ED present. Maybe it's time for a few of you to recommend agenda items for the upcoming board meeting.
3. Begin to make the Autocrat feel just a bit uncomfortable. It is possible that the Autocrat will thaw a bit — maybe they thought they were the only one who was willing to do things. Or maybe not. Maybe they will just get angry. To this I say: So what? Because if you sit idly by and lose a five-star staff leader, that will cause a great deal more upheaval in your organization than a bad temper from an Autocrat. Here's the deal: you joined the board because of your deep sense of responsibility. Time to put it to good use. Be part of the solution.

The Board Chair on Steroids

This is different from a five-star board chair. As I mentioned in Chapter 3, a five-star board member is a leader, a mentor, a facilitator. He is someone who builds a strong team of board members, each given the opportunity to lead and contribute.

Symptoms

This board chair ("Steroids") always feels it's just easier to do it themself. If they do ask a board member to draft something or create a plan, they'll spend hours rewriting something that was 85% "there" to make it, in their mind, an A+. In so doing, their fellow board member feels undermined and wonders why they bothered.

This happens with the Executive Director as well. But the ED knows how hard Steroids works. So what if the high performance of the board rests largely on one person's shoulders? As long as the board is doing its thing, the ED won't worry that others are disengaged or M.I.A.

Challenges

Board leadership pipeline is dormant. No one steps up because no one needs to. The ED will likely be very frustrated but much less of a flight risk. The board *is* delivering for the organization — through the "steroid" approach of a single individual. The biggest challenge in this scenario is that the board chair job looks absolutely impossible and so replacing Steroids is going to be really tough.

Antidote

The antidote to this scenario is very similar to that for the Autocrat scenario, but easier. The power dynamic is part of Steroid's hardwiring, but not in a dysfunctional way, so the approach can be more positive and collaborative as strong board members can actually *discuss* a higher level of engagement. And typically, Steroids wants what is best for the organization and will, upon reflection and with discussion, understand that the board chair job must seem doable in order for someone who can't toss 150% of their time at the organization but can still be a first-rate board leader to step up.

The Weakest Link

Walk into a board room with a meeting "run" by The Weakest Link, or "Link" for short, and here's the first thing you will notice. You will have absolutely no idea who the board chair is.

Symptoms

Board meetings are poorly run. Link is typically insecure, passive, and not very strategic. Biggest personalities and loudest voices rule the day. Link will allow a board discussion to go on forever and right into the weeds.

Challenges

This board chair drives the board crazy. Almost every other board member knows they could do a better job but this would mean volunteering. Typically Link either was the lone volunteer or the only one who could be persuaded. Board members are not pushed to do their best. And neither is the Executive Director. The ED does not have the strategic thought partner she needs. Link doesn't ask good questions, lets the ED totally run the show (which is fine if the ED is a rock star but a massive liability if the ED's performance is a problem). Link does not anticipate problems or anticipate what the board know.

Typically, a strong ED will actually find Link appealing (*"Link" leaves me alone so I can do my job without interference from a board that is not helping me anyway*). Your big risk here is not that your ED will scram; instead, your risk is that you lose the checks and balances that an effective board chair provides. A weak board chair can lead to a weak and ineffective board. It puts the organization in a very vulnerable position for the board not to take its responsibility to provide strong oversight seriously. This profile may in fact be the scariest.

Antidote

As board members, you actually voted for Link! Maybe you didn't realize Link would be so weak? I'm not buying it. People don't change their stripes that easily. Tell the truth. The board needed a chair, and you weren't willing. Or you didn't work to persuade someone to do it and offer your own leadership on a committee as support. So inaction leads to the election of Link. They couldn't do much harm, right?

Wrong.

Link must be supported and quickly. And, of course, the board needs to find a strong replacement to stand in the wings. A group of like-minded board members needs to talk and figure out how to reduce the liability of the chair. This group is either formally created like the Executive Committee or informally created with a small group of folks who understand that the board needs leadership and Link isn't the one to provide it. It must also be accompanied by the understanding of and a commitment to building board leadership to ensure that folks like Link do not ever find their way onto the board chair ballot.

OK, so staff leaders, do you feel wildly validated? Hang on. Because now it's your turn.

WHEN THE STAFF LEADER ISN'T LEADING

A formal evaluation and a set of annual goals either met or not are the keys to determining whether the board needs to make the toughest call it makes — to terminate an executive director. And as I mentioned earlier, so few boards do these well if at all. So boards often just simply don't know for sure or do not have the kind of documentation needed for either a Performance Improvement Plan or a termination with cause.

Compound this with a board that either is clueless or chooses to be. So much of these issues are systemic, aren't they? A poorly recruited board without a clear understanding of its responsibilities or a reluctant board chair may not ask the right kinds of questions that will unearth the performance issues. The board may simply be too disengaged to see them, or as I see in many cases, board members just choose to ignore the problems they do see. Maybe some board members see but not all of them. Maybe the board chair sees clearly but can get no forward motion to make the tough call.

There is one last pattern I've seen that I want to add to this mix. I cover making a new hire in the upcoming section,

"Making a Great Hire," but boards are often *overly* protective of their new leaders. They have gone through a time-consuming process and become deeply invested in the outcome. The selection of an executive director is perhaps the single most visible reflection on a nonprofit board's' ability to govern. The board's *need* for the new ED to be a rock star is very high, and this need can lead a board to making excuses and identifying other possible sources of the problems.

As a result of this stewpot of issues, EDs who should be terminated are not *managed out* by way of setting and sharpening focus on shorter term goals and performing more frequent evaluations. Fewer EDs are terminated in a timely fashion, and the slow pace means bigger challenges to clean up for the new sheriff in town. More good staff members leave to go work for more capable leaders. And most important, your ability to educate or advocate for your clients is severely diminished.

And if all this is not a strong argument for intentional recruitment, the addition of human resource expertise to your organization and a formal evaluation process, then I really don't know what is.

Let's have a look at a few different scenarios that should propel a board to take action and some advice on how to proceed.

The Bad Hire

Dear Joan,

I'm really torn. Three months ago, we hired a new Executive Director. I was the candidate's biggest advocate. Yes, the vote went in his favor but it was not unanimous. As the board chair, I have been managing and providing oversight and there have been signs from Day 1 that our new ED has challenges. Even staff has been sending cryptic signals to me that point to trouble. We were told he was strong in finance but now I've heard he barely knows Excel. We have the budget for him to hire an assistant and I think that will help but he hasn't even started the process. His board report at his first board meeting made everyone very nervous — it was scattered and there was a lot of complaining and blaming about what he had not accomplished. He never developed a 90-day plan. And yet I find myself defending him. Am I just covering for him? Or justifying my own advocacy for his hiring? One day I feel like he needs to go and the next I feel like he just needs more resources.

Signed,

On the Fence

Dear Fence,

Based on the little I have to go on here, you should come down off the fence. This ED has got to go and you need to let go of your personal investment in his hire. There is something way bigger at stake than your ego. Yes, the organization's reputation will take a hit, but it should. Sounds like, for whatever reason, you made a hiring mistake.

Symptoms

See *Dear Joan* in the preceding section. And, by the way, the board chair in the above letter probably knows only the half of it. When you make a hiring mistake, the problems begin to surface in all sorts of ways. You start to see smoke. Maybe even a few licks of flames. Trust me, there is more where that came from. But here are a few 90-day markers.

- Do they know the finances of your organization cold?
- Have they made a direct solicitation for a donation from an individual?

- Have they met with the 25 most important stakeholders in the organization to introduce themself and share their vision?
- Do they have a really good read on staff?
- At their first board meeting, did they present a 90-day plan?
- Have they been in regular communication with the board, bi-weekly emails for example, to share successes and updates and to enlist board support in specific ways?

If the answers to most of these questions is "no," I would suggest that Bad Hire is in the house.

Challenges

I have no interest in insulting your intelligence, so I won't list all the reasons that Bad Hire can hurt your organization, but there's something important to say. Problems are clear really quickly. I will spend an hour on the phone with a prospective client who is seeking coaching as a new ED. In that hour, I can tell. I can tell if you have a potential Rock Star or Bad Hire. It has to do with tone, with authenticity, with the clarity of purpose I hear in the voice and in what they say. Board members see it too, if they allow themselves to do so.

The idea that you made a mistake will feel awful and fearful. The fear is the worst part. The fear that your credibility as a board will be greatly damaged with a failed hire and that as a result, the credibility of the organization and its work will be lessened in the eyes of those you serve and those who fund.

You and your type A board members will come up with a hundred justifications. You'll supervise more closely. You'll provide scaffolding — maybe a coach. You see some signs of turnaround. Or at least they will feel like signs. Because you want to see them so badly. Because another search feels so overwhelming. Maybe you can make this work.

Can I let you in on another secret I think board members don't know? From the outside looking in, the board takes a bigger credibility hit when it waits. Donors meet with the ED and wonder if the board "gets it." Colleagues in your sector will meet him and wonder if the board "gets it." And the longer you wait, the less your stakeholders will believe that you "get it." And that's the biggest problem of all to the credibility of the board and your organization — that stakeholders believe that the board doesn't see what is so obvious to them.

Antidote

Board members should fan out and casually connect with varying stakeholders as soon as something just doesn't feel right. Do this as a stewardship effort (this is important with anyone you hire). It's time for reconnaissance and external validation.

Next, in that first meeting with the new ED and the chair, ask the ED how they intend to tackle the first 90 days. You should receive a thoughtful answer, you should be asked for input and you should be told that you are going to get something in writing for the two of you to review together. If this does not happen, then ask for one. Use this deliverable to assess who you have in the driver's seat.

Next, be sure the board is holding tight to the reins of board recruitment. Please! If this new ED builds the board the wrong way (and if they are a Bad Hire, they might), they will pack it with allies. Allies who will vote in their favor on issues that matter. Oh, like voting to fire them, for example.

At the 90-day mark, the Executive Committee should go into executive session and have a candid conversation (yet another place that pro bono HR consultant could come in handy). I promise you that you will have more clues than you think you do. Especially if you as board members do some stewardship of stakeholders for feedback.

If you think this is a failed hire, create a plan to develop a paper trail. Put the ED on the equivalent of a Performance Improvement Plan. If you have a full-on Bad Hire, they will not meet the goals you set in the plan. And then the process of cutting bait can begin.

One last piece of advice on this topic: Bring the search committee back together and appreciate the heck out of them. They will need moral support; they spent a ton of time on this and will feel like failures. And then gently, ever so gently, begin a conversation about whether there were clues in the process. You need to learn so you get it right next time.

Toast EDs

Baby boomers are retiring from nonprofit leadership roles in droves. Sometimes they are rock stars and you are devastated at the prospect of losing them. Sometimes they are no longer hitting on all their pistons. And sometimes it is just time for a new kind of leadership.

Symptoms

They haven't had an innovative idea in some time, they really don't have the energy to make needed changes (asking folks off the bus or bringing new folks onto the bus), and the organization becomes somewhat dormant. The board pushes for something new and keeps pushing. The resistance is either clear or passive. The organization is often still doing great work but the board finds itself seeing missed opportunities at every turn.

Challenges

Obvious. Frustrated board members — some who came with a lot of energy for innovation move on. Someone running out the clock is not pushing hard enough. And sometimes, the ED with the long tenure is not savvy in social marketing and digital engagement and does not see it as a priority.

Antidote

One answer is of course to wait it out. The work continues to be of high quality. And yet there is a growing recognition that your clients and donors deserve more. Another option is to push harder for change, turning the heat up and sending messages of all sorts that more is expected. The ED might accelerate a departure timetable. The third option is to work closely with the ED to create scenarios, projects, and initiatives that reenergize the leader. I have seen highly innovative, five-star leaders who have been in their jobs for years and when I ask the recipe, I inevitably hear "I feel like my job is always different — I have had so many opportunities to re-invent myself." If the ED is receptive, this can be an effective antidote.

The Founder Who Sticks Around Too Long

Now this is a different kettle of fish from the other staff leader challenges. The symptoms and challenges are clear. The antidote requires the strongest board of all. And in the ultimate irony, a founder has so much power in an organization that the board *follows* and does not lead. I'm sure you have had the pleasure of reading *Make Way for Ducklings* to a young child. Think about the mother duck leading her duckling across the street. Get the idea? The founder is the leader of all the board ducklings and this means a weak board — at a point in which a strong board is never more critical.

Symptoms

"Responsibility without authority" is the key symptom. Folks are given roles and responsibilities but decisions really rest with the founder. The organization is built around the founder and not around the mission. This is true of the board recruitment and often staff as well. Lastly, people come to work because of the cache and charisma of the founder. For some it wears off and there are others who become long-suffering #2s who work so hard to keep the team on track.

Challenges

A very long list here and it begins with staff attrition. Generally those who found organizations (and this is true in the for-profit as well as the nonprofit sectors) are visionaries, leaders, the folks with the big ideas. They are infrequently the folks who can execute or manage. And processes like strategic planning feel cumbersome and limiting to the founder.

Antidote

The only antidote that I have ever seen work is the development of a strong board with new voices and faces that are not personally tied to the founder. If this board can begin to hold the founder accountable, there is hope. Money is another way to change the dynamic. If the organization is given a grant to do strategic planning and the board and staff are accountable to an external force (and one who is writing a big check), change is possible and the founder can be brought into alignment with the rest of the organization around a new road map.

But, make no mistake, this is no easy feat. Sometimes, the very best thing for the organization is to work with the founder to create some other kind of role that takes him out of the day-to-day operation of the organization (and NOT ON THE BOARD!). This requires the board turning up the heat on the founder and then a great deal of diplomacy and finesse. It doesn't sound easy, does it? Not gonna lie; it's not. It's worth a shot if you believe in the mission of the organization and the sustainability of the organization with the founder in some lesser role.

Having done a deep dive into the profiles of leaders who present real challenges to your organization, shall we focus on another scenario — the leader you want to stay forever leaves *you*.

THE FIVE-STAR STAFF LEADER CALLS IT QUITS

The scenario a board dreads. Early on in this person's tenure, you know you have struck gold. Have a glance back at Chapter 1 and review the superpowers of nonprofit leadership. You will see those superpowers in your leader. You hope it will last forever. And then it doesn't. It was a helluva ride, but all good things. . .

Just to clarify, this five-star scenario could also be the departure of a founder. There is overlap. When founder Robin Steinberg chose to move on from Bronx Defenders, an organization providing holistic public defense, the Board needed to come to grips with the loss of gold. But as you'll read in a bit, there was a plan because Robin had given thought to succession. Stay with me.

As I mentioned, this is the one transition that rocks an organization to its core. The five-star leader is often beloved. Their presence helps recruit staff and board members who want to be part of this winning team. This leader understands that it takes a village to build a five-star nonprofit — a strong board, the right staff, engaged volunteers, donors who are informed and appreciated and a program strategy that is smart, impactful, and measurable. With this leader, everyone really does feel lucky to be a member of this village. I've seen it. It's kind of magical.

Let's talk about the elements that will ensure the smoothest transition.

I had a picture of what a new kind of contribution to the nonprofit sector could look like.

An ED Contract

Please tell me you were smart enough as an organization to offer your rock star a contract. And please tell me that it was a negotiation process that was fair and honored the contributions of your amazing leader, providing whatever incentives you could offer to ensure retention.

Let's say you didn't screw it up. In this contract, you provided an incentive to your rock star to stay with you and work right up to the last day. Perhaps a month of salary for every year of service if they stay through the end of their contract (can you imagine working full throttle as an ED and shopping for a new gig? Me neither).

The contract should also include a date by which the ED is required to make her intentions known. I happen to like a 6-month date before the end of the contract. Others think 9 months or a year are appropriate. Under the right circumstances and for the right reasons, 9 months or a year can work, but beware of the challenge of the lame duck ED Regardless of the notice period, the ED needs to inform the board leadership of her intention of engaging in new contract negotiations.

I took my contract seriously and knew that 6-month date cold. Being the planner I am, my process began much earlier — at least a year before even the 6-month contract trigger date.

I needed time, and I did my due diligence. A big dose of soul searching and lots of conversation with my wife, and then with my five-star board chair, thought partner, and trusted friend.

I reached a decision not to renew because of several reasons. First and foremost, my wife and I decided that one of us needed to be at home to advocate for our three kids' turbulent ride through junior high and high school. Next, I never wanted to be perceived to have overstayed my welcome to the potential detriment of the organization. And last, I was sure I had another good chapter or two (or 11 in the case of this book) left in me.

Thoughtful Transition Planning

Rock star EDs, founders, and long-tenured leaders need to begin both the tactical and the emotional transition process several years in advance. Rachael Gibson, a Senior Consultant at Raffa-Marcum's Nonprofit & Social Sector Group, is a colleague in the sector and a kindred spirit about transitions. She has worked with founders and long tenure leaders up to three years in advance of their departure to ready the leader and work with the board to strengthen it to be able to withstand the turbulence of change.

I also do this work and I do hope that organizations with founders and rock stars have or find resources to bring in outside counsel. It can make for a smoother transition and mitigate a great number of common mistakes that organizational leadership can make.

Outside counsel can also help create a very *very* detailed roll-out plan — from a strategy to transfer ownership of relationships from the strong rock star across the board and staff, to messaging strategy for each stakeholder group, to a very thoughtfully considered rollout of the information both internally and externally. This outside counsel can also provide an organization with clear pros and cons about the continued involvement of the leader after she steps down. (Hint: Board members seem to be willing to do most anything to keep the rock star involved and often think a formal role, like board service, makes sense. This could be the biggest thing that ties the hands of a new leader to set their own course.)

> Leadership transitions —whether someone chooses to step off the bus and on to a new adventure or you recognize that your constituents need and deserve leadership they are not getting — are one of the top most destabilizing events in a nonprofit's trajectory.

It bears repeating. Leadership transitions —whether someone chooses to step off the bus and on to a new adventure or you recognize that your constituents need and deserve leadership they are not getting — are one of the top most destabilizing events in a nonprofit's trajectory. And demanding the best at the staff and board level, making tough decisions when you have to, and managing the departures of those you wish would stay — these are as important jobs as any a nonprofit board does.

And your organization will be judged as much by the "how" (the process and communication) as it will by who fills the shoes.

Folks pay a lot of attention. Because for those who care deeply about your mission, there is so much riding on the choices you make and how you make them.

MAKING A GREAT HIRE

I am never short on points of view but in this section, I've got *lots* of them. Let me take them one by one.

The Biggest Mistake Boards Make

Either on their own or with the support of a search firm, the field is narrowed to three finalists. The process has been time-consuming, and now it is decision time. The committee knows in its heart that the candidates are strong but not a rock star is among them. There are two choices: keep the search open and broaden the candidate pool, or select the best of three (or what I call, *the best of a mediocre lot*). The primary motivations are twofold (and I get them both): first, a long transition with no full-time leader in place makes an organization vulnerable, and second, the committee lacks the appetite to reopen the search.

I've never seen this strategy pay off. Your clients, your organization, your donors — they all expect better than mediocre. And well they should.

A Strong Search Committee

Select the best and the brightest, and if there is not HR expertise on your board, find it outside and add it to the committee. You might want someone who is a retired nonprofit ED, who has in fact done the job. A strong committee is smart enough not to belabor the crafting of a job description. I often find this piece comical. A committee will spend 2 or 3 months getting the kitchen sink in to the description when the words "Messiah Wanted!" will do.

Building a Strong, Large, and Diverse Pool of Prospects

Anxiety and a scarcity mindset can fast-track this portion of the search or delegate it completely to a firm without offering sufficient guidance or creative input. This is a place for *maximum investment* in exchange for *maximum return.*

A Thoughtful Strategy to Contend with Internal Candidates

A five-star leader will have a written succession plan with notes about potential internal candidates as well as external folks to consider. Often a leader is clear (and adamant) about an internal candidate who should succeed them. In concept it is fantastic that the leader has given this thought. Unless the executive *expects their pick to be the anointed successor.*

This can present a path of least resistance or, more strongly, be seen as a wonderful thing that the ED has cultivated a successor. But. But. The board *must* own the choice. The board must believe it has hired the best person.

Different organizations make different choices. Alex Roque was the Development Director of the Ali Forney Center, an organization that provides shelter and support for homeless LGBTQ youth in NYC. The founder, the remarkable Carl Siciliano, believed that hiring Alex was a no brainer. The board wanted to own the choice and put Alex through a number of intense interviews and completed the process seeing what Carl saw. They felt no need for a national search and are thrilled to have Alex as their new leader.

When Robin Steinberg stepped down as the founder of Bronx Defenders, she was clear that Justine Olderman would be the ideal new CEO. The board did not disagree but opted for a national search with an outside firm. After a national search, Justine rose to the top. What was the point of all that? Well, now Justine knows she has the enthusiastic support of the board and never has to wonder whether the board selected her because that is what Robin wanted.

THE ON-DECK CIRCLE

If you have ever served on a board, there has been that executive session once a year without staff that focuses on this topic. And the topic is always described just this bluntly: "We need to talk about what happens if Joan gets hit by a bus."

> The topic is always described just this bluntly: "We need to talk about what happens if Joan gets hit by a bus."

Not only is it deeply offensive to anyone who has experienced the imaginable loss of a friend or family member this way, but also it ends up being this conversation you have so that you can say that you have had it. I have never found them to be helpful. Not long ago I finally figured out why.

Boards are not only asking the wrong question, but going about it all wrong. Of course they mean well. The topic, however you slice and dice it, is about the board's duty to consider succession planning. The problem is that the topic gets discussed through the lens of crisis.

At the risk of alienating Mets fans, I am an unabashed New York Yankee fan. I went to college in the Bronx and cut just a few classes in the spring before finals to head to the stadium.

Now, you don't have to be a baseball fan to appreciate the accomplishments of one of the greatest athletes in my lifetime, Yankee shortstop Derek Jeter. (And as an aside, what makes him a great athlete were his leadership attributes on the team and in the sport). The management couldn't just wait until Jeter decided to announce his retirement; they needed to plan and be ready. The organization scouted and identified a replacement well before Jeter made it official. It's time for nonprofits to think in this vein.

Rather than framing succession planning through a crisis lens, organizations need to talk regularly with the ED (in executive session). Who are the rock stars? Possible successors? Are they folks that, with professional development, can grow into a more senior spot?

Why isn't *that* the conversation the board is having with the ED? Tell us about your staff. How do we retain the rock stars? What skills and attributes can we build that could turn them into organizational leadership material? Should we invest in a coach for her?

It's time for nonprofits to take a different approach to succession planning. Create an intentional process, and please don't treat it like crisis management. Build a farm team of board and staff, recruit folks with potential, groom them. Give them leadership opportunities and evaluate. And of course the board should be taking *exactly* the same approach.

Of all the antidotes included here about stability during transition, this may be the most important one of all. Build a stable, effective organization with great people, and I guarantee you the transition will be stable too. And your communities and donors will appreciate and respect you for maintaining stability where others simply cannot.

SETTING A NEW EXECUTIVE DIRECTOR UP TO SUCCEED

You may remember that in our discussion of "copilots" in Chapter 3, my co-chair / copilots resigned *at my first board meeting*. David Huebner and Peggy Brady were a key part of the draw of stepping into the unknown land of nonprofits — I had done my homework on them and believed they would be just the right partners to lead the organization into its new future. But they did not think so.

A good deal of my work is serving as an executive coach for new CEOs with a particular expertise on CEOs following long-tenured leaders and through this work I have learned that David and Peggy were two of the most self-aware board leaders I have had the privilege to know. As you may recall, they told me that they had led the board during a tumultuous time that required them to manage the executive director closely. They believed it would be hard for them to be different co-chairs and I deserved partners who would give me the space needed to lead and manage effectively.

Earlier in this chapter, I mentioned that as soon as a leader announces she will be leaving, the power shifts to the board. The board navigates the transition to the best of its ability and then leads a search. That search process can be one of the best bonding experiences for a board, creating a real sense of shared purpose, sometimes for the first time for a board, and very often the first time that this sense of purpose is about "following the leader."

Then the new person arrives. If the new leader is following a founder or someone retiring after a long tenure, she will unearth what I call "dust bunnies" and sometimes "dust bunnies on the dust bunnies." Some of these will be about systems and processes that require updating; others could be much deeper problems. And if there has been a tumultuous departure or even a scandal, the new leader will have organizational trust and culture issues to contend with, and we all know that culture issues can swallow smart strategy whole.

What is the appropriate level of engagement during the first weeks and months of a new leader's tenure? The pendulum tends to swing in one of two ways:

"OK, New CEO. Take it From Here. We are Exhausted."

In this approach, the board sees its active engagement as a temporary state until a new leader arrives that it can follow.

The board crushed the search, hiring the rock star the clients deserve, and it can now go into hibernation for a while. Or for the foreseeable future.

A new CEO needs an actively engaged board and will not be successful without one. A board "engine" stuck in neutral will be an *obstacle* to success. The board is not out of the way. *It's actually in the way by thinking it should get out of the way!*

"We *Have* to Stay Close Because [*Insert Good Reason Here*]."

Let's say the leader is coming in on cleanup duty following a failed leadership tenure. Maybe the board knew about the mess all along, or maybe it kind of knew but the depth of the mess was really not very clear until late in the game.

My role throughout this book is to connect all the dots to illustrate the root causes of challenges. I am convinced that the more you understand their root causes, the more of these challenges you can preempt, thereby setting up your organization to succeed.

In this case, a disengaged board, recruited without understanding the big "why" and recruited without intention, is not a strong board, and it can miss big challenges. That said, once it is all clear and the board needs to find a leader, they can't imagine letting go. This board sees the mess created by the last executive director and perhaps even has some guilt about letting it go on too long. And this board is determined to stay close.

In this (also common) scenario, the new leader feels totally micromanaged. The new leader wants to be her rock star self and the board is focused on the branches on the limbs of the tree. Forget about seeing the forest (a key board role).

Getting It Right

This is where investing early on in the copilot relationship is key. Remember our friend Carlos De La Rosa and Roseanne Siino from Lindsay Wildlife Experience and the time they spent talking about personal values and getting to really understand and appreciate one another? That was about building trust. Building trust is the antidote to the two scenarios above: the board that disengages after hiring a new ED and the one that micromanages him. This antidote points organizations toward shared leadership.

Both parties will need to be self-aware and thoughtful. A new CEO who dismisses the board's hyper-engagement and does not honor the battles it has fought does so at their own peril. A new CEO who starts nagging the hibernating board from day 1 to get out and raise money does so at the organization's peril.

The first 90 days of a new tenure will tell much of the story. If it involves real relationship building with a solid set of 90-day goals (that will be imperfect because they will be written by the new ED with zero response from the board *or* will be overly edited by a board still focused on branches), the prognosis is quite good. If the ED is an effective relationship builder and communicator and reads folks well (remember, as covered in Chapter 1, it's leadership *attributes* that really matter), your new ED will honor a micromanaging board and focus on how to communicate early and often in a way that calms your new board down and builds trust. And most important, a new ED will begin to educate the board about its role as ambassadors, as strategists, as stewards — the early days of a new tenure are the perfect time for board members to be sharing the good news, bragging a bit about the new executive, and building a bigger army of folks who are excited to know and do more for this wonderful organization.

> The first 90 days of a new tenure will tell much of the story.

One last thing: New leaders are wise to build quick wins into the first 90-day plan. Affirms the board's choice and builds trust. Win-win.

WHAT LEADERS DO DURING VULNERABLE TIMES

During the early months of the COVID-19 pandemic, I looked for leadership wherever I could. I needed someone to tell me the truth, but I needed it to sound reassuring, confident, and empathetic. I found myself looking to a 39-year-old woman from New Zealand, Prime Minister Jacinda Ardern, for the leadership I needed. That we all needed.

She was authentic, accessible, and empathetic. She held press conferences and Facebook Lives from her living room. She moved swiftly and, as I covered in Chapter 9, she kept the main thing the main thing, and the main thing was keeping the people of New Zealand as safe as she possibly could. In a move that stole my heart, she made a public statement near Easter to alert kids all throughout the country that the Easter Bunny (and the Tooth Fairy!) had been designated "essential workers" although the health crisis may slow them down a bit.

Nothing in my lifetime will ever compare to COVID-19. That said, moments of vulnerability in a country or in an organization demand leadership. And when the vulnerability has been created by the exit or absence of leadership as it is during a staff leadership transition, leadership is even more necessary, and it will need to come from a different source.

A nonprofit in a leadership transition is different from a transition in a for-profit company. It's all that passion I've spoken about — that's the ingredient that makes nonprofits more than a little messy. Staff, board, donors, and volunteers are not just looking for a CEO who can run the show; they are looking for a leader who can inspire confidence, run the show, and help them envision a future that is better as a result of their shared investments. Think about Emily Klehm from South Suburban Humane Society in Chicago Heights. You can run a shelter, or you can dream big and secure a $6 million grant to build a campus for people to help pets and for pets to help people.

Transitions call for board leadership in a way that few other moments in the lifespan of a nonprofit do. And it's not just about the search and the task of finding a new Executive Director. It's about leading an anxious community and assuring them that "you've got this."

> Transitions call for board leadership in a way that few other moments in the lifespan of a nonprofit do.

You also must pay special attention to communication. Stewarding all the folks who matter in your organization should be a priority for a group of board members, different from the search committee. Boards often think that communicating about the search is the important job. Of course that is important. But the strongest organizations nurture the members of their community, reminding them the work continues, sharing successes, and instilling in them confidence that there really isn't a gap in leadership at all.

And if you can assure them that the Tooth Fairy is still making the rounds, all the better.

"I'm feeling in control, powerful, and so lucky to have this job.
Do you think that's a side effect of the new meds?"

Chapter 11   You Are
the Champions

I know who you are. I write to you, and for you, every week.
You are clients. You are the folks I support in the Nonprofit
Leadership Lab. You are fellow staff leaders. You are board colleagues of mine, and board members I worked to recruit. You
educate our young people, you deliver meals, and you work
to cure illnesses and fight the stigma often associated with
them. You fight for equality for women, people of color, and
LGBTQ folks. You provide beds to the homeless and put battered women back on their feet. You are storytellers who do not
allow us to forget. You protect our lands, and you navigate a
complex world for those who are new here. You remind society
of the power of religion and remind us of the power of deep
faith. You bring music, theatre, and dance to us and in so doing
make us think, make us feel, and lift us up.

Yes that's it: You lift us up — each and every one of you. And
you stand shoulder to shoulder with over 12 million colleagues

who head to work at a nonprofit every day, each of you doing your part to repair the world. You also stand shoulder to shoulder with over 60 million people who give of their time to causes they care about. Studies tell us that roughly 25% of Americans engage in some kind of volunteer work.

It's quite a big tribe. I like the word *tribe*. So often I hear staff and board leaders talk about being overwhelmed and feeling alone, and I wish more of them felt that sense of tribe.

You are hardly alone. You are in the best of company — noble company. And with every passing year, it feels like the world needs you more than ever. So many aspects of our society are broken, and it gives me great hope to know that you are all out there, chipping away at the solutions that will lift us all up.

The work is hard, I know. I've been in the trenches. I've read hate mail. I've missed more than my share of school plays. I read it in the mail I receive and I see it in the eyes of my clients: optimism on one hand and stress and exhaustion on the other. It feels like every decision matters — *a lot*. It feels like so much is riding on your ability to make an impact.

Not long ago, I spent two weeks at a health boot camp for people of a certain age and learned the value of taking good care of yourself. I learned about the value of something else, too: interval training. In interval training, you work hard (*really* hard) and then you take a short break. Then you repeat the process. I learned that interval training makes you stronger. Maybe you knew that, but this was headline news to me.

> Interval training makes you stronger.

The trajectory of certain jobs looks like the one shown in Figure 11.1, with peaks, lulls, and plateaus.

And then you can see the pace of the nonprofit world in Figure 11.2. *Everything* matters *all the time.*

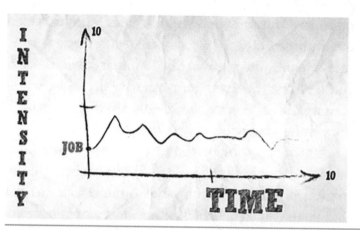

FIGURE 11.1 The trajectory of a normal career.

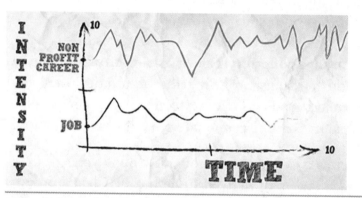

FIGURE 11.2 The trajectory of a nonprofit career.

I wish someone had told me all this back in 1997 — that I would never work so hard or care so much. That I would feel like I was letting the whole world down if I took a break. That interval train-

> A "sprinter's pace" is unsustainable because the issues the nonprofit sector addresses are of the "marathon" variety.

ing makes you stronger. That a "sprinter's pace" is unsustainable because the issues the nonprofit sector addresses are of the "marathon" variety.

If I understood all this, maybe I wouldn't have almost killed my development director.

For all these reasons, my fellow tribe members, I decided to write this book. Actually, it was more than a decision. I was *compelled*. Just as I am of service to each of my clients, I believe that this book can be of service to you, the reader.

Leading a nonprofit is a tough and often thankless job (and for board leaders, it's *unpaid*, to boot). It is my fondest hope that this book has offered you both philosophical and tactical takeaways that enable you to feel less alone and more effective.

In an effort to help tidy up the messy world of the nonprofit, here are some sound bites worth keeping in mind as you continue to fight the good fight:

- **A highly effective nonprofit is like a first-rate, twin-engine jet.**

  Board and staff must work together in a model of shared leadership and partnership. Alone, neither can manage, plan, or grow resources in the passionate pursuit of your mission.

- **Your power as a leader comes from all around you.**

  It takes a village to run a five-star nonprofit. Clients, donors, volunteers — a diverse group of people who have value to add must be engaged. You are not alone. Look around you, and look to Kermit the Frog for inspiration. (See Chapter 1.)

- **Learn to tell a helluva story about your work.**

  Fewer elements of the human culture are more primitive than the narrative. And although talking about your organization should be an easy task, it turns out that it's mighty tough. Practice, get it right, and get people at "Hello."

- **Take the time to ask the tough questions.**

  If the term *strategic planning* causes you to break out in a rash, don't use it. Instead, dedicate time with your "village" to pose the tough strategic questions you must answer in order to create the most expedient and effective route to the fulfillment of your mission.

- **Your love for your organization and its work must trump your fear of asking.**

  No color commentary is needed here.

- **Manage people in 3D.**

  Take the time to get to know and understand the motives and aspirations of your fellow board members, your staff, and those closest to the organization. Ask them to tell you why this work matters. Give them a voice. Trust me: It will inspire *you* when your people bring *all* of themselves to the work.

- **Anticipate.**

  Remember my earlier comment in this chapter about interval training? The break you take after working hard doesn't have to be a walk around the block or a long weekend. It can also mean taking a break from your role as firefighter to allow for *planning*. This kind of break can certainly make you stronger and can enable you to weather the storms that will surely come your way.

- **Maintain a firm and compassionate grasp on the organization during a transition.**

  A change in leadership is more destabilizing than you might assume, especially on the staff side. Take this transition seriously and ensure that your board is as strong and effective as it can possibly be. Then you can recruit the best leaders and retain them, and your star staff, for the long haul.

Let me say one last thing: It's a privilege to have a leadership role in a nonprofit. It's a joy to have the opportunity to dedicate your skills, life experience, time, energy, and passion to a cause you care deeply about.

That said, the work is tough and often thankless. And so I will end with these two words:

Thank you.

Bibliography

PREFACE

McKeever, Brice (November 2018). The Nonprofit Sector in Brief 2018: Public Charites, Giving, and Volunteering. https://nccs.urban.org/publication/nonprofit-sector-brief-2018#the-nonprofit-sector-in-brief-2018-public-charites-giving-and-volunteering.

Duckworth, Angela (2019). *Grit*. Vermilion.

contributor/i, Joan Garry. Too Many Boards Abuse Their Power. Let's Change That. *The Chronicle of Philanthropy* (24 September 2019). https://www.philanthropy.com/article/Too-Many-Boards-Abuse-Their/247206.

CHAPTER 1: THE SUPERPOWERS OF NONPROFIT LEADERSHIP

Collins, Jim (2005). *From Good to Great in the Social Sector: Why Business Thinking is Not the Answer*. New York: HarperCollins. Print.

Hesselbein, Frances (2002). *Hesselbein on Leadership*. San Francisco: Jossey-Bass. Print.

Robert, Henry M. (1907). *Pocket Manual of Robert's Rules of Order for Deliberative Assemblies*. Northbrook, IL: Scott Foresman. Print.

CHAPTER 2: YOU'VE GOT TO GET ME AT HELLO

Heath, Chip, and Heath, Dan (2007). *Made to Stick: Why Some Ideas Survive and Others Die*. New York: Random House. Print.

Steinbeck, John (2002). *East of Eden*. New York: Penguin. Print.

This is the HBR article: https://hbr.org/2007/03/made-to-stick-by-chip-heath-an

CHAPTER 4: WHY BOARDS MATTER

Taylor, Barbara E. et al. (2013). *Governance as Leadership: Reframing the Work of Nonprofit Boards*. Hoboken, NJ: Wiley.

Trower, Cathy Ann (2013). *The Practitioner's Guide to Governance as Leadership: Building High-Performing Nonprofit Boards*. San Francisco, CA: Jossey-Bass.

Ingram, Richard T. (2015). *Ten Basic Responsibilities of Nonprofit Boards*. Washington, DC: BoardSource.

Hamblin, James. The physiological power of altruism. *The Atlantic*. Atlantic Media Company, 30 December 2015. Web. 25 October 2016. https://www.theatlantic.com/health/archive/2015/12/altruism-for-a-better-body/422280.

Garry, Joan (2016). A template for a great board orientation. *Joan Garry Nonprofit Leadership* (15 December 2016), blog.joangarry.com/board-orientation-template.

CHAPTER 5: THE KEY IS NOT IN THE ANSWERS. IT'S IN THE QUESTIONS

Eisenhower, Dwight D. (1957). Remarks at the National Defense Executive Reserve Conference (14 November 1957). Online by Gerhard Peters and John T. Woolley, The American Presidency Project. https://www.presidency.ucsb.edu/documents/remarks-the-national-defense-executive-reserve-conference.

O'Donovan, Dana, and Flower, Noah R. The strategic plan is dead. Long live strategy. *The Strategic Plan Is Dead. Long Live Strategy.* N.p., 10 January 2013. Web. 24 October 2016. https://ssir.org/articles/entry/the_strategic_plan_is_dead._long_live_strategy.

CHAPTER 7: MANAGING THE PAID AND THE UNPAID

Sinek, Simon (2009). *Start with Why: How Great Leaders Inspire Everyone to Take Action.* New York: Portfolio. Print.

Pink, Daniel H. (2018). *Drive: The Surprising Truth about What Motivates Us.* Edinburgh, UK: Canongate Books.

Ep 12: Community Organizing [PODCAST]. *Joan Garry Nonprofit Leadership,* 20 May 2016. www.joangarry.com/ep-12-community-organizing-caroline-samponaro-podcast.

Darr, Renelle (2017). Council post: The new workplace: Where meaning and purpose are more important than ever. *Forbes, Forbes Magazine,* 13 September 2017. www.forbes.com/sites/forbescoachescouncil/2017/09/13/the-new-workplace-where-meaning-and-purpose-are-more-important-than-ever/#785e7bd85a46.

CHAPTER 8: THE SMALL AND THE MIGHTY

Salamon, Lester M. and Newhouse, Chelsea L. (2019). The 2019 nonprofit employment report, Nonprofit Economic Data Bulletin no. 47. (Baltimore: Johns Hopkins Center for Civil Society Studies, January 2019). ccss.jhu.edu.

Morris, George et al. (2018). *The Financial Health of the United States Nonprofit Sector*. Guidestar.

Hamilton, Sarah (2019). Council post: The nonprofit sector is growing: Why nonprofits should act now to leverage their position. *Forbes, Forbes Magazine*, 2 October 2019. www.forbes.com/sites/forbescoachescouncil/2019/10/02/the-nonprofit-sector-is-growing-why-nonprofits-should-act-now-to-leverage-their-position/#713136657b52.

Kopp, Wendy (2011). *One Day, All Children . . .: the Unlikely Triumph of Teach for America and What I Learned Along the Way*. New York: PublicAffairs.

Janus, Kathleen K. (2018). *Social Startup Success: How the Best Non-profits Launch, Scale Up, and Make a Difference*. Cambridge, MA: Da Capo Press.

CHAPTER 9: WHEN IT HITS THE FAN

Goodman, J. David (2014). DNA confirms body parts belong to missing boy with autism. *New York Times*, 22 January 2014: *A16*. Print.

AP. Greenpeace Loses $5.2 Million on Currency Trading. *USA Today*. Gannett, 16 June 2014. Web. 25 October 2016. http://www.usatoday.com/story/news/nation/2014/06/16/greenpeace-loses-millions/10568731.

Yardley, Jim (2016). Tower of logs collapses at Texas A&M, *killing 11*. *New York Times* (18 November 1999). *Web.* 25 October 2016. http://www.nytimes.com/1999/11/19/us/tower-of-logs-collapses-at-texas-a-m-killing-11.html.

Drape, Joe (2012). Sandusky guilty of sexual abuse of 10 young boys. *New York Times* (23 June 2012): *A1*. Print.

Orlando Shooting — *The New York Times*. N.p., 20 June 2016. Web. 25 October 2016. http://www.nytimes.com/news-event/2016-orlando-shooting.

Crisis Intel & Reports — Institute for Crisis Management. N.p., n.d. Web. 25 October 2016. http://crisisconsultant.com/crisis-intel-reports.

Fearn-Banks, Kathleen (2011). *Crisis Communications: A Casebook Approach*. 4th Edition. Mahwah, NJ: Erlbaum. Print.

Fink, Steven (2013). *Crisis Communications: The Definitive Guide to Managing The Message.* New York: McGraw Hill. Print. (pps 138-179).

Bonk, Kathy and Tynes, Emily (2008). *Strategic Communications for Nonprofits.* San Francisco, CA: Jossey Bass. Print.

Kruse, Kevin (2012). Stephen Covey: 10 quotes that can change your life. *Forbes.* Forbes Magazine, 16 July 2012. Web. 24 October 2016. http://www.forbes.com/sites/kevinkruse/2012/07/16/the-7-habits.

CHAPTER 10: HELLO, I MUST BE GOING

Branson, Tom (2020). Nonprofit employee retention. ExactHire. 22 January 2020. www.exacthire.com/blog/workforce-management/nonprofit-employee-retention.

Sergeant, Adrian, and Day, Harriet (2018). A study of nonprofit leadership in the US and its impending crisis. The Concord Leadership Group. https://concordleadershipgroup.com/report.

Index